The WEB DESIGN WOW! BOOK

Showcasing the Best of On-Screen Communication

Jack Davis & Susan Merritt

with Linnea Dayton, Wow! Book Series Editor

PEACHPIT
PRESS

The Web Design Wow! Book

Jack Davis and Susan Merritt
Find us on the World Wide Web at: www.wowbooks.com

Peachpit Press
1249 Eighth Street
Berkeley, CA 94710
(510) 524-2178 phone
(510) 524-2221 fax

Find us on the World Wide Web at: www.peachpit.com and www.wowbooks.com

Peachpit Press is a division of Addison Wesley Longman.

Series editor: Linnea Dayton
Cover design and illustration: Jack Davis
Book design: Jill Davis
Editing: Linnea Dayton
Index: Jackie Estrada
Production: Jill Davis
wowbooks.com Web site: Tommy Yune

This book was typeset using the Stone Serif and Stone Sans families. It was composed in PageMaker 6.0. Final output was computer to plate.

ISBN 0-201-88678-2

9 8 7 6

Printed and bound in the United States of America.

The WEB DESIGN WOW! BOOK

Showcasing the Best of On-Screen Communication

Berkeley,USA:
Peachpit Press, 1998

CD IN THE BACK OF THE BOOK

 WITH
CD-ROM

To our parents Frank and Mary
and Sam and Barbara
for the gifts of
love, life, and creativity.

—Jack and Jill Davis

To my parents Charlie and Sarah,
for their love and guidance,
and my husband Calvin and our son Danne,
for their patience and support.

—Susan Merritt

Contents

Acknowledgments

This book would not have been possible without a great deal of support. First, we would like to extend a big thanks to the Wow! series editor, Linnea Dayton, whose incredible eye for detail and sense of clarity guided us every step of the way, and to Jill Davis, our talented book designer and producer, whose award-winning work makes this book shine. And to the folks at Peachpit Press, especially Jeanne Woodward, Victor Gavenda, and Nancy Aldrich-Ruenzel, whose continual support for this book fueled our enthusiasm.

We are thankful to Kathy Davis who conducted some of the Gallery interviews; to Linda Heida, who transcribed the taped interviews and helped with contacting contributors and organizing the information for the Appendix and Index; and to Jonathan Parker, production artist extraordinaire, for his participation in the book's earlier stages. Thanks also to the people who assisted us with the many details, including Danny DeBate, Lisa King, Catherine Lorenzo, Katherine Reisen, Barbara Ursich, and Danne Woo. And to the friends, family, colleagues, and co-workers who stood by us along the way.

Finally, we wish to express our sincere gratitude to the individuals, companies, and organizations who have allowed us to interview them and who gave us permission to include their work in this book and to share their experience, knowledge, and expertise with our readers; their names and contact information are listed in the Appendix.

—*Jack Davis and Susan Merritt*

In addition, I would like to thank San Diego State University for the opportunity to take a sabbatical leave to begin this book, and especially Fred Orth, Director of the School of Art, Design and Art History, Joyce Gattas, Dean of the College of Professional Studies and Fine Arts, and Hayes Anderson, Associate Dean, for their continued support of technology in the arts.

I am especially grateful to my graduate students Russ Prior and Jeff Uhlik for pushing the boundaries; to Jenny Woo and Chris Woo, who, by example, have inspired me to take risks and have taught me the value of following my own dreams; to Miriam Erb for attentively listening and always asking the right questions; and to Rebecca and Arthur Joseph for their invaluable friendship and their never-ending words of encouragement.

—*Susan Merritt*

Heartfelt thanks to all our "partners in crime" who have encouraged and supported us during the course of this project and whose influences will always be felt in our lives: Steve and Lisa King; John and Robbie Schulz; Jorgé Castellanos; Geno Andrews; Tommy Yune. Finally, we are grateful to Granma Malena, who gave immeasurable love and attention to the kids when we had deadlines to meet.

—*Jack and Jill Davis*

Nothing clears away the creative cobwebs like being inspired by the successful work of others.

Welcome

Welcome to *The Web Design Wow! Book*, a showcase of successful Web sites and other interactive projects that we present here to inspire you and to show you how talented professionals have tackled the new challenges of interface design and interactivity. Current technology imposes certain limits on on-screen design: Things have to look good at a much lower resolution than designers are accustomed to in printed work. And the slower-than-the-speed-of-light rates at which data can be moved from one part of the globe to another over the Internet make it crucial to make the audiovisual components of the message as compact as possible. For these reasons and many others new delivery platforms such as the Web require new kinds of solutions to age-old design problems. But they also offer new design opportunities related to the integration of text, graphics, motion, and sound, and the ability to link these elements dynamically.

Today compact file size is all-important for quick access to information from the Web. But data transfer technologies are changing very quickly—too quickly for Web designers not to take inspiration from the years of more complex interactive communications designed to be delivered by CD-ROM, floppy disk, or kiosk. So along with Web sites, you'll find examples in this book of interface designs from these media as well.

Enjoy!

There are as many different ways of designing for interactivity as there are designers (entier.com; myrrh.com; iqvc.com, see page 196). This book showcases a few hundred interface solutions with the idea that we learn best by example.

Telling a compelling story is what communication is all about. And the capabilities of the Web are a new and powerful asset in sharing our stories with others throughout the world, like this story of one family's struggle with AIDS. (startribune.com/aids, see page 160)

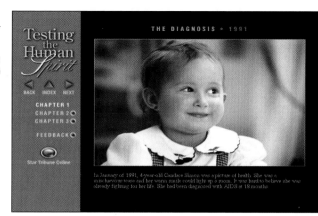

With on-screen communication, the interface is the conduit through which the interactive story flows.

Introduction

What Is an Interface?

The *interface* is the part of a tool or technology with which the user interacts. For a screwdriver, it's the handle. For a bicycle, it's the seat, handlebars, pedals, and gear levers. For a Web site, it's a crafted communication environment that houses the site's content and the navigation devices the user needs to get to the content. The design goal for an interface is to clarify the content offered by the site and to "dish it out" effectively. For example,

- If the Web site (or other interactive venue) is designed as a tool—to allow visitors to get the tech support information they seek or to buy tickets to ride the commuter train—the interface should be virtually transparent, so it doesn't get in the way as users set about getting what they came for.

- If the site's primary goal is education, the interface needs to be engaging enough to encourage participation and learning.

- If the site is intended to promote or sell a product or service, the interface has a big role to play in making it easy for potential buyers to get the information they need to make a decision. It also has to help motivate them to take action, and it needs to provide a way for them to place orders, either online or off.

The Designer's Role

The designers of today's interactive interfaces are the latest in a long line of artists and craftspeople who take the philosophical, the conceptual, and the physical and transform them into packets of communication that inspire, teach, or sell to an audience. Like the ancient Chinese painter-poets, the troubadours, minstrels, and jesters of the Middle Ages, or the novelists and ad writers of more modern times, interface designers package thoughts and information so that they can be transported, shared, considered, debated, and acted upon.

When putting together Web sites, designers don't work in a vacuum. They usually have a lot of help from people who are expert at developing the content and implementing the relevant technologies. So instead of providing click-and-drag recipes for using the multitudes of programs typically required to prepare a Web site, CD-ROM, or other interactive project, this

Powerful design is about shaping information and sharing experiences in such a way that the user is drawn into the interactive conversation as an active participant—rather than left as a passive recipient at the end of a wire. (designory.com, see page 88)

Immediate access to information is what the Web is all about. The key is to make that access straightforward and intuitive and to provide the user with a sense of control. (landor.com, see page 76)

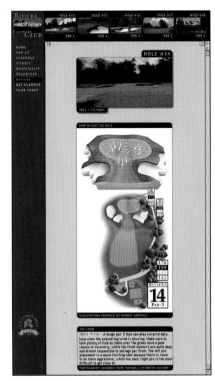

A Web site's style and its supporting message of upscale sophistication, homespun quality, or cutting-edge hipness, play a major role in shaping a personality that will be remembered by the user long after specific tidbits of information are forgotten. (ussenioropen98.com)

Chapters 1, 2, and 3 give an overview of some of the design opportunities and production issues that are important in designing for the screen.

Each chapter ends with a Gallery of screens from additional Web sites, with captions that include insights from their creators.

book focuses on *designing* the interface so the bells and whistles of the technology always complement the communication goals of the site.

How To Use This Book

As a tool for problem-solving and inspiration, this book is designed for a "flip and focus" approach: With your design problem in mind, flip through the pages until you see a solution that catches your eye, and then stop and read about it.

If you'd like to take a more structured approach to the subject of interface design, starting with an overview of the entire process, you can begin by reading Chapters 1 through 3 (see A, above left). You'll find reminders about design fundamentals and designer-client-producer interactions, extended and par-ticularized for the interface design process and Web site development. Since it's commonly understood that Web site addresses usually have the "www." prefix as part of their URL, most Web site references in this book have been listed without it; be sure to include the complete **"http://www."** prefix if required by your browser when you visit a site re-ferred to in this book. You'll find active links to these sites at the Web Design Wow! Book section of **wowbooks.com.**

In Chapters 4 through 10 you'll find case studies (see B, at right) of outstand-ing interface design projects, grouped according to communication goals, with chapters on marketing, entertainment, tools and applications, education and training, publishing, portfolios and pre-sentations, and sales. Each case study presents the concepts behind the design, examples of screen layouts, a map of screen organization (see C, above right), insights and strategies from the creators, and a brief listing of the human resources, hard-ware, and software (see D, at right) used to carry out the project. At the end of each chapter is a Gallery section with additional inspiring examples of screen design (see E, left).

At the back of the book is the Appendix, with credits and contact information for the interfaces included in the opening chapters, case studies, and Galleries. To locate a particular topic in the text, use the Index at the very end of the book.

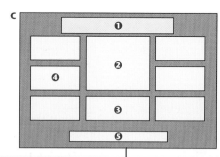

Each project includes a screen diagram with an accompanying legend that highlights the components of the interface. Yellow signifies an interface's navigation elements, blue is used for informational elements (photo-graphs, text, and so on), and gray shows background areas.

STATS AND SOFTWARE

An 8-member development team that included representatives from Lynx Golf, DigitalFacades, and DDB Needham Los Angeles worked 9 months to plan, develop content, and design and produce the Lynx Golf Web site. Software included BBEdit, Illustrator, and Photoshop run-ning on Macs. **lynxgolf.com**

Chapters 4 through 10 present double-page summaries of specific interactive projects, above, along with a condensed list of some of the resources used in their creation, left.

1 An Overview of the Production Process

CONCEPT

Time, Money, and Talent **14**

The Communication Challenge **15**

Identifying the Audience **16**

Shaping the Solution **17**

Determining the Content **18**

DESIGN

Choosing the Appropriate Technologies **19**

Establishing a Unified Metaphor, Personality, or Style **20**

Mapping Out Organization and Navigation **22**

Storyboarding the Dynamics **23**

Creating a Prototype **24**

PRODUCTION

Gathering the Assets and Setting Standards **25**

Processing, Integrating, and Archiving **26**

Assembling, Coding, Programming **27**

Testing, Refining, and Retesting **28**

MARKETING

Getting the Word Out **29**

Gallery **30**

It pays to know the road before you start the trip—especially if you're the one driving the bus.

WHETHER YOU'RE ABOUT TO EMBARK on designing your own online portfolio or you're leading a client by the hand into the uncharted territory of developing an elaborate corporate Web site, it's good to understand the potential and anticipate the pitfalls before you get very far down the road. On the next 16 pages you'll find a general checklist of possible stages or steps you can follow in designing and producing Web sites and other dynamically interactive communication pieces. Not all stages will apply to all projects, but these pages present the lay of the land so you can intelligently chart your journey—or the journey your clients are paying you to take them on—which can make the difference between taking charge of a project and keeping it on track, or hanging on for dear life as the project careens out of control.

What a Concept!

Just as in print media, the first stage of a Web design project is developing the concept. It's here at the beginning of the project that you have to answer some essential questions: Why is this Web site needed? Who will it need to communicate with? How can the communication be achieved most effectively? What do you want visitors to the site to take away with them? And when should the Web site be done? Is this the time to embark on a big interactive project, or will it take awhile for you or the client to gather the necessary resources or personnel? Once you've answered these questions, you'll be well on your way to arriving at a focused solution.

Design

During the design phase, you'll choose technologies that make sense for the project, based on what you've decided about who the audience is, how best to communicate with them, and what you want them to walk away with. This is also the time for mapping out the organization of the site and figuring out how visitors will navigate it. Storyboards and prototypes can help you make sure your ideas will work. No matter how good a concept you come up with and what kind of whiz-bang technologies you use to support it, if visitors can't figure out how to get to what they want, they'll soon become bored, confused, or frustrated.

Production

The production phase involves assembling the text, images, audio, and navigation elements you planned in the design phase and integrating them with the code to make them work. In other words, "building out" the site—constructing the environment, installing the attractions, stocking the stores, posting directional signs, and turning on the lights. How well you manage the production phase can determine whether your site becomes a successful, welcoming center of design, information, and commerce, or just another stop along the road to somewhere else.

Marketing

If you want people to come to the virtual concert of information you've designed and produced as your Web site, you'll have to let them know it exists. You can have the most beautiful or eloquent or dynamic or insightful or educational or practical or entertaining center of communication on the Web, and if no one knows it's there, you might as well be singing in the shower. So putting your site on the map and promoting it as a must-see destination is vitally important for every Web project.

Having the resources you need is half the battle. And if you don't win this half, the second half could get gory.

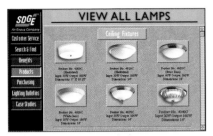

The more than 600 pages in this utility company's Web site **(sdge.com, see page 82)** offer users a wide range of services, from help with fixture selections to virtual reality facility tours. The company quickly realized that this project's scope would require not only a design firm's expertise to produce the site, but also a second resource for writing specialized code.

PARTNERING WITH YOUR CLIENT

To produce a winning Web site, you and your client must share the same goals and objectives. So throughout the book, you'll find the two terms "you" and "your client" used interchangeably. In some cases, you'll be your own client. In the other cases, when you (as designer) will be acting on behalf of your client, it's important to establish clear communication and a comfortable working relationship, and to **make sure you get the client's written approval at critical points in the project**—especially those points where the next step will lead to a significant change in the final product or will require a substantial expenditure of time or money.

Time, Money, and Talent

As you begin the work of developing a concept, it's a good idea to take inventory of your resources, and the resources of your client. What do you have available that will help you bring the project in on time, on target, and within budget? This inventory helps answer the "when" question: "Is this an appropriate time to undertake this project?"

Developing a Web site takes some combination of time, money, experience, and expertise. Lacking one or two of these resources, you may find that you can make up the difference by adding more of the others.

Time

Everything about designing and producing an interactive project takes time. There's the time it takes to learn what works on the Web and how to combine it with other interactive media; time to learn how to translate the rules of good design into success on-screen; time to learn the basic tools of site production. If you're starting out with a new client, you'll need time to learn who the audience will be and how to appeal to that audience in this medium. You'll need time to educate your client about what you're doing and how the process works. And you'll need time to experiment. It's important to make sure that both you and your client understand how much development time the Web site is likely to take, how much of your learning time the client will be paying for, and how much of the client's time will be required in addition to the work you'll be doing.

Money and Talent

To some degree, what you and your client lack in time can be made up in money and talent. If you have, or can hire, Web expertise, the job will go faster. And you can be confident that your creative time is being spent on a practical solution, not on risky explorations or reinventing the wheel. It may be worth it to hire subcontractors for programming, animation, and even static Web graphics. Paying for experienced talent is one of the ways to help protect yourself from failing or having to start over. And you're almost certain to learn something from the expert's example, so for the next job you'll have more experience in-house.

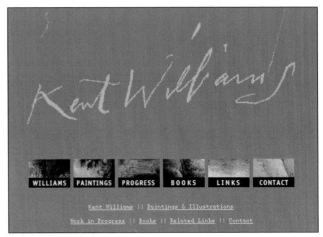

This artist's elegant portfolio was designed to be an informative and inspirational promotion tool. Even though new works in progress are added regularly, the site requires only minimal attention and upkeep. **(spearedpeanut.com/artist/kentwilliams.html, see page 183)**

After this Web site for a leading computer game developer **(presto.com, see page 30)** was designed and produced in-house, the maintenance of the site was turned over to an outside firm that could dedicate the necessary time and resources to keep it current and running smoothly.

To hit the target, you have to know what it is, and how to keep yourself from being distracted from it.

The Communication Challenge

Answering the question "Why is this Web site needed?" is really a two-part endeavor. The first part is targeting the problem you want the Web site to help solve. For instance, does your client's brand lack the name recognition that motivates people to pick the product off the shelf? Is the customer service department overrun with phone calls from people who want information that could easily be delivered online? Is the firm often over-stocked with one kind of widget or another?

Being Problem-Specific

In identifying the need, it's important to be as specific as possible about what your target is, and to define it in a way that will let you assess whether your best shot is producing a hit or a miss. You may think sales should go up 10% within a month. Or the average wait time in the customer service telephone queue should be cut by a fourth. Or "x" amount of widgets should be cleared out of the warehouse this quarter. The better you are at defining the desired target, the better you'll be at developing a solution that works, and recognizing when it doesn't work. (And the happier both you and your client are likely to be.)

Choosing the Right Delivery Method

The second aspect of the "why" question is "Why the Web?" Eager design firms and their clients sometimes turn to new media for the "cool" factor. But the Web might not be the best arrow for hitting your particular target. Ask yourself whether the Web is the most accessible, most powerful, and most cost-effective way to get the specific results you want from your audience. If not, pull another arrow out of the quiver. For many design problems, the print medium is still the best at hitting the bulls-eye; it's still the most portable and most intuitive. Perhaps a CD-ROM is more appropriate if your message doesn't change and is graphics-intensive, and your audience is clearly identified. But if you need instant access and dynamic interaction, or if each individual customer just needs an individual "page" of information from an encyclopedic database, or if you know that your potential buyers visit the Internet on a regular basis, a Web site is probably part of the perfect solution.

The primary goal of this online stock photography site (**digitalstock.com, see page 202**) is to provide quick-and-easy search capabilities of its constantly expanding resources. Users must be able to get immediate feedback on their request for images based on their needs so they can follow through by downloading low-resolution images or high-resolution finals, or by ordering complete CD-ROM collections.

This car manufacturer's Internet presence (**toyota.com, see page 86**) has taken the "online brochure" to new heights. Besides all the traditional collateral materials that are instantly accessible to users, the site also dedicates certain areas to dealer services, an owner's club, and a lifestyles webzine, designed to hold the user's interest and keep visitors coming back.

First came direct-mail catalogs, then TV shopping, and now the ultimate in instant gratification—online malls. One of the main challenges in Web-based commerce is generating confidence—in the stability of the seller, in the support behind the product, and in the sales transaction itself. This site focuses much of its design attention on a warm and cozy living-room environment that helps to make the shopper feel comfortable and confident (**iqvc.com, see page 196**).

You can't please all of the people all of the time. So aim to be wildly successful with your key audience, and don't worry about the rest.

As the name epicurious suggests, this Web site is aimed at those with discriminating taste. Featuring the best in travel, food, and wine, epicurious.com is actually two sites in one: Epicurious Travel and Epicurious Food. **(epicurious.com, see page 154)**

Identifying the Audience

Once you've figured out why you or your client needs a Web site—in other words, you've identified the "itch"—the next step is to figure out who, exactly, you're going to get to "scratch" it. What kinds of individuals make up the group that will buy the overstocked widgets, download the information instead of tying up corporate phone lines, or make your client's brand name a household word?

The Demographics You Need

You need to determine the audience of the Web site that you're targeting (1) so that you can make your design solution as relevant and aesthetically compelling to your particular viewers as possible, and (2) so that you can, with the site's content, work out a trade—a sort of "I'll scratch your back, if you'll scratch mine" proposition. The "scratch" that the Web site will offer its visitors could be anything from useful information to pure entertaining distraction.

To develop the right scratch—not only *what* to communicate, but *how*—you must anticipate the *visitor's* itch. To do that, it pays to have some basic information about these visitors: age, sex, education, and income, for instance. Beyond that, you may also want to know some specifics that will make your message more focused and compelling, such as their hobbies, what other media they use, what Web sites they regularly visit, what print publications they read, and what television programs they watch.

For purely technical reasons that will affect how you produce and deliver the elements that make up your site, you'll also need some practical information about the equipment your audience uses to connect to the Web: What computer platforms, monitor setups, operating systems, and Web browsers do they use? What connection speed is typical when they log on to the Net?

Where To Get the Info

Clients should be able to tell you much of what you need to know about the audience who buys their products or uses their services. If they don't have concrete information it may be time to hire a marketing firm that can perform focus-group testing or develop surveys and questionnaires. For basic demographics on Internet users, try the Graphics, Visualization, and Usability Center, a Web site of Georgia Institute of Technology's College of Computing: **cc.gatech.edu/gvu/user_surveys/**.

Developed for students in grades K–12 in conjunction with The National Geographic Society's Annual Geography Awareness Week **(nationalgeographic.com, see page 130),** Fantastic Forest uses colorful illustrations, an adventure game format, and sounds of the forest to provide students with an entertaining way to learn about forest habitats.

What better way to hit a broad market with a lighthearted product than with a characterization of the viewers themselves? If you are going to sell underwear on the Web, as the Joe Boxer site does **(joeboxer.com, see page 203),** it's best not to take yourself too seriously, augmenting the shopping experience with a heaping dose of entertainment.

What specifics will the visitor remember if interviewed five minutes after leaving your site? And more important, how will that experience affect that person's opinions or actions?

Shaping the Solution

When you understand both what your client wants to "sell" and who is likely to be "buying," you're ready to begin shaping the communication experience that your Web site will provide to visitors. In other words, it's time to begin working on "How?"— How will you present the information so your audience will benefit from it, and how will you provide a call to action that gets them to follow through promptly, either online or off?

Designing the Communication Environment

If your client needs to improve brand awareness, then your strategy will be to ensure that visitors leave the Web site with the knowledge that your client's brand is equal to or better than the competition. A way to accomplish this goal, depending on your audience, may be to create a site that exudes sophistication, or establishes technical expertise, or celebrates its own cutting-edge hipness. On the other hand, if your client sells widgets, and the audience consists of "show me" types, presenting a corporate personality will take a back seat to demonstrating the features, functions, and benefits of the products. For a nonprofit organization, or even for the customer support division of a for-profit business, the environment you design will be different still—one that ensures that the information and resources that your visitors seek are easily accessible. You may want the site to provide downloadable information, link to other useful sites, or encourage visitors to take action offline.

Shaping and Reshaping

You can't just design a site, hand it over to your clients or their Webmasters, and walk away. To be successful, a Web site—more than almost any other kind of communication experience today—requires continual re-evaluation. Built into your site's design should be (1) a way to assess whether you're attracting the audience you want to reach and whether visitors are indeed getting your message and responding to the call to action, and (2) a plan for updating or making any changes that are needed. Your plan should stay focused on the goal and use all available resources to present and support the response (the action you want the user to take, or the opinion you want to foster) as directly as possible.

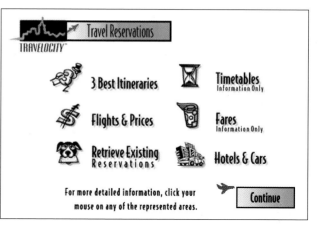

This online travel agency **(travelocity.com, see page 200)** breaks up its interface options into straightforward on-screen directions and simple, clearly labeled category icons. The obvious differentiation between areas that lead to a purchase and those where a visitor can go strictly for information only helps alleviate the fears of users who see doing business on the Web as risky or otherwise problematic.

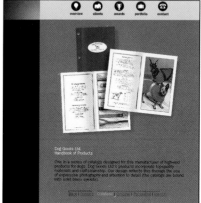

A straightforward grid system, color scheme, and set of navigation options provide an effective backdrop for this design firm's Web site **(pivotdesign.com)**, focusing attention on the projects the firm has created for its clients.

Among the design features of this cable television channel's Web site (discovery.com, see page 94), two are particularly responsible for keeping the site focused and successful: (1) It's simple and intuitive for viewers to use, with easy access to past and current topics and specials; and (2) it's relatively easy for the production team to update and expand.

Once you have the big picture, it's easy to make out the details.

Determining the Content

Once you know what the communication landscape of your Web site will look like, you can get down to the architect's job of deciding how to "build it out." You've planned a project that will attract the audience you want to reach, and you've identified generally what you want visitors to take away with them and how you want to call them to action. Now it's time to think about what content you'll need to deliver in order to accomplish those goals, and what will be the best combination of media to use as the delivery system.

Organizing Information

The primary message, or content, that you want to deliver online may be almost identical to what's already being delivered by the client in print, or on radio, CD-ROM, or TV, and you may be able to reinforce that message—and also save time and money—by repurposing existing materials in your Web-building plans. But if you take graphics and promotional text from print brochures, sound from a radio spot, or product specifications from a company database, you'll want to reshape this content to take advantage of the Web's opportunities for interaction. For example, you can use hypertext links to "layer" any supporting (but nonessential) content, such as biographies of corporate officers, to a "deeper" part of the site. That way the information will be available to those who are interested, but it won't interrupt the flow of the typical visitor's cruise through the site. Here's another example: Unlike a radio commercial, audio on the Web can be available on demand; the message may actually "stick" longer if the visitor has to take some action—like clicking a button—to request it.

The Other Kind of Content

The client's message isn't the only content that's important to a Web site. Web visitors are certainly not a captive audience. They're never farther than a click away from leaving your online "neighborhood," perhaps never to return. Part of a Web site's content, therefore, has to be designed to give people the added value they seek—to keep them at the site long enough to get the message, or to bring them back for future visits, so you can

The Sci-Fi Channel (**scifi.com, see page 104**) wanted to extend its brand identity and augment its television presence. So it developed a Web site where viewers could log on and tune in. Users can check programming schedules, visit the retail store, or simply get more information about their favorite sci-fi programs.

In this Web site for J. Walter Thompson (**jwtworld.com, see page 74**) visitors try their hand at advertising when they play The Ad Game, an entertaining feature that adds value to the Web site's user experience.

reinforce the message or update it. In exchange for the time they spend at your site, visitors want information they can apply, tools they can use, beauty they can enjoy, games they can play, "freebies" they can download, or links to other interesting sites they can visit.

Technology Is Not Content

With the need for added value and the constantly changing technology of the Internet, it can be tempting to show off your up-to-the-minute technological prowess by embellishing a Web site with bells and whistles. But too many bells and whistles can make a site's content harder to get to. Keep in mind that nothing that you build into the Web experience should dilute or detract from your goal for the site. Any dynamic interaction that you plan into a site—even a site with the biggest budget in Web history—should always support and reinforce the primary content.

The Allstar webzine (**allstarmag.com, see page 167**) organizes its content strictly for online use rather than repurposing it as a print cousin. In addition to reading the online music magazine, users can browse through a store of related items, or tune into the sister music site.

Technology is at its best when it makes information more accessible, more engaging, and more memorable.

Although this firm (bluewaters.com) specializes in creating the latest in digital video, it chose to communicate its marketing message using large, readable type punctuated with relevant imagery in a rebus-like format. This opening screen is engaging and creates the desire to continue learning about the company's product.

The opening animation for this design firm's Web site (pivotdesign.com) is a simple animated GIF that plays off the meaning of the company name and makes it more memorable. Since GIF animations are accessible to all popular browsers, there's no need for plug-ins or browser extensions.

Choosing the Appropriate Technologies

With the concept for the Web site clearly in mind, you can move on to the concrete and practical aspects of designing the site. One of these tasks is selecting the kinds of online media you'll incorporate.

What Technology Can Do

Motion, sound, interactivity, and the standard well-designed static graphics, can help engage visitors in your site, and can also earn it a place in their memories and bring them back to enjoy it again. But with Web technology changing at a mind-boggling pace—from advancing computer capabilities to warring browsers to increasing throughput speed, plug-in mania, and new animation techniques—it's quite a trick to choose the most reliable tools for making your message accessible.

Matching the Technology to the Audience

Keep your target audience clearly in mind when it comes to choosing specific media types (text, animation, video, audio, virtual reality, and so on) and the technologies to deliver them (frames, supplemental plug-ins, Java applets, and searchable databases, for instance). If your product is high-tech and your audience is made up of early adopters of technology, then using all the latest online gadgets may be appropriate. The technology itself may be part of the appeal of the site, and potential site visitors are likely to have the computer horsepower and the plug-ins to make the technology work correctly.

On the other hand, if your product or service appeals to a more general audience, then using the latest technology could isolate your site from visitors who aren't well-equipped to experience it. It might even irritate a sizable fraction of your audience because, with the equipment they have, your site will be sluggish, unreliable, or intimidating. If you were an architect and designing a house, you probably wouldn't recommend a computerized five-zone environmental-control system with a 120-page user guide if a simple thermostat would do the job. So why use a Shockwave animation, which requires a browser plug-in to see it, when a GIF animation, which works automatically with the most commonly used browsers, will do the trick? As

technology changes, you can substitute other technologies for "Shockwave" and "GIF" in the previous sentence, but the fundamental question remains the same. In general, it's much easier to get into trouble by using too much cutting-edge technology than too little.

The use of QuickTime VR (apple.com) helps sell clothing in a virtual environment. Although it's more work to implement VR technology in a Web site, it completes the virtual shopping spree by increasing the potential buyer's "tactile" experience.

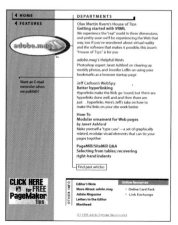

This online magazine (adobemag.com) uses PDF (portable document format) files created in a WYSIWYG page layout program and exported to Acrobat to present many of its articles. This format allows for hypertext links, the seamless integration of graphics, extensive searches, and the ability to view the document on any computer, but requires that files be downloaded and viewed with a special "reader" plug-in.

The best hand tools are effective, intuitive, and unbreakable. And when used, they feel like comfortable extensions of one's own body.

This site for recording artist Miss Angie (myrrh.com/missangie) allows the user to get up close and personal by providing insights into the musician's sources of inspiration.

This prototype of an electronics manufacturer's splash screen (Pioneer, Japan, Kazumoto Yokouchi) uses a device metaphor, complete with faux speaker grilles, to add a tangible feel to a site that is designed to respond quickly to the user's every request.

Establishing a Unified Metaphor, Personality, or Style

The design of an interface flows from its audience and its purpose—for instance, to educate, promote, or sell. Once the concept for a Web site has been developed, it's time to design the front end, the "instrument panel" or "storefront" that you'll use to deliver the site's content to its visitors. In designing the experience, it's essential to choose a metaphor, personality, or style that unifies the content and supports and clarifies the communication. Your goal is to develop an interface that's as direct, useful, engaging, and memorable as it can be. The challenge is to design something *useful* that people also *enjoy using*.

Choosing a Metaphor

One of the most effective ways of communicating is to use the familiar to explain the unfamiliar. And one way to do that is with a *metaphor*—a figure of speech, or an entire constructed environment, in which one thing is spoken of or represented as if it were another. For instance, the opening description on this page of what makes a useful hand tool, rather than being a literal description, is a metaphor that was put on the page to help communicate how the interactive components of an on-screen interface have to work in order to succeed. As another example, the Web itself is a metaphor for a network of connected institutions, individuals, and information.

If your site design uses a metaphor, it will provide a sort of physical reality for the mental space that visitors inhabit while they are there. So pick a metaphor—a printed page, an appliance, or the interior of a retail store, for example—that supports and strengthens the concept and communication process, and in no way distracts from it.

As you make your choice, consider not only how well the metaphor will work to carry your message and appeal to your audience, but also whether your budget, expertise, and other resources will allow you to carry it through effectively, and whether the metaphor is one that you'll be able to use consistently for all aspects of the communication site. Web cruisers will appreciate it if your site doesn't change the rules in the middle of the game.

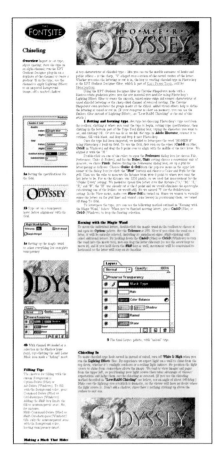

Using a flat, white page metaphor is a sensible choice for this educational site (fontsite.com, see page 146) that focuses on typography and design. Emphasis is on a clean layout and simple graphics, a good idea both for teaching effective design and for down-loading quickly.

Personality

If you don't use a physical metaphor to unify your site, it will still need its own unique identity and personality. Will the delivery of your information be "flavored" funny, techy, hip, grungy, or formal? Two Web sites developed with very similar layouts but with different personalities can provide entirely different experiences. Again, be consistent. If major parts of your site have some fairly sobering information to present, a humorous personality that works for some parts of the site may have to be scrapped in favor of a more formal personality—one that won't have to be altered in order to avoid confusing the message when the visitor gets to the central information.

The dramatic nature of this newspaper's online version (**startribune.com/aids, see page 160**) of a story about a family struck with AIDS required a sensitive approach. Black-and-white photographs and monochromatic graphics and navigation elements allow the focus to remain on the humanity of the issue, rather than the technology that delivers it.

The large type and silhouetted graphics of this online lifestyle magazine (**giantrobot.com, see page 50**), and the intentional absence of dimensional navigation elements, put it in a printed page metaphor, with an emphasis on directness and simplicity.

Style

A third contributor to the flavor of your Web site's interface design is its style—its layout, graphics, typefaces, colors, and so on. The layout of the site needs to be flexible enough to support changing content and different media types. This requires an underlying grid that at least defines areas for site or company identification, navigation elements, text, and imagery. In addition, alignment within these areas should be consistent. For instance, don't center some elements but align others left. (In general, left or right alignment supports a grid better and reads better than centering, and therefore is the better "default" design choice.) Even beyond the basic grid, always look for ways to align, and thus relate, elements to one another.

One way to characterize an interface is by the dimensionality of its graphics: 2D, "2½D," or 3D. The 2D style is similar to the printed page, with its emphasis on a structured organization of text and graphics on a flat surface. An example of the 2½D style is the beveled button, a navigation element that appears raised and clickable. Using this approach you can easily make it clear which parts of the interface are interactive. The 3D style defines a virtual three-dimensional space, where images of real-world environments and objects are used for navigation and information access.

Typically, dimensionality is closely tied with the metaphor used for the site. For instance, a newspaper or magazine metaphor is best represented in a 2D style. A 2½D style works well for an instrument panel or appliance metaphor. A 3D style can involve anything from illustrations that fake perspective to a render-on-the-fly virtual reality (VRML) representation that lets the visitor move freely through a complex environ-

In this CD-ROM about the history of the universe (*The Cartoon History of the Universe*, **see page 128**), the virtual 3D library and the Professor (the help agent shown on the flying monitor) serve as educational metaphors. To carry the interface personality further, users travel through history in the time machine, at right, a navigation device that effectively draws the user in as an active participant.

ment. But metaphor and style don't have to match perfectly. For instance, a three-dimensional metaphor such as a house can also be presented in a 2D graphical style, as a blueprint or cross-sectional drawing showing different rooms.

Like metaphor and personality, style should be consistent throughout the site. Visitors are likely to be confused if you use drop-shadowed 2D icons for the main navigation elements in one part of the site and then switch to beveled buttons or 3D elements somewhere else.

This promotional floppy-disk-based font sampler from the TreacyFaces digital type foundry begins with an animation of a 3D type specimen book that opens and enlarges to reveal details. The book metaphor alludes to the quality and craft-manship of the pre-computer days of typographic design. (**treacyfaces.com**)

By now, the novelty of "I wonder what will happen if I click this?" has worn off for most people. Organized, intuitive, and approachable will win out over scattered, mysterious, and cryptic almost every time.

Mapping Out Organization and Navigation

Most people approach a Web site with two questions in mind: "What's here for me? And how do I get to it?" In general, if a site doesn't answer these two questions immediately, visitors will be on their way to other destinations. But if they are confident that the site's content is useful, entertaining, or inspiring and they feel they have control over the process of getting to it, they're likely to stay and visit, and also come back in the future.

Shallow or Deep?

When you organize the information in a Web site, you'll feel the tension between wanting to make lots of options available on the surface so visitors don't have to do a lot of digging (a *shallow* site), and wanting to give visitors a head start on sorting out what's important, by prioritizing the information so that specific topics are layered beneath general categories (a *deep* site). In general, there should be no more than six to ten main options available on-screen at one time. Having more choices than that creates confusion, so you don't want the site to be excessively shallow. On the other hand, a visitor should be able to get to any point within the site in two or three clicks, which tends to keep the site from getting too deep. No matter how complex or seemingly simple the site, a map, directory, or navigate-by-menu section is an essential resource that provides an overview of the entire site and allows the visitor to move around comfortably and feel in control.

The Path of Least Resistance

It's up to the designer or producer to organize a site's content and create a navigation system so a typical visitor will experience the most direct and logical presentation of information the site has

It is essential to graphically represent a site's structure and organization, whether organized vertically like the tree structure, top, **(grants.com, see page 70)**, or presented radially like the hub of a wheel, below, **(jwtworld.com, see page 74)**. A site map should be descriptive, showing where each element is in relation to other elements. And it should be active—all visible on-screen elements should be *hot,* or clickable, navigation devices.

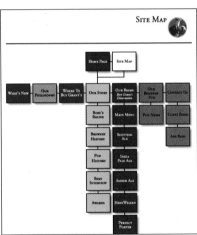

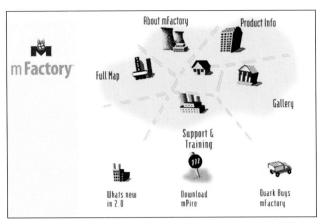

In the mFactory Web site **(mfactory.com, see page 176),** which effectively uses a simplified city plan as its metaphor, the house (home page) is surrounded by various buildings (general categories), while urban objects that represent changing options are kept separate at the bottom of the screen.

This site map **(sbg.com, see page 64)** has six main options surrounding its central "home." The contents of the two deepest sections (Partners and Portfolios) are listed individually off to the side, saving time by allowing direct access to the subsections.

to offer. No one knows better than the designer the best way to experience the site. Make this "golden path" obvious to users without *forcing* them into a linear presentation. Just like patrons at a theme park, visitors to a Web site must be given the freedom to explore and to choose where they want to go next. But just like the elements that shape the choices in a theme park (the walkways, sights, sounds, and even smells), a Web site's attractions (organization, layout, animations, prompts, and so on) should beckon the visitor along an optimized track.

Let Them Know Before They Go

Navigational choices should be intuitive, so visitors don't have to wonder "What will happen if I click this?" Links should be clear and useful, and visitors shouldn't be left stranded, with no clear way to get back to where they were before the last click.

The storyboard is the first test of whether your "tripod" of content, organization, and navigation can stand on its own.

Storyboarding the Dynamics

The storyboard is a device used to lay out the main sections and interactivity of a site. You'll start with the splash screen or home page and proceed through the information the site provides, showing how it is accessed and continuing to the point where the visitor receives the payoff. The user might not necessarily be finished with the site after receiving the payoff, but the designer and client must be confident that at some point in the user's interaction with the site the message has been delivered and understood.

Telling the Story

Through storyboarding, you'll answer the question "How does this site work?" for everyone on the design team. Using quick sketches to represent the graphical elements and brief summaries to stand in for the text, you can illustrate the individual pages or elements of the site and their relationships to one another. The pages—perhaps represented on large sticky notes so relationships and organization can easily be changed—can be tacked to a wall or spread out on a large table. In the process of setting up the storyboard to show how a user moves through the site, interacts with it, and provides input, it will become apparent where the weak points are, and you'll know whether there are major holes in the design and whether everyone on the team is "watching the same movie."

Picking It Apart

Part of the storyboarding process involves challenging your design and looking for possible gaps in the story. After your pages are in place, start exploring all the ways you can think of that a typical user *might* want to access the content. Ask yourself whether the content or organization can be simplified, made more intuitive or powerful. Play the role of the visitor who is genuinely interested in what your site has to offer but who is a nonconformist, an independent thinker, a wanderer—the guy who typically cuts across the lawn to get from point A to point B, rather than staying on the sidewalk. Are the links you've planned appropriate for this kind of visitor as well as for linear thinkers? Will the links keep visitors within the site until they reach the payoff point—downloading the information they need, ordering a widget, or mentally moving your client's brand upward in the ranks of its competitors? Or will the links distract the visitor away from the site and down a different path? Keep modifying the storyboard—removing or adding pages and moving them around to change relationships—until you're satisfied that the dynamic interaction of your site is at its most intuitive and engaging.

From a rough napkin sketch to a wall covered with sticky notes and string, there are many methods of visualizing the possible categories and relationships of information within an interactive project. The main goal is to ensure that the content is coherent and that all the trails through the forest are safe, complete, and clearly marked.

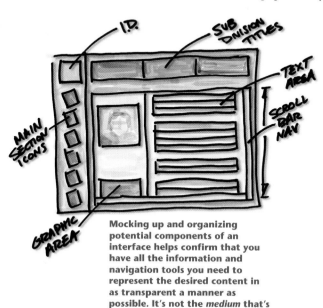

Mocking up and organizing potential components of an interface helps confirm that you have all the information and navigation tools you need to represent the desired content in as transparent a manner as possible. It's not the *medium* that's important—it's the *message*.

Remember the old axiom about planning: "Measure twice, cut once."

Sometimes you only need to take the prototype as far as is required to test your design concept.

Creating a Prototype

Taking what you learned from the storyboarding exercise, you can now make the second measurement in the "measure twice, cut once" approach to interface design. At this point you'll mock up the interface using representational navigation elements, text, and images, so you can present it—on the computer—to the uninitiated.

Making It Real

Your on-screen prototype can be as simple as a digital "slide show" with one of the creators at the controls, responding to audience prompts. Or it can be as complex as a prototyped interactive "shell" that a user can operate alone. The idea is to develop the material just enough to check whether the experience you have so carefully orchestrated will achieve the result you intended, before you commit the time and resources to produce the final layouts, text, illustrations, animations, audio, or virtual environments you may have in mind, not to mention the coding or programming that will make it all work.

Present your prototype to a mixed audience—insiders (invite the design team and the client) and outsiders (pick friends and colleagues who aren't afraid to criticize). As they explore the site, look for navigation and information ambiguities—any "What does this do?" or "So now what?" kinds of questions. As you did in the storyboarding phase, look for ways to streamline—to shorten paths and eliminate nonessential elements. Also keep your eyes open for production pitfalls, elements that were difficult to prototype and will be more difficult to execute in final form, or ideas that were easy to prototype but will be perhaps too complex to actually implement. Consider, too, the cost of updating the site and keeping the quality of the changes up to the standards set by the first edition. After the audience has had a chance to experience the entire prototype, take a deep breath, cross your fingers, and ask them to explain in their own words what they thought the goal of the site was, what the main thrust of the content was, and

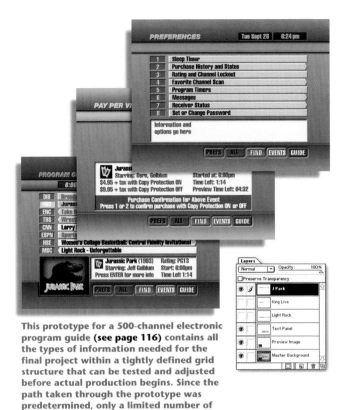

This prototype for a 500-channel electronic program guide **(see page 116)** contains all the types of information needed for the final project within a tightly defined grid structure that can be tested and adjusted before actual production begins. Since the path taken through the prototype was predetermined, only a limited number of button states had to be illustrated, as seen here, in the Photoshop Layers Palette.

One of the first challenges at the prototype stage of a Web site is the development of a layout grid that's flexible enough to hold all the potential navigation and information elements, yet structured enough to create the necessary visual continuity. In this case, this utility company's foundational grid incorporates both straight and curved guides **(Melbourne Water)**.

what action they felt compelled to take at the end of the interactive experience.

Playing It Safe

It may take a revision or two to fine-tune the prototype before it hits the predetermined target. But when you reach that point, it's a good time to cover yourself by asking the client for another sign off, accepting the prototype as the plan for the site and agreeing to pay for any client-requested future additions or revisions beyond the scope of what was agreed upon. From here on in the project, it will be harder and more expensive to make changes. So you need to make sure there is agreement on how you will proceed and who will pay for departures from the agreed-upon plan.

Any amount of time that you invest up front in establishing an organized system for design, approval, processing, and integration of assets will pay back a hundredfold later on when the going gets tough.

Gathering the Assets and Setting Standards

The next step in the process of developing the project is to determine where you will get the content, or *assets* (all the elements—text, visuals, and audio—that make up the final project) to develop the prototype into the real product. As you gather some materials and plan to create or buy others, it will be important to develop standards for the way the assets will look and sound, and how everything will be approved, processed, delivered, and backed up, during both development and final archiving.

Rounding Up Assets

As mentioned before, it's likely that some of the materials you need can be "repurposed" from existing sources—for instance, text, and even graphics stored in digital form, from brochures, annual reports, or other printed products. What can't be found will have to be created or purchased. You may be prepared to originate graphics and text, but you may also want to buy rights to assets that are currently beyond your capabilities, like animation, music, or custom code.

Once you have a clear idea of where the assets will come from, you should be able to predict their cost. This is another point at which you'll want the client to sign off on plans for the project.

Setting and Implementing Standards

To end up with a cohesive Web site, it's important to establish clear standards for content, and make sure everyone understands and follows them. One way to do this is with a *standards manual*, a document that sets up guidelines to guarantee a consistent look and feel. This manual should spell out the specific colors, typefaces, icon characteristics, illustration techniques, photograph treatments, and layout elements (windows, panels, frames, grids, and so on) that will be used in the project. It should prescribe how existing material will be treated as it's repurposed, and how new material will be designed, illustrated, photographed, digitized, recorded, coded, and archived. One

Cooktek's online marketing site (cooktek.com, see page 65) uses product photography and informational text borrowed from existing printed collateral material as the basis for its content. This content is optimized for both on-screen display and quick download.

Establishing a set of design standards, as was done for Myrrh Records music label and magazine site (myrrh.com), helps designers maintain visual consistency, thereby allowing for easier and quicker image creation, and reducing the likelihood of last-minute changes.

way to ensure that elements will be treated consistently is to develop and use *macros,* or miniprograms, such as Photoshop's Actions, to apply the same treatment to multiple elements.

And remember, with so many different processes and standards involved in a site, it's essential that the project have a manager, a point person responsible for orchestrating all the people, assets, and technologies involved in project development.

What the assembly line did for the Model T—bringing standardization, quality, and affordability to the masses—it can also do for the laborious job of asset finishing.

Utilities like the Photoshop plug-in, above, and the stand-alone application, below, that optimizes JPEG and GIF files for the Web are invaluable tools when speed, control, and consistency are important—and they are always important with projects of any significant size.

Processing, Integrating, and Archiving

Asset *processing* involves making sure that your visual and audio content is optimized for both high quality and quick download. *Integration* means combining different elements into their final form, like synchronizing animations with their accompanying sounds or applying tags and naming conventions to the assets so that when coding is completed, they will all appear as expected. *Archiving* is the final backup of all assets.

Processing

In the struggle to maintain asset quality while compressing file size, the goal is to create a system that works consistently and is easily accessible. With bandwidth increasing so that more can be downloaded in less time, and browsers and compression schemes improving almost daily, it takes diligent effort to make sure you're taking advantage of the best of the available quality and compression compromises (the balance between making the graphic as high in quality as possible and as tightly compressed as possible). Choose applications and utilities designed to optimize quality and file size and to ensure that exactly the same series of treatments is applied to all related elements.

Integrating

The integrating process involves applying formatting tags to text, naming graphics correctly, and providing details like "alt" tags (which enable users to see a text-based label in each graphics placeholder before it downloads). If you are a neophyte to the process, look to your Web site host or the person responsible for coding your site to provide you with appropriate text tags and naming conventions. Just as for a print project you would check with your printer about trapping specifications or standards for converting image files from RGB to CMYK, be sure to check with your site host about how your assets should be delivered. The host should also be able to tell you what the options are for testing the site before turning it loose on the Internet and for tracking the "traffic" to see how many people visit the site once it's posted and where they tend to go within it.

Processing and integrating assets are more complex for some projects than for others. This CD-ROM first-person role-playing game *(The Journeyman Project 3: Legacy of Time)* uses photorealistic 3D animation and advanced bluescreen techniques to synthesize virtual worlds and epic adventures. Creating the environments in Electric Image, compositing them with the live actors in After Effects, and adding elaborate special effects from Photoshop (all before even starting the optimizing process of rendering the scenes to QuickTime) took extensive planning.

Archiving

During site development you'll need backup procedures and a naming scheme that makes it clear which is the current version of each asset. There should also be a standardized system for archiving the final version of all the assets. The archive will serve both for repurposing and as a form of insurance in case some technological disaster happens. Unfortunately, backing up precious assets is too often relegated to "when we get around to it"—and disaster often strikes before we get around to it.

The programming stage is when life is breathed into the monster, and when care must be taken to ensure that no neck bolts or hairline stitches are left visible.

Assembling, Coding, Programming

It's at the point when the assets are assembled and linked with appropriate code that the whole becomes greater than the sum of its parts. This is the stage of the project where the browser wars, plug-in options, and computer idiosyncrasies can bring even the most battle-hardened Web warriors to their knees.

Keeping the Goal in Mind

As your site is assembled, remember to stay focused on communicating what the visitor needs to take away from the site and on making the visit as positive an experience as possible. If you're in doubt about how far to push the technology and your capabilities with it, keep in mind that simplicity is often best. This approach will not only reduce your own frustration level but will also work toward making the site accessible to the lowest common denominator of hardware and software within your target audience.

Taming the Technology

Although Web technology changes constantly, there are a few rules of thumb that continue to be helpful: Be cautious of "1.0" software. Often, being an early adopter means offering yourself (and your client) as late-round "beta testers" as the bugs get worked out of what will eventually be a perfectly wonderful program. Avoid the guinea pig stage—if these new ideas work, they will make it to the mainstream, usually after a round or two of refinement, and you can adopt them then.

Use software that works and has a track record, including bits of code from existing sites, which you can analyze and adapt. Remember to get in touch with the masters who have produced the code you like, tell them of your admiration, and start up a dialog. When designing for the Web it's important to have allies with whom you can trade tips and techniques.

Books also help. Although books on the nuts and bolts of putting together Web sites change almost as quickly as the technology, you can keep an eye out for the latest editions of useful titles by expert authors.

Integrating live frame-grabs from a hundred remote locations into a subscriber-based Web site—all before breakfast, seven days a week—necessitates a serious streamlining of the assembling and programming process. Here custom code and a simplified interface help to meet the need (**surfcheck.com, see page 120**).

Incorporating interactive games (even the most elementary ones based on simple moving icons, trivia, or memory tests) into a site can add an entertainment value that may be worth the added time and troubleshooting that will be inevitable while programming them (**joeboxer.com, see page 203**).

This musician's section (**myrrh.com/amygrant**) within the Myrrh Records Web site can afford new opportunities for dynamic interaction because it takes advantage of Flash technology. This object-oriented software produces graphics, sound, and animation that download quickly.

A kilobyte of prevention is worth a megabyte of cure.

This educational site (nationalgeographic.com, see page 147) uses QuickTime VR to provide a user-directed virtual walkthrough of an elaborate 3D environment. If the user does not have the QTVR extension installed, then the individual views of the rooms can still be viewed, but without the dynamic 360° interaction. It's important to make sure that if a desired piece of software is not available, or is not working right, the asset will not "break" and stop the viewer's use of the site, or worse yet, crash the user's system.

Testing, Refining, and Retesting

Testing your completed Web site is like going to the doctor for a checkup—it may be embarrassing and a little uncomfortable, but it sure beats a debilitating surprise later on. Whether it's incompatibility with a particular browser, images that look bad on-screen or don't even appear, or links that don't work, it's always better to discover the problems with your creation *before* you post your site on the Web for all the wide world to see.

Round One

The first round of testing can be a "friendly" internal test, with your "site" stored on local hard drives rather than on an external server. Try as many different browsers, plug-in scenarios, and computer platforms as your audience is likely to be using. The goal here is to check for links that don't work, graphics inappropriately saved, and layouts or type that look different from the way you intended. Fix any problems, and then take another look. Remember, this is your chance to "change your answers before you turn your paper in to the teacher."

Round Two

Now that your site is working, show it to a group of "outsiders" who are inexperienced or critical or both—possibly the same ones who picked your prototype apart—and see what works for them. Are content and navigation still clear? Have gaps developed in the logic of how the user moves around, or are resources missing that visitors have been led to expect to find at the site? And, finally, one last time, is there anywhere things can be streamlined or simplified? Fix what you can without going overboard in time or resources, and move on to the next round of testing.

Round Three

Final testing takes place after the site has been uploaded to the host server but before it has been posted for all to see. Now you can test various access speeds and try out the full range of browsers, plug-ins, and system configurations your target audience might use. Be sure to try older versions of hardware and browser software. At this stage you'll also find out if your site was relying on extra resources that were stored on your hard disk

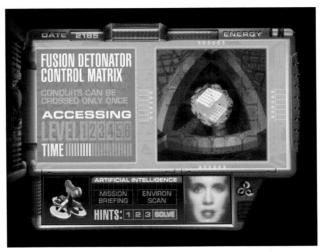

The more elaborate the interactivity, as in this deactivation game from *The Journeyman Project: Pegasus Prime* (presto.com, see page 98), the greater the possibility that the user will stumble over that one-in-a-hundred combination of "clicking this, typing that, and going there" that causes the unforeseen gremlin to arise. Testing of a project should increase exponentially with the number of possible choices within it.

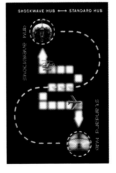

Having two versions of a site (qaswa.com, see page 180) is one way of getting around the problem of what to do with users who are not equipped with the minimum system requirements of your target audience, but who still want to help themselves to the benefits of your information. Many users, even with cutting-edge technologies available, prefer the faster load times of the "decaffeinated" version of a site.

and therefore were available in rounds one and two but are not available now that the apron strings have been cut. Take what you find in the way of incompatibilities, broken layouts, or unacceptable performance, and try to compensate—by reducing your reliance on the latest technology, or emphasizing the hardware and software requirements stated on the splash screen. If you can't bear to give up the bells and whistles and don't want to restrict your audience to those whose systems can handle them, you can still create a simpler version of the site and give people the option to choose between versions when they enter.

If nobody knows your new address, it'll be a pretty boring housewarming party.

Here are some of the many awards out there to capture and pin onto your site's lapel. For a list of 150 of the most interesting awards, try the Web site **contestnetwork.com.** And for help submitting your site for awards or for trading links and banner ads, try **accusubmit.com** or **award-it.com.**

Getting the Word Out

After all the planning, designing, producing, testing, and refining, your site will be ready to go online, where all can visit it. With a zillion sites out there and a hundred bazillion linked pages within them, your site could be harder for Web cruisers to find than the proverbial needle in a haystack. But with a little effort, you can dramatically improve the likelihood that your audience will find your site and therefore get your message.

Registering
Register your site with the appropriate online directories and search engines, so that anyone searching for a specific topic that your site covers will find you. A *directory,* either general or specialized, will usually list your site only if you make the effort to get it listed. *Search engines,* on the other hand, use automated "agents" to examine sites to determine what they are about, and then automatically add the sites to their giant databases.

To find out what directories and search engines exist with whom you might want to register, check the directory Web site **directoryguide.com.** You can register with directories and search engines one at a time by emailing a brief description (usually 250 characters or less; for tips on optimizing your site for search engines, check the Web page **submit-it.com/subopt.htm**). Some service providers offer a registration service for the sites they host, or you can use services like **submit-it.com** and **register-it.com**. If these two services don't cover some of the more specialized directories you want to reach, you still may have to contact those directories individually.

Trading Links
Links provide a way for people who are visiting related sites to find yours. You can start by working out reciprocal arrangements with sites that would benefit from being linked to yours. And whenever it's appropriate, establish a link from the credits page of your client's site back to your site—it's a very effective form of "satisfied customer" advertising.

Seeking Awards
Submit your site for awards. Even if you don't display all your awards on your site, the awarding sites will typically link to

If possible, arrange with your clients to establish links from their Web sites to your own site **(spearedpeanut.com/ artist/kentwilliams.html, see page 183).** It's one of the best ways to direct admirers of your work back to the source.

yours. Do some prospecting: Start with sites singled out for excellence by a guide that lists "cool sites," such as the well-known Yahoo site **(yahoo.com/picks).** Check those sites for other awards, and any time you notice another one, follow the link back to the awarding site and find out how to submit your site for consideration.

Using Ads—Online and Off
Many Web sites now sell banner ads; others will provide a link if you pay for it. Either may be worthwhile if the site that will display the ad is one that your audience visits often.

You can also use offline media to advertise the existence of your site. Start by including your Web address on all stationery, from letterhead to business cards, in your annual reports and brochures, in all advertising including TV spots, and on signage and company vehicles.

Starting the Buzz
Use all the avenues you and your client can think of to let people know there's a new site out there with a new service or a new angle. Put out a press release that includes a screen dump, with the aim of getting the image of your site in front of as many people as possible, whether through Web-specific magazines, computer sections of newspapers, glossy design journals, or technology-touting TV and radio shows. Mention the site in any conference or trade show appearance that you make. Participating in online special interest groups (SIGs) or chat rooms, where you or your clients freely share knowledge, can provide an opportunity to plug the Web site when people ask where they can find out more.

Like the Web sites of many creative companies, **presto.com** wears several hats. Designed to sell the richly illustrated and animated games that Presto develops, the site also provides technical support for those who have already bought the products. It presents information about the company and posts help-wanted ads when new team members are needed.

The dark backgrounds that are carried throughout the site are appropriate for displaying Presto's products, which fall within the science fiction realm and are highly graphical. Occasional text appears in small blocks, reversed out of the black background. "If our goal was to deliver a lot of information via text," says designer Tommy Yune, "we'd use black text on white pages instead. The design has to fit the communication goal."

In tailoring the site's presentation to its target audience, the Presto team realized that the home page would need to appeal to a fairly broad audience—in terms of both interest and computer equipment. In contrast, some of the internal pages could be targeted more narrowly, since the products they presented were designed to run on specific platforms, and the site designers could assume that most of the visitors who made their way to one of those pages would have at least the hardware and software needed for the game. So, for instance, no frame technology was used on this opening page, since not all site visitors would have the browsers necessary to view frames. But frames were used to organize content elsewhere in the site when the audience for the product being presented would probably be equipped to handle them. The graphical main menu on the home page was constructed as a JPEG *image map*—a single full-color graphic with several active areas that serve as buttons—because it would download faster than a dozen or more separate button graphics. The JPEG is progressive, coming into view in stages, blurred at first, to keep visitors engaged and interested until the final sharp image has finished downloading.

"We figure the home page has to 'hook' people into the site quickly," says Yune, "or they'll leave. But once they're engaged and interested, they're willing to wait for longer downloads."

The design of the Smucker's Web site (smucker.com)—from its content to the choice of graphic components and typefaces—supports the company's goal of extending and preserving brand equity. The antique style and "family" feel of the site's graphics reinforce the brand's essence—simplicity and dependability, harkening back to the old-fashioned appeal of toast and jam in the morning. "We tried to make every element, from the Clarendon type to the sepia-toned photographs from the Smucker's archives, contribute to the old-fashioned sense of the site," says designer Tim Irvine of Giant Step.

A visitor to the site can find information about all the Smucker's product lines, down to the nutrition facts about each individual product. In 1997 the site also celebrated the company's 100th anniversary by incorporating an illustrated history of Smucker's.

Technologically, the Smucker's site is relatively low-key. As a front door to the site, a quick-to-download animation shows the evolution of the jelly jar. Starting from the first products in 1897, a series of animated transitions brings the visitor up to the present design. Like the interactive Smucker's Jelly Quiz, upper right, the animation isn't so much a display of bells and whistles as an attempt to engage the visitor. "Neither the client nor we found it necessary to push the envelope of the technology," reports Giant Step's Melisa Vázquez. "In fact, it would have seemed contradictory to the brand essence."

The personality of the site may be old-fashioned, but the Smucker's company and the designers were eager to make good use of current Web technology. Smucker's is a partner in the Supermarket Shopping Network. "So if you want to put together a shopping list online," says Vázquez, "you can add items from the Smucker's site to your shopping cart and then connect to a shopping site where you can do your online ordering." The link is the Grocery Shopping button, right below the 100-year-anniversary logo on the home page shown here, above left.

2 An Interface Checklist

Interface Styles and Metaphors **34**

Backgrounds and Textures **36**

Buttons and Controls **37**

Contents and Directory **38**

Splash, Setup, and Help **39**

Windows, Panels, and Frames **40**

Typography **41**

Images **42**

Animation **43**

Video **44**

Music, Voice, and Sound Effects **45**

Virtual Reality **46**

Feedback and Response **47**

Input **48**

Layered Information and Nested Navigation **49**

Gallery **50**

For interactive information design, the interface components—and the technologies behind them—are the canvas, paints, and picture frames that are used to meet the communication challenge.

HAVING THE APPROPRIATE INGREDIENTS and a knowledge of how to use them makes the difference between a marginal cook and a masterful chef. So it is with new media. This chapter pinpoints 15 possible "ingredients" and tells what each one can contribute to a "gourmet" interface—Web or otherwise.

The trick to choosing technologies, navigational elements, and graphic techniques is to continually ask yourself whether your choice furthers the main communication goal. No matter how cool the "face" on your project may be, does it add to or detract from the content? On the following pages, you'll find hundreds of different interface components to inspire you. It's up to you to determine which types are appropriate for a particular application, and how your audience will go about using them.

Whether an interface element is appropriate or not depends on a number of factors. First, does it significantly help the communication process? Second, do you have the resources to create, process, and program the element? And third, is there a similar component or technology that could enhance the communication experience in a more elegant or cost-effective manner?

In the creative process you'll have to consider all the issues of art, technology, cognitive psychology, and marketing. Throughout this book, you will see examples of how others have successfully grappled with them.

The metaphor that's used in designing an interface not only affects the project's personality but also determines how the information will be accessed and whether the user will be drawn into the process.

Interface Styles and Metaphors

The Medium and the Message

Once a designer and client have decided on the most powerful, accessible, and memorable concept for solving the client's particular communication problem, the next job is to determine how to shape that solution into a unified experience. These pages show many such communication challenges being solved in different ways. But in the examples shown, the method of delivering the information and the media used to present it supports rather than detracts from the message itself.

2D, 2½D, and 3D Interface Design

As mentioned in Chapter 1, one way to categorize interface styles is to sort them into three simplified types. First, the 2D interface is closest to print communication, where elements are represented flat on the screen and navigation elements are distinguished from their information counterparts by clear labeling. This style is often found in interactive publications, corporate communications, or anywhere else that information needs to be presented without distractions and where exploration is not an intended feature of the communication process.

A second extremely popular interface style is 2½D. This is the familiar "beveled button" approach, where the navigation elements appear to be raised off the screen by a simulated interaction of light and shadow. The idea is to represent mechanical buttons that can be pressed to make things happen. This metaphor is connected to the world of electronic appliances, such as televisions, stereos, and VCRs.

Graphics capabilities of most computers are growing fast, and *bandwidth*, how much and how fast information can be transferred from one place to another, is also increasing rapidly. So more and more interfaces are employing the 2½D style, whose realistic-looking navigation elements and backgrounds usually require bigger files than a strictly 2D interface. Although 2½D design has been used, overused, and sometimes abused, it's still one of the most effective methods, for the simple reason that it has such a strong connection to our tangible world. The benefit to the user of being able to tell at a glance which

This marketing and portfolio site expresses its company's unique style and personality with a combination of surrealistic imagery, hand-labeled buttons, and humorous animations (**boxtop.com**). The small screen at the bottom with an animation of the company's logo, for instance, moves left and right, caught in an endless tug-of-war.

This imaginative book publisher's site (**klutz.com**) uses a tree-house metaphor, with rooms that showcase its various book titles. To move through the site the user climbs up and down the ladder. Clicking on the appropriate furniture in the room places an order or links to associated educational sites.

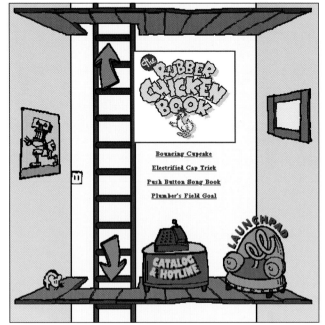

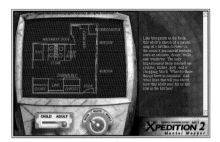

This section of an educational site (**nationalgeographic.com, see page 147**) uses a fanciful TV metaphor to present its content. It also pulls the student into the presentation with the allure of a gadget with lots of switches and knobs.

This training program for oil-rig workers (*Leave It to SEEMIS*, see page 138) uses a 3D virtual living room metaphor to coax the student through tedious technical information. The TV guide is the directory, the TV itself zooms up and fills the entire screen to deliver the course information, and the telephone rings to quiz the participant on what has been learned.

Although the interface elements used in this TV channel's Web site (sundancechannel.com, see page 84) are presented flat—without embossing or shadowing—dimensionality is achieved by overlapping typography, varying type size, and adding subtle glows and transparent color effects.

While text and illustrations are used minimally in this online portfolio, it is visually striking because of the application of color and negative space (secondstory.com). A simple layout with consistently placed frames helps focus attention on the "storytelling" that this company does for its clients.

This interactive reference tool on the human body (*How Your Body Works*, see page 132) has dozens of hot spots where a simple rollover of the cursor reveals the title of the area of interest. A click then zooms the viewer into that area, where the topic is presented with video clips, animations, and elaborate interactive explorations.

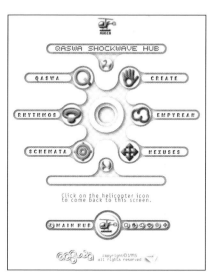

To help lift its navigation elements visually off the background, this company's online portfolio (qaswa.com, see page 180) borrows from the look and feel of embossed 2½D images on transparent Photoshop layers.

elements on the screen are for navigation and which ones are strictly for the delivery of information can't be overstated. If a user, intent on finding information, has to search or guess to figure out which elements are functional and which ones are not, then the communication process is hindered.

The third method of presenting information in interactive media is the 3D interface style. In this case the screen becomes a window into a virtual space where "hot" elements are represented as common physical objects. In these kinds of projects, the emphasis is usually on exploration, rather than simple data access. The 3D approach has the advantage of drawing users into the experience, allowing them to feel that if it were not for their interaction, many golden treasures would be left undiscovered.

A potential hazard with 3D interfaces is that the metaphor can become confusing for the user, and the very concept that was designed to encourage exploration can become a point of frustration for someone who only wants to get in, learn something specific, and then get out. But the 3D style is becoming more and more popular as virtual reality tools such as the 360-degree image panoramas of QuickTime VR or the render-on-the-fly technologies of Virtual Reality Markup Language (VRML) become more accessible.

This photographer's portfolio site (pdn-pix. com/mastermichel, see page 184) is the epitome of elegant simplicity, with its minimalist hand drawn controls and dynamic use of color.

Setting the graphic tone of a screen with a foundation background layer is the first step in the long process of building up the information elements.

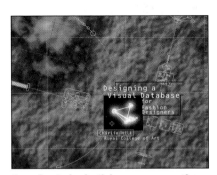

An animated celestial map serves as the backdrop for this CD-ROM design journal *(The American Center for Design Journal, see page 156).* Moving the cursor over a cryptic diagram reveals a summary of the selected project. Users click to move into the project area, or move the cursor to one of the four edges to pan the map to another destination.

Backgrounds and Textures

Laying a Foundation

Once an overall metaphor or style has been determined for a particular project, the background becomes the visual foundation for all the other graphics. Whether the interactive experience of the viewer is going to be friendly, high-tech, or ethereal is determined in large part by the background graphics. Presentation backgrounds were once only solid colors or simple color gradations. Now there are no limits to the imagery, style, and techniques that can be used to create a background. One consideration in background design that's related more to current technology than to aesthetics is the factor of file size—files can never be too small or download too quickly.

Technology Versus Art

For many projects, concerns about throughput and file size may be the determining factor that influences how project designers create background graphics. Tiled patterns or simplified graphics with large areas of flat color take advantage of lossless compression technologies using run-length-encoding in file formats such as GIF and PNG (portable network graphics; pronounced "ping").

This interactive corporate overview uses a background of sky to support a surreal series of floating doors that serve as access points to areas of interest in this promotional CD-ROM for **Clement Mok Designs.** The simple but intriguing concept for this table of contents begs the question, "What's behind the closed doors?"

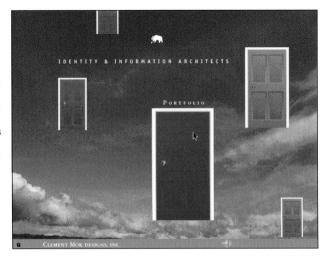

This historical CD-ROM *(Victoria Buildings and Builders)* uses changing background textures to help differentiate at a glance the many sections of the project, while keeping its main navigational elements anchored at the four corners and top and bottom center.

For this stock-music CD *(HiRez Audio)* a simple abstract background was created by applying noise and motion blur filters to a 50% gray screen. This background was then embossed to give the translucent button effect.

One of the most creative communication opportunities is the design and integration of intuitive and practical controls for the user to work and play with.

Here are examples of three possible *states* of an active button: (1) the *rest* state of inactivity; (2) the *rollover* state that shows a clickable point (a rollover can also bring up the title of the button above or below it); (3) the *active* or *mouse-down* state; upon release of the mouse button the action is started. Another option sometimes used (but not shown here) is the *ghosted* state, which shows that the button is presently inactive and unavailable for selection.

Buttons and Controls

To Bevel or Not To Bevel

Until recently, it was taken for granted that beveled buttons with embossed type or icons were the main methods for controlling an interactive presentation. But now the idea of what constitutes a navigation tool encompasses practically anything that can be imagined. With such a dramatic range of imagery for navigation and information access—some of which can be ambiguous—it's often helpful to clarify the control's purpose by putting its title under or over the button or by making the title appear on or near the button when the cursor rolls over it.

Button Mechanics

Whether buttons are 2-, 2½- or 3-dimensional, technology permitting they should be designed with two or more states. The first state, common to all buttons, is the dormant, or *rest*, state— the way the button looks when it's waiting to be activated. The second state, which most buttons have, is the *active* state—the button looks different once it's clicked, and the change can even be accompanied by a sound effect. A third, intermediate, state is the *rollover* state, a highlighted condition that happens any time the cursor moves over a clickable button or is sent to it by using an arrow or tab key. This in-between state can be used to help the user keep track of where the cursor is, to make a button say "push me," or to have the title of the button appear for clarification.

Software developer MetaCreations **(Bryce 2, see page 110)** is famous for its innovative interfaces, whose uniquely designed tools and controls pull the user in to explore the program.

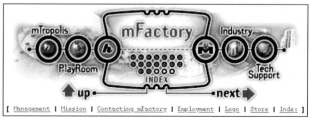

Including hypertext links at the bottom of a Web page in addition to the graphic controls ensures that all users will be able to navigate the site **(mfactory.com, see page 176).**

The navigation controls for Studio Archetype's Web site **(studioarchetype.com)** serve a dual purpose. They not only show the available options, but each also serves as a labeled tab for the currently active section.

gallery

magazine

interaction

Shadows add dimension and provide an easy way to distinguish between elements that provide choices (as shown here) and those that simply illustrate ideas **(surfermag.com, see page 162).**

These variations on the beveled button maintain a unified look and feel by using a circular shape and an understated color scheme, and by making sure the iconographic style and line weights are kept consistent **(pmdraid.com).**

The most important screens in an interactive project are a clear and complete home page and an accompanying directory or site map These allow the user to feel grounded and secure within the potential labyrinth of information.

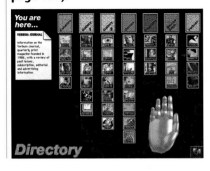

Contents and Directory

You Can't Beat Books!

For a Web site to be successful, its overall scope and main sections need to be quickly and easily understood by the user. Printed publications are usually quite good at presenting such an overview. With a table of contents and pages that you can flip through in moments, it's easy to gauge the size, scope, and style of a book or magazine. So in many cases print is still the most flexible and practical medium for delivery of linear information.

Topics and Subtopics

Borrowing from books, most sites use a table of contents screen as the foundation or "home" from which the viewer will venture forth into the maze of information. This screen usually lists the major divisions of the project, just as a printed table of contents lists the chapters of a book or the features and departments in a magazine.

At least equally important is an overall directory, an expanded table of contents, or map, of the entire interactive piece. This directory makes available not only all the main "chapters" but also subsections and sometimes even finer divisions. The idea is that from this one location the user can go to any other point in the piece with one or two clicks, rather than descending level by level through layers of information, never quite sure whether the journey will lead to the destination that houses the sought-after data.

This corporate Web site (adobe.com, see page 68) uses two labeled horizontal bars to list all the main sections of the site. The selected main section title remains present and highlighted as the user moves down into a subsection of the site, which also has its own horizontal navigation bar. This hierarchy shows at a glance exactly where you are.

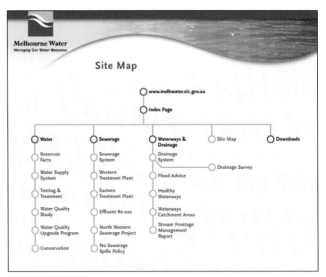

A simple "subway" map shows the organization of this utility company's Web site prototype (**Melbourne Water**) and enables users to quickly understand the scope of the site and navigate through its contents.

The three main destinations—Index, Home, and Contact— are presented as simple labels and are always available on each page in the lower right corner of this design firm's Web site (kuester.com). When Index is selected, instead of changing to an entirely different screen, only the central information panel changes and is replaced with a short text-based overview of the five main subsections, bottom.

When the interface is complex, it's the user's right—and the designer's responsibility—to have Help available on-screen.

Splash, Setup, and Help

The First Impression

Often a victim of the frantic rush at the end of the production process, the initial splash screen (with accompanying setup instructions), and the Help system sometimes don't get the design attention they deserve. This is too bad, because it's the splash screen that offers the first taste of what the interactive experience is going to be like. And without clear instructions on how to use any unique features of the product or site (including links to any necessary browser extensions), the user is doomed to a lonely trial-and-error attempt to get the darn thing to work.

Always by Your Side

Accessible from anywhere in the program, interactive Help explains how the interface works, sometimes down to the last slider or button. Help can come in many forms; from *balloons*, explanatory tags that pop up when the cursor rolls over some screen feature, to a personable *video agent*, or *talking head*, who provides a practical guiding hand. Building technical support into the setup screen or the online help is likely to be a big benefit to the user. It's also likely to please the client by cutting down on the number of phone calls from frustrated users trying to figure out the company's new resource.

To help install the basic files needed to run this educational CD-ROM *(The Cartoon History of the Universe,* **see page 128), an installer program (1) searches the user's system for possible conflicts with extensions, inits, and currently running applications; (2) moves the potentially conflicting software temporarily; and (3) puts it back in place when the installation is finished. This transfers the burden of conflict resolution to custom software, rather than leaving it to trial-and-error sleuthing by the user.**

Bold, colorful graphics and typography combined with humorous and sometimes sassy remarks (from cyberspace drinking buddies) establish a casual attitude on the Kahlúa Web site's introductory screen (kahlua.com). The message and specific beverage are continually swapped out so visitors returning even minutes later will find a different welcoming statement and Kahlúa cocktail awaiting them. A disclaimer for viewers younger than the drinking age also appears on the splash screen, as well as the thoughtful and practical notice that turning off the audio portion of the presentation will help with slower computers.

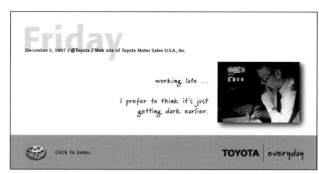

Starting off each entrance to this car manufacturer's site (toyota.com, see page 86) with the current date and a quote-of-the-day makes users immediately feel like they have come to a place that's dedicated to current information and a unique personal experience. Contributing to a feeling of familiarity, the splash screen displays the two main components of the corporate identity, which are also used in both print and TV campaigns— a graphic symbol, a logo, and a familiar slogan.

This design firm's Web site (cow.com) provides a good example of how to immediately grab a user's attention and engage the imagination. A set of children's blocks illustrates the company name. The blocks rearrange themselves daily, and the greeting changes, so the site always keeps a fresh face before the public.

Information can't be left to simply float about on the screen. It has to be put in context, framed in windows and panels that are tied consistently and clearly to an underlying grid.

One primary goal of design is to create a unified whole that's more than the sum of its parts. This unity, or visual *gestalt*, can be derived by grouping objects with similar functions together and keeping their styles consistent. For example, here are four ways to organize six buttons with two distinct functions.

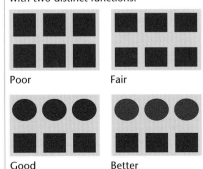

Poor   Fair

Good   Better

Windows, Panels, and Frames

The Framework
Information overload—which characterizes this turning of the century—has the potential to mushroom out of control in interactive media projects. Just like the printed page, a Web site interface benefits from an underlying grid that organizes all the on-screen windows, panels, and frames. This layout grid for the main areas of information needs to be flexible enough to accommodate a wide variety of different information types (like scrolling blocks of body copy, video clips, spot illustrations, and order forms), yet rigid enough to provide a consistent skeleton that unifies the design.

Grouping
In their most effective state, all the elements of an interface work together. Applying grouping principles of similarity and proximity, the designer visually organizes information and creates a unified whole for the communication process. Unifying the appearance of similar functions and grounding them to a foundational grid (using consistent windows or frames), will make navigation more intuitive for the user, and the project's content will be more accessible. This organization supports ease of use by moving the process of recognizing elements and their purposes from the left side of the brain (analytical) to the right side (intuitive).

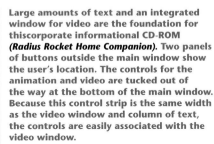

Relying on an underlying grid for its organization, the U.S. Senior Open 98 Web site (**usseenioropen98.com**) displays a number of different kinds of information about the event simultaneously. This site takes advantage of both horizontally and vertically scrolling windows, as well as a fixed navigation frame on the left to maintain organization, clarity, and consistency. To add a unique touch, the corners of the rectangles are rounded, like the PGA Senior Tour logo. Type size and color help to prioritize information.

Large amounts of text and an integrated window for video are the foundation for thiscorporate informational CD-ROM (*Radius Rocket Home Companion*). Two panels of buttons outside the main window show the user's location. The controls for the animation and video are tucked out of the way at the bottom of the main window. Because this control strip is the same width as the video window and column of text, the controls are easily associated with the video window.

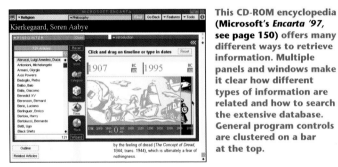

This CD-ROM encyclopedia (Microsoft's *Encarta '97,* see page 150) offers many different ways to retrieve information. Multiple panels and windows make it clear how different types of information are related and how to search the extensive database. General program controls are clustered on a bar at the top.

The CD-ROM version of Larry Gonick's 350-page comic book *The Cartoon History of the Universe* (see page 128) also uses the traditional panels of the comic strip format, even though the stories are framed within a panel of high-tech controls and interactive animations.

Typography and pixels— a marriage made in . . . ?

TYPE ON-SCREEN: A NECESSITY

When selecting a typeface for on-screen text blocks, consider these suggestions: (1) Use the largest typeface that works— if possible, stick with 10- to 12-point or larger. (2) Use a typeface whose lower-case letters have a large x-height. (3) Whenever possible, follow the professional design standards of the printed page—enough leading (line spacing), correct word breaks (which should be kept to a minimum), and no widows (a short single word on a line by itself at the end of a paragraph). (4) Keep the number of different typefaces to a minimum.

As more designers use the computer screen as the final destination for their work, more font suppliers are creating type specifically for on-screen purposes. Above are 12-point samples of Adobe's Web-optimized typefaces Minion (the serif typeface at the top) and Myriad (the two sans serif samples). Notice the large body size of the lowercase letters. The smooth antialiased samples on the left are typical of type rendered as a graphic, while the aliased versions on the right are charac-teristic of "live" editable text.

Typography

Making Text the Best It Can Be

One of the biggest challenges of working in a screen-based environment is conveying a lot of information through the use of typography. With only 72 pixels per inch in standard computer monitors, the potential for jagged and hard-to-read text is high. A 10-point letter (usually the smallest size that's used for body copy) typically uses only 10 pixels vertically to determine its strokes and serifs, if it has any, and even fewer pixels horizontally. With this in mind, there are two important principles for preparing text for the screen: First, write the copy in the form of short, concise paragraphs much as you would write captions. Second, integrate *hypertext links* whenever text is getting too long or too specific for the typical user. Also, there's a big plus for the user if an interactive presentation allows text to be copied so it can be pasted into other working documents.

Different Strokes: Display Type

For display typography, the best way currently to get large, smooth-edged type is to render it in a pixel-based program like Photoshop or Painter and then bring it into the interactive environment as a graphic, just like an illustration. This can increase file size significantly over live text, but it assures that the beautiful letterforms stay beautiful and that type styles will be maintained, no matter what System or browser users employ. (If your site is already using a plug-in like Flash as a standard, then converting any large display type outlines in a program like Illustrator or FreeHand will also allow it to be displayed accurately and with antialiasing.)

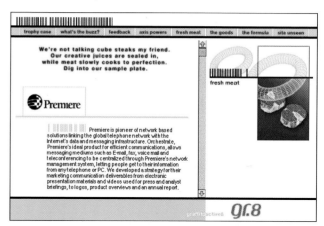

This subtle glow of color calls attention to the antialiased intro-ductory text type in this design firm's Web site (gr8.com, see page 187). The body copy below is kept live so it can be quickly updated, so it remains in an aliased typeface that's available on the user's computer.

The main navigation tools in this CD-ROM magazine (*Verbum Interactive*, see page 164) are in the lower right corner and allow the user to move between major sections. The story control panel, grounded to the bottom of the main text panel, has buttons for printing the article, and for moving forward and back within the text, and includes the current page number). A small running man icon shows whether any animations are associated with the article. A shrink-and-expand box gives the user control of the text block's size and position on-screen.

On the home page of the Sundance Film Festival 1998 Web site (sundancefilm.com, see page 84), large sans serif headline type, which interacts with the fine lines of a Mondrianlike grid, was created as a graphic to retain the integrity of the type. Type size and bright warm colors are used to show emphasis.

From cave paintings to Photoshop files, mankind has told stories and communicated concepts through pictures for centuries.

These graphics were originally created for a book and then later repurposed for use in this publisher's Web site (**klutz.com**). The flat areas of color lend themselves very well to the compression algorithms of the GIF format.

Images

You Say "Tomato" . . .

In theory, as long as the communication is clear, there's no limit to the variety of imagery that can be used to help the viewer see the information in an interactive presentation. Images can be realistic, symbolic, or abstract, created in any style or with any technique and then adapted for viewing on-screen. But in practice, planning the imagery for a Web site usually involves a compromise between the desire to choose a concept that's creative and takes full advantage of the beauty of the medium, and the drive to make good, economical use of resources already available, not to mention the challenge to make the graphical end result as quick to download as possible.

Where Does It All Come From?

The images for an interactive presentation can be created from scratch, assembled from stock art or photography, or adapted from existing material. In any case, images must always be specially formatted for the low-resolution, narrow-bandwidth environment of the Internet. As the examples in this book show, there are many different paths to pleasing results, depending on whether the imagery is in the form of line art, flat-color graphics, or continuous-tone imagery such as photos or paintings.

These dynamic spot illustrations by John Lycette for Carbon's interactive puzzle **Paper Machine** show the attention to detail and creative thought that can go into even the smallest elements. Click on the numbers (right) to fold the paper airplane; when it's complete, it flies away.

These spot illustrations by Steven Salerno for the J. Walter Thompson Web site typify the overall style of the advertising agency's site (**jwtworld.com**, see page 74) and are actually navigation elements. Playful and expressive, they show just how far interactive multimedia has come from the days when simple shapes and spartan iconography were the only design elements used for navigating presentation interfaces.

The whimsical **Bettmann Archive** screensaver uses 20 images from the extensive collection, which are cut into four horizontal strips and randomly reassemble to create thousands of amusing combinations. Eventually the four segments of one image come together to complete a single face and the Bettmann name appears on-screen to promote the Archive.

To help unify the increasingly diverse images that are needed in the Discovery Channel's Web site (**discovery.com**, see page 94) to illustrate upcoming and current programming, designers use a consistent grid with maximum and minimum size descriptions and a simple rule-and-text label.

As a modern-day sage once said, "A picture is worth a thousand words, but if it moves, shheeee-it!"

Not all "animations" have to move. Consider, for example, this demonstration of how to make someone believe a muffin can bounce. This sequence of images from a publisher's Web site (**klutz.com**) shows sample illustrations from the publications it offers for sale. These images show that paramount in communicating motion is not necessarily the motion itself but the communication of a concept in a way that's appropriate, engaging and memorable.

Animation

Why Animate?

One of the chief principles of storytelling, especially in cinematography is "show, don't tell" what you want to convey. It's dramatically more memorable to *see* a concept demonstrated than to hear or read a description of it. With animation, even more brainpower and imagination are brought to bear, so a user's understanding and recall can both increase dramatically.

Before Going Off Half-Cocked . . .

Adding extensive animation to an interactive presentation or Web site can be expensive, in both money and time. So before you commit these resources to animation, it pays to ask yourself three questions about your project: Will animation improve the delivery of the type of information you need to convey? Are sufficient resources—production budget, researched content, and capable talent—available for building the animations? And will it be reasonably quick and easy for the user to download and playback the animation? If the answer to any of these questions is "no," the cost of animating may outweigh the benefits for that particular project. A series of step-by-step illustrations may do just as well, with less cost for both the developer and the user.

Which Technology This Week?

Motion on the Web and methods to deliver it change and improve constantly. One relatively new advance being added to the staples of simple GIF animations and QuickTime movies is vector-based graphics treatment like that used in Macromedia's Flash, which describes imagery as mathematical shapes, or *vectors*, that can be animated on the fly rather than drawn frame-by-frame and pixel-by-pixel as in raster-based animation. Vector animations can be dramatically smaller in file size and can be scaled dynamically without degrading the quality of the image. To download plug-ins and to see a live demonstration, check out **real.com** or **macromedia.com/flash.** Or, you can download the plug-ins from *The Web Design Wow! Book* companion CD-ROM located in the back of this book.

This bookseller's Web site (**barnesandnoble.com**) uses Flash software and its vector-based animation format for promotional teasers. This method of describing moving graphics allows for quick download times because only the mathematical descriptions of the shapes, fills, colors, and motion paths are downloaded, and only when these tiny files reach the user's computer are they converted to pixels. The vector-based nature of this technology also allows for on-the-fly scaling of the design for different screen resolutions.

These *sprites,* or animated objects, are from the 3D-based environment of the **Leave It to SEEMIS** interface **(see page 138)** and are shown in their different states of ringing. One of the first steps in animating sprites for interactivity is to figure out how many states are needed in order to present the action effectively.

In this opening series of screens on the **Clement Mok Designs** interactive CD-ROM portfolio, three definitions for the word *architecture* go in and out of focus one at a time while a voice-over reads them in turn. The combination of well-chosen words, superimposed imagery, simple animation, and voice-over makes this a very effective animated opening segment.

Video on the Web has the potential to dramatically add to the communication process. Even on a computer screen, there's something captivating about a live encounter.

Video

Shooting for the Little Screen

With the addition of interactive video clips, the personality, credibility, clarity, and human interest of a presentation goes up dramatically. Even in small windows, videos of live people are a dramatic improvement over text explanations or *voice-overs*, narration by an unseen speaker.

Although video clips may be viewed at a small frame size and limited frame rate, the filming and digitization quality of the original video should be at a professional level. The days of shooting with home video cameras using table lamps perched nearby for lighting are long gone.

Here are some things to consider when shooting talking heads for the small screen: (1) Use theatrical actors—their training in delivery and subtle exaggeration suits tiny windows and slow frame rates well. (2) Change camera angles regularly for extended clips, just like the evening news. (3) Incorporate the spokesperson into the presentation as if he or she were talking solely to the individual user.

Too Much of a Good Thing

Like on-screen text, video in multimedia can be overdone. Just as too much body copy can be painful to read because of the low resolution of the computer screen, too much linear video, no matter what the quality or how fast it can be streamed over the Internet, can be frustrating when a person is expecting a more interactive experience. Whenever appropriate, break up the videos into short segments, "paragraphs" that contain a single concept.

When it comes to how a project displays and controls video, the possibilities are endless. In this role-playing game (*The Journeyman Project: Pegasus Prime,* see page 98), the shape of the video window has been distorted to fit into an imaginary overhead display, while another video stream is composited into the background.

The challenge in the *Interactive Roundtable* CD-ROM project was to create an interactive panel discussion in which the viewer actually seems to direct the discussion between the speakers (see page 136). Here the user can select from several topics and choose a speaker to reply to the question, or let any of the panelists ask his own question, which can then be answered by other panelists. This back-and-forth use of video based upon an extensive database of questions and answers makes excellent use of the strengths of multimedia.

Past experience with video leads us to think that this kind of imagery has to be presented in a horizontal rectangular format with a 3:4 aspect ratio. But there's nothing inherent in the video playback process that says this must be the case (though keeping its dimensions to increments of 16 pixels can sometimes help with playback). In the *Herman Miller Aeron Chair* presentation, top, and the *Surfology 101* CD-ROM, small video windows have been vignetted on backgrounds whose color and texture match the main background of the screen. This technique incorporates the video seamlessly into the background so the elements on the screen, including the text overlay, are unified.

All you need to do is watch your favorite movie with the volume turned down to realize the powerful impact that carefully crafted music, voice, and sound effects have on the communication process.

Music, Voice, and Sound Effects

If a Web Page Falls in the Forest . . .

There are many roles for sound in interactive design: Sound effects and spoken words can deliver essential information; music or environmental sound can weave an audio texture, strengthening the emotion and personality that underlies a concept; and sound can fill in a gap in the action while something is downloading or the site is waiting for the user to respond.

Making It Sound Good

It's hard to ignore bad sound. Viewers are less likely to be distracted if the color is a little off or the type is pixelated than if the sound is scratchy or muffled. But for a designer, getting good sound can be one of the most daunting tasks in multi-media. Many of the elements that go into a project—illustrations, photographs, diagrams, and typography—are familiar to designers because of their experience with the printed page. Even animation and video are largely visual—pictures in motion. But sound and music pull interactivity into a completely new dimension, one that requires a different kind of expertise.

There are many fine "clip" music resources and sound effects available, but nothing can compete with music that's professionally composed, performed, and recorded solely to support and strengthen the concepts behind a unique on-screen project.

Some of the most elaborate uses of music, voice, and sound effects in the digital realm can be found in interactive adventure games, like *The Journeyman Project 2: Buried in Time* (see page 92). As in any movie, the soundtrack creates the mood, clues the viewer to what's currently happening on-screen, and creates anticipation about what's coming next. These same storytelling and cinematic principles can also be used effectively in a corporate presentation or an online encyclopedia.

By using streaming audio technology, such as RealAudio, the Sci-Fi Channel's Web site (**scifi.com, see page 104**) is able to offer dozens of long-playing radio dramas on demand, opening up an entirely new avenue of broadcasting.

If project developers choose not to use audio that streams continually off the Net, another option is to offer short specific clips that can be downloaded and played back separately, as in the Testing the Human Spirit section of the *Star Tribune* site, above (**startribune.com/aids, see page 160**). Downloading bypasses the need for additional browser plug-ins to receive streaming audio, but it also takes the audio out of the integrated interactive experience.

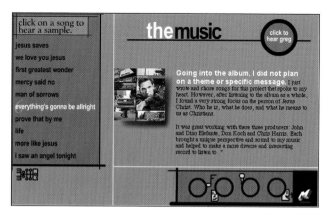

The Myrrh Records (**myrrh.com**) uses the extensive sound capabilities of Flash to include background musics and sound effects, and also to let the user play song clips and artist interviews on demand.

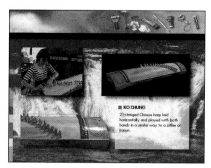

To introduce unusual instruments from around the world the *Xplora1* (see page 102) shows a video of a musician playing an instrument, along with a still photograph and a written description of that instrument. It also lets the viewer play the instrument and hear its unique sounds. This interactivity and immediacy encourage the quest for similar satisfying and creative experiences.

Although virtual reality is still in its infancy, it's likely to become one of the most potent communication tools ever devised.

Apple's QuickTime VR technology is used here in this *Herman Miller Aeron Chair* presentation to let the viewer freely spin a three-dimensional model of the Aeron chair, a new ergonomic office chair. Letting users actually "get their hands on" a product can add dramatically to understanding and to marketing success.

Interactive adventure games like *The Journeyman Project* (see page 98) that use prerendered 3D graphics and animations set a new standard for realism. Now corporate communications, marketing, and educational CD-ROM titles and Web sites also put these techniques to extensive use.

Virtual Reality

Cyberspace, the Final Frontier

Three kinds of technologies are used to simulate the experience of moving around in a virtual space: *rendering-on-the-fly, prerendered,* and *interactive panoramas.* With the render-on-the-fly method, images of the environment are rendered as the viewer moves around in real time, determining what part of an environment to look at simply by pointing a cursor, moving a joy stick, or operating a head set or data glove. The imagery usually isn't very detailed, since it is being generated while you watch. VRML (virtual reality markup language) uses the render-on-the-fly method.

A second method of creating the impression of motion through a space is to prerender a series of images simulating a walkthrough in a 3D environment, and then play these images back as an animation once the user chooses a particular path. These prerendered walkthroughs allow for an incredible amount of realistic detail in the scene but lack the spontaneity inherent in rendered-on-the-fly scenarios, where there is no predetermined path through the environment.

The third way of imitating spatial reality is through technology like QuickTime VR, in which a series of photos or rendered views of a scene are stitched together into a seamless 360-degree panoramic "cylinder" or "sphere," to give the viewer the sense of standing within the environment. QuickTime VR and its counterparts can also create environments where the viewer is stationary and an object rotates on its own axis, as if the person were turning it, and looking at it from different angles.

Speed, Flexibility, or Realism

Virtual reality can add dramatically to the first-person experience of interactive communication. And as the technologies improve, we'll continue to get closer to the "holodeck" we all long for. For now, render-on-the-fly offers the most freedom and flexibility, and the best playback speeds on the Web. Prerendered movies give viewers photorealistic glimpses into nonexistent worlds, and 360-degree panoramas provide dramatic (and relatively easy) ways to add to the sense of being there that citizens of the Net can enjoy.

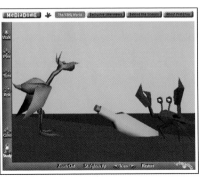

With the popularity of interactive adventures like *The Journeyman Project* and *Myst,* the virtual environment experience is being used more and more in original storytelling as in this ongoing VRML cartoon adventure, Driftwood, by Protozoa (**protozoa.com**).
copyright Protozoa 1998

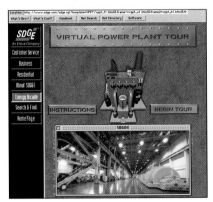

The San Diego Gas & Electric Web site (**sdge.com**, see page 82) uses QuickTime VR to allow the viewer to explore a power plant's generator which would otherwise be off-limits to the general public.

We live in a physical world where each action generates a reaction. So feedback is vital to making the experience feel real.

LAYERS IN ACTION

To allow for flexibility in designing and redesigning interface components in Photoshop, always keep your background, your main design elements, and all your navigation buttons (and their different states) on separate layers.

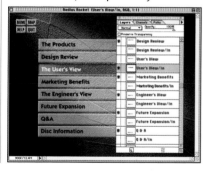

Feedback and Response

What Have I Done?

When people click a button or make a choice on-screen, they want some kind of feedback that lets them know that their request has been acknowledged and that something will happen as a result. Many of the familiar multimedia responses are imitations of real-world counterparts—a switch makes a clicking sound, a light flashes on, a dimensional button goes from its "outie" to its "innie" state, a border is highlighted, type changes color, or a status line reports on download progress.

Where Am I? And Where Have I Been?

For centuries, running heads at the top of the page in books have identified the chapter title, acting as immediately accessible location markers. Bookmarks or dog-eared page corners have marked the places where readers want to return. Multimedia users need similar guideposts so they won't unwittingly cover the same territory again, and so they can revisit an especially interesting spot. Transferring the memory burden from user to computer whenever possible is important to a successful interface. For example, the Web's standard procedure of changing the color of underlined hot text that has already been clicked on, especially where multiple words on different pages link to the same destination, establishes a "been there, done that" trail for the site visitor to use as a reference.

The table of contents for an educational Web site (**cccnet.com, see page 144**) uses enlarged versions of section icons with an added drop shadow to instantly show users where they are in the scope of the presentation.

The sliders on this interactive machine in the virtual world of Xpedition Hall (**nationalgeographic.com, see page 147**) make users feel confident that their actions will elicit a response because the device metaphor is familiar.

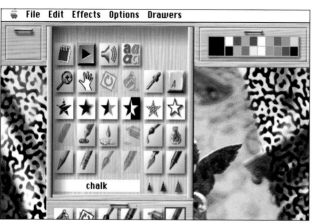

Aside from the depressed dimensional button on a tool panel or a change in the cursor, most software applications offer very little response to tell the user a viable tool has been chosen. This interface from a popular paint program, **Art Dabbler (see page 112)**, uses animated pull-out drawers and associated sound effects to let artists know they're in a friendly, familiar space—one that will immediately respond to their requests.

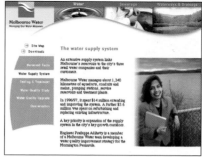

The Melbourne Water utility company's prototype site (**Melbourne Water**) emphasizes the currently opened section by screening back the headline labels of the two nonactive sections and turning their normally full-color graphics into duotones. The background color for the title of the subsection currently being viewed, on the left-hand side, changes to match the main background.

In a truly interactive presentation, the user can not only acquire sought-after information, but also request individualized interaction.

The Mackerel Web site has a button designed as a 2¢ postage stamp, which

leads to an area where users can give their feedback, or "two cents' worth." **(mackerel.com, see page 174)**

Input

Two-Way Communication

To move from a linear slide show to a truly interactive communication experience, there must be some way for users to make their interests and preferences known. Without some method of input, users realize that nothing about their experience is unique. They quickly figure out that all the facts, figures, information, and experiences they encounter are the same ones anyone else viewing the project would experience. But with the simple addition of preferences, a feedback questionnaire, or a search function, the experience can be made to feel individually tailored and unique.

Beyond Pushing Buttons

User input can be for ordering, testing, diagnosing, or setting up preferred methods of accessing information. Any of these opportunities for participation or customizing the interaction can significantly improve the electronic communication experience.

By starting off the communication experience with a congenial "How Do You Feel?," the Kahlúa Web site **(kahlua.com)** immediately gets the user involved as a participant, not just a viewer. The approach here is to use the smiley face buttons as a mood meter, allowing for personalized interaction without getting bogged down in unnecessary technology or text-based responses. Voice-overs prompt you to finish your drink, to choose an area to visit, far right, or to surf the Net using the search engine provided on Kahlúa's navigation tool. If you use the search feature, the tool and drink travel with you as you surf.

Allowing visitors to forward gems of information found at a favorite site to Web-linked buddies via a built-in email service is a great way of adding value to a site, as well as pulling in new users **(epicurious.com, see page 154).**

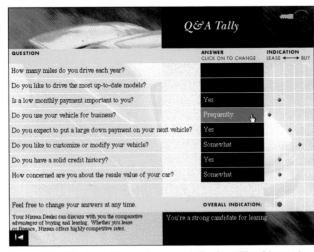

Even a simplified question-and-answer tally sheet like this one in the *Nissan Interactive* presentation **(see page 80)** goes a long way toward increasing the user's feeling of control in determining what sorts of information are presented.

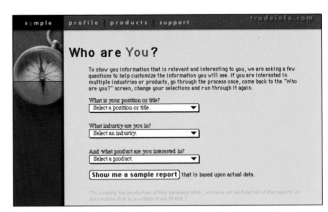

There are many benefits to getting a profile of users as they interact with your site—from market research, to supplying customers with product updates, to customizing the presentation experience itself. This information supply firm **(tradeinfo.com)** uses a short multiple-choice interview and the resulting industry report to tailor a presentation of the benefits of its services for potential clients.

To avoid visual information overload, elements that aren't essential at the moment can be tucked away.

Layered Information and Nested Navigation

I Want It When I Want It—But Not Before

Because of the nonlinear searching that computers do so easily, multimedia is one of the best methods yet invented for communicating an extensive, complex body of information. But prioritizing and linking are not new approaches to organizing knowledge. Layered information has been around for a long time—footnotes and end notes in a book, for example. The idea is to make related or supporting information about a particular subject easy to find when the user wants it, but to tuck it out of the way until then, so it doesn't interfere with the main flow of communication. In interactive presentations, layering reduces screen clutter, which makes it easier for the user to see the major choices that are available at the moment.

The main navigation buttons in an electronic magazine (*Verbum Interactive*, see page 164) are the three squares at the right end of the power bar, above. Clicking the leftmost of these three buttons activates the bar, which extends to reveal buttons for the seven sections of the publication. Clicking any of these buttons opens a pop-up menu that shows the articles available within that section. A great deal of navigation information is packed economically into a series of small buttons.

A Guided Journey

Layering or submerging information until it's needed works for navigation as well as for information content. As mentioned in Chapter 1, just as the planners of theme parks direct visitors along particular routes with signage, sound, color, even the architecture of the pathways and the smells that waft through the air, so interface designers should layer navigation clues to guide people to what's likely to be the most direct and rewarding path through the multimedia experience. And yet full access to any destination must be available at all times—just as theme park visitors can choose to go off the beaten path and explore on their own. For complex site maps or directories, pull-down or pop-up menus are effective tools for layering navigational choices. Choosing from pull-down or pop-up menus requires a three-step mousing process of click, drag, and release, but menus can hold a large number of destinations within a very small space.

By putting as many small thumbnail samples as possible on-screen at once, the TreacyFaces Web site (**treacyfaces.com**) lets users quickly compare options before focusing on a specific typeface for a closer view.

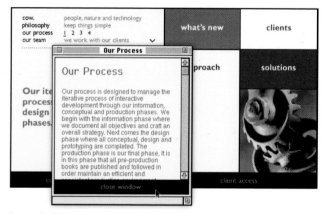

Instead of jumping visitors around to different areas of the site as they request information, the design firm Cow brings the information to them in manageable amounts (**cow.com**). Small overlapping windows pop up with details, then are put away when the user is finished with them.

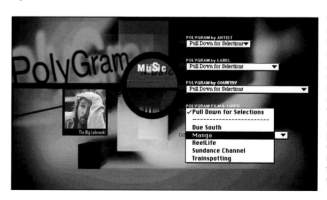

The many destinations within the Polygram Web site (**polygram.com**) were organized into five main sections, each of which was then divided into smaller subsections with pull-down menus. Thus the home page remains simple and practical, rather than overwhelming with too many options fighting for attention at one time.

The Giant Robot site (**giantrobot.com**) was designed to complement and help promote the original print version of the magazine. A cultural magazine directed to young, hip Asian Americans, the print version had existed long before the Web site. But the response to the online version among readers was so positive that editor Ed Nakamura and designer David H. K. Yu have been developing new aspects of the online version.

Much of the content of the Giant Robot site is repurposed from the printed magazine, though the site has more illustrations, and the text is sometimes shortened. One advantage of the Web site is that past issues of the printed magazine can be made available on-screen.

The emphasis at the Giant Robot site is on content rather than technology, though interactivity is provided through email so that visitors can correspond with the magazine's staff. Plans for the future include new sections of the online magazine that aren't in the printed version, and perhaps sound and video.

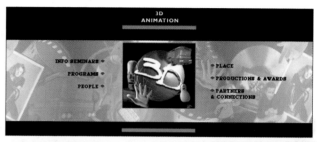

The **Vancouver Film School** (VFS) Web site (**vfs.com**) is designed to market the courses available at the school and to educate people about the wide range of programs the school provides. Broader in scope than its name indicates, the school makes an effort through the Web site to let people know that its subject areas extend to multimedia, 3D animation, classical animation, and acting.

"A second goal of the site," says Susan Janzen, Web site administrator, "is to provide a venue where students of the school can display their talents and what they have learned. Students can use it as an online resumé, portfolio, or calling card when they've finished their courses and are looking for work." The site also provides a way for students to communicate directly with instructors.

The VFS site has evolved through three previous designs (near right), to arrive at the current home page (above), with each new design getting simpler, requiring fewer clicks for visitors to get where they want to go. To unify the site, its color scheme is maintained throughout, and to cut download time while giving each section's opening screen its own unique look, the background stays the same while a small central element changes (far right).

"We use a bit of Java to brighten up the site," says Janzen, "but we leave a lot of the high-tech components to the students, so they can show off what they've learned. We do use QuickTime VR to allow prospective students to view our multimedia labs. But animation, video, and audio are found mostly in student projects and galleries."

3 Five Design Reminders

We all benefit from having our work critiqued, but better to have it done in the soft light of concept introspection than in the harsh glare of product failure.

WITH THE WIDESPREAD USE OF CD-ROMS and the popularity of the World Wide Web, communicators finally have the audience—the critical mass—to attract the courageous clients, the talented designers, and the insightful publishers away from their print-only caves and into the world of communicating via the screen.

Theme Parks and Chat Shows

In working with interactive media, designers look to the familiar, the established—things they've designed, or at least observed, before—to use as a jumping-off place. Is the interactive project designed as if it were a coffee-table book? Or is the process more like putting together a conference room slide presentation? Maybe it's closer to producing a TV documentary or talk show. Interactive media can incorporate aspects of all of these methods of communicating information: Print, TV, slides, movies, music videos, and even theme parks are all sources of inspiration for the creative process of designing on-screen experiences.

Pinned to the Wall

What follows in this chapter are some reminders that cross over the various interface metaphors and get back to basic principles of good design and effective communication. If you studied design in college or art school, you can think of these reminders as words from that all-too-honest professor, spoken to you as

your final project hung on the wall for all to critique. Words that you knew you should have spoken to yourself beforehand about whether your project achieved its communication goals and whether it took full advantage of all the applicable principles of good design.

So in the early stages of any interface design project, pin your concept on the proverbial corkboard. Stand back a few feet and play the design devil's advocate. Now's the time to trim away the nonessentials, refocus on the goals, and fine-tune the visuals, before you really have to show your project to the world.

No matter how well-crafted the bow and arrow, you don't hit a bull's-eye by looking away from the target.

The Speared Peanut Web site (spearedpeanut.com, see page 182) uses a simple yet elegant framework to present the capabilities of the firm. It's clear that the goal of this site is to focus attention on the company's capabilities, rather than on elaborate bells and whistles that could possibly confuse the medium with the message.

Communicate with *Clarity*

What's the Point?

What would the response be if a person who had just interacted with your project were to be asked "What was the point—the purpose—of what you were just working with?" Could that person concisely state the idea or feeling or call to action that you wanted users to come away with when you set out to design the project? Clarity is crucial. In this culture where people flip channels and surf the Web at the speed of light, hunting for that next nugget of information or entertainment, you can't afford to be ambiguous.

Three Chances To Win

Every person who interacts with your presentation will take a somewhat unique approach. But in general you have three opportunities to hook your audience. To put it another way, there are three hurdles of trust that a user needs to be helped over before he or she will invest much time or attention in the work you've so painstakingly crafted. Each one of these obstacles potentially has a time limit associated with it, and if you can't win the user over in time, there's always another Web site just a click away, and there's always room for another dusty CD-ROM on the shelf.

Within the first second it must be clear to the user that your project is useful and well-crafted. If your splash screen or home page is ugly or doesn't load properly, for instance, you will already have lost many of the high-strung cyber hunters out there. That first impression is all-important. You need a hook that will make the viewer say "This could be *rewarding*, this is *quality*; I'll be taken care of here."

Now, with that first hurdle crossed, you may have another 10 seconds to convince the person whose hand is on the mouse that your presentation is *easy to use*. If the user can't quickly grasp "how things work," you've tripped well before getting to the finish line.

If you've made it to this point successfully, however, you may actually have a whole minute to convince the user that you have

This online retail section of the Kahlúa Web site (kahlua.com) could have been more conventionally designed with structured frames and lengthy text descriptions as in printed catalogs. But the designers instead chose a spontaneous and lighthearted style that complements the overall personality of the site, with loosely drawn artwork, bold colors, humorous copywriting, and illustrated type reminiscent of clothing labels. The site doesn't provide online sales, but the telephone number is prominently placed to make ordering products offline easy.

In order to give a positive first impression, the **Melbourne Water** utility company, which focuses on sewage and drainage issues, chose to use a beautiful and symbolic photographic collage of the water cycle and simple navigation labeling system for its prototype Web site's splash screen. The clear organization and thoughtful illustrations portray the benefits of water resource management, and thereby reconfirm the company's organization, high standards, and efficiency.

Travelocity, an online travel agency **(travelocity.com, see page 200)** has a very simple and inviting home page, that introduces the main sections of the site using color-coding that follows through all subsequent pages.

The main menu for a promotional presentation (*The Mackerel Stack*, **see page 172**) identifies the company, the main components of the presentation, and its purpose right up front, presenting the menu title, clearly labeled buttons leading to the main sections, and a direct call to action: "Please select."

This prototype electronic TV program guide **(see page 116)** uses a familiar chart format to organize a lot of information. It not only provides descriptions of particular shows, but also tells whether a TV show has started prior to, or will continue after, the current time slot. This information, along with some artificial intelligence capabilities that select potentially interesting shows for the individual viewer based on previously input preferences, allows users to make informed choices as they embark on their channel-surfing adventures.

This online marketing brochure and sales tool for Lynx golf **(lynxgolf.com, see page 78)** uses photographic imagery to designate hot areas that lead to further information. These well-chosen photos, coupled with clear labeling, constitute a common syntax that makes options clear and makes it easy to choose where you want to go.

interesting content and that he or she can get to it directly, without a lot of gymnastics. If your audience makes it this far, they're usually hooked. And later, when they've finished their visit, if you were to ask, they would hopefully be able to express clearly what you wanted them to take away from the experience.

Use a Common Syntax

For your interface to be clear, you need to use imagery and symbols that are easily understood by everyone who's likely to use it. Just as it's now part of most people's technological vocabulary that a VCR button with double-left-facing triangles on it will rewind a video tape, most users of interactive media know that the antiquated bent arrow carriage return symbol means "take me back where I just came from" in a multimedia project. Whatever the design of the tools used for navigating or accessing information, whether they are traditional and tested or new and original, they must provide the clear foundation that will facilitate the interaction between human and machine.

Know Before You Go

There is one school of thought in interface development (let's call it *Mystian*) that says that what people love about multimedia is the exploration—the anticipation of "not knowing what's around the bend." While this may be true for certain entertainment titles, for most interactive projects it's better to let users know where they will end up before you lead them down a certain path.

What are some ways to enable informed navigation instead of blind exploration? Try using cropped picture icons to give a hint of the potential destination, or designate an area for text that, upon a rollover of the related button, gives a brief title or summary of where this hot spot leads. The idea here is to clarify by whatever means possible not only how one moves around a project but also what is available once a person gets there.

There's nothing more disconcerting in life than finding that something familiar has changed for no apparent reason.

Keep a Visual, Conceptual, and Mechanical *Consistency*

How Consistency Helps

The human mind constantly searches for patterns—organizing, analyzing, categorizing, and combining the things it observes, always striving to find the unified whole that means more than the sum of the parts. If the mind can't find that sought-after unity in what it's focusing on, its tendency is to look elsewhere. This is why it's vital that the information architect organize and present all the experiences that make up an interactive presentation or Web site in a way that makes it easier, not harder, for the mind to do what it does naturally.

One of the most obvious ways of making it easier to see the whole is to group objects with similar functions together—by using both *proximity*, which creates patterns and associations that can be easily understood and remembered, and *similarity*, which relates objects by characteristics like shape, style, or color. Any time you spend at the beginning of the design process refining the grid and the style guidelines that are the foundation for this organization will pay off tremendously when production is hot and heavy and the myriad of different content elements need to be integrated into a whole.

This prototype site promoting the Sydney Design Conference keeps the event title consistently placed at the top of the page, and the current section's title is always locked in position at the left edge. Once the visitor proceeds past the home page, top, the table of contents moves to the lower right corner and becomes a navigation device. This navigation structure, along with repeated design elements and the optimal use of white space, creates an approachable and contemporary on-screen environment.

The EnviroLink Web site **(envirolink.com, see page 152) uses icons carved on stones to symbolize its sections and topics. The cluster of overlapping stones forms a unified navigation device that rests on the negative space of the vertical panel. This pile of stones is an elegant solution for keeping navigation options available, yet out of the way.**

This original layout for the home page of the Web site of this popular TV channel (discovery.com, see page 94) uses an obvious grid to organize the graphics that provide access to the site's different sections. These buttons are grouped together in a row at the bottom of the screen and are all represented by photographs of round objects to associate with the image of the earth used to identify the channel.

A Web site's navigation tools can be made consistent even if you start with a diverse collection of graphics or imagery. For example, the three photos below were unified, as shown in the bottom row, by (1) cropping within a consistent shape, (2) reducing color to a mono-chromatic color table, (3) replacing the backgrounds, (4) applying a glow, and (5) adding a drop shadow. Developing such standard treatments and instructing all artists to adhere to them will maintain consistency and also help manage a task force that may be called upon when new graphics or photos are needed.

Navigation and Information Access

An essential principle in organizing an interface is that all similar tools used for navigating and accessing information should stay consistent. They must be consistent not only in where they are located on the screen, but also in their labeling, in their different action states, and in any sounds associated with them. For example, if animations are turned on by clicking a simple icon in one instance, they should not be accessed by a text button or hot word in another.

Coordinating Your Style

To give a coherent personality to your project, all the elements of style that make it unique should be coordinated. Sometimes this can be difficult when there is a large production team, especially if team members are working in several locations. But taking the time to develop interface standards that nail down in detail the specific ways that the elements of the project will be presented will allow for faster production and fewer surprises. Artwork and other media that can benefit from detailed, unify-ing style guidelines include iconography (specify styles, sizes, line widths, colors, and button states), photography (include cropping specifications, special effects, and color depth), frames, borders, windows (call out dimensions, textures, colors, and placement), sounds (specify spot sounds that accompany ac-tions, ambient sounds or music for different sections, volume levels, and sampling rates), and file formats (compression set-tings and naming conventions).

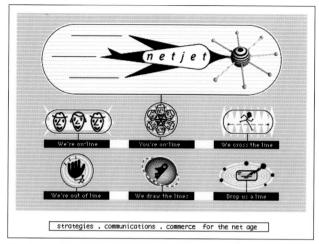

The design firm NetJet's Web site (**netjet.com**) uses a consistent humorous style, not only in its illustrative icons, but also in its copywriting. The creative use of the word "line" in each of the section titles provides continuity while the playful icons draw the user into exploration of the site.

The photographic collages on the left side of the screen, which make up the framework of **Classic Photographic Image Objects'** floppy disk–based promotional slide show, stay consistent from screen to screen with only the right-hand portion of the display changing over time.

A recognizable logo and color-coded photo-graphic imagery related to the site's section titles greet the user on the splash screen of the **Museum of Victoria's** Web site prototype. The color-coding and use of the museum logo are continued throughout the site, as is the blending photographic treatments.

Balancing between consistency and contrast is like walking a tightrope. It offers the possibility of exhilarating success but it's also fraught with the potential for disaster.

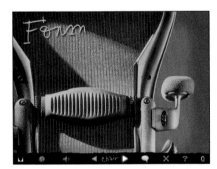

The **Herman Miller** CD-ROM presentation uses a combination of extreme close-up photographs for the opening section images, in contrast to the interior shots, which were taken with a wider perspective and are more diagrammatic. Adding to the contrast, duotones are used in the opening section but full-color images run throughout the subsequent screens of the presentation.

Take Advantage of *Contrast*

Road Warriors

No matter the content of a presentation, without a dynamic use of contrasting elements the mind tends to first gloss over the information, then lose interest in exploring, then finally leave and go on vacation. With the incredible overload of information that bombards us all day, including the thousands of competing images and sound bites that we wade through to get the information we really want, designers must make sure that the experience they are presenting doesn't get lost in the stop-and-go traffic of the information superhighway. That's why engaging the user with just the right dynamic tension of visuals, space, and sounds is so important in creating an effective presentation.

The challenge here is to make sure that contrasting elements are energizing rather than annoying, that a user's mind is intrigued, not confused. A word of caution: Sometimes this play of elements against one another calls for violating some of the design dogma of the past—but not blindly. It's always best to

The Iomega Web site (**iomega.com, see page 202**) uses a magazine metaphor with plenty of white space, dynamic photography, bold iconography, and extensive navigation options to create a home page that's both easy on the eyes and practical.

The **ReZ.n8** animation and design firm's portfolio disc uses three contrasting panels: a black column, left, that houses the minimalist navigation tools; a large white panel, right, used to display information; and a center area for highly expressive Illustrations—in this case, a portrait of one of the company founders superimposed with a dynamic texture of typography. Interesting typographic contrast is used throughout, as seen in the navigation element in the lower right corner of this screen: horizontal and vertical, serif and sans serif, positive and negative.

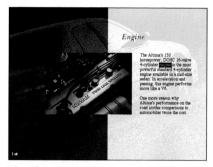

The **Nissan Interactive** presentation **(see page 80)** contrasts a 1-bit dark-and-light background image with an overlapping, full-color beauty shot of a portion of the car. This contrasting use of positive and negative space, black-and-white and color photography, and reversed-out text in the body copy creates an efficient and dynamic design.

understand the rules and their importance to communication before stretching or even breaking them.

Contrasting Visual Types

One of the best ways to create dynamic tension is to contrast different flavors of design elements. You can do this simply by using a 20-point extra bold sans serif typeface, such as Helvetica Black, for titles and a 12-point lighter serif face, such as Century Schoolbook, for the body text. Or this contrast could be taken to an extreme by reversing that 12-point body copy out of a portion of a 300-point Helvetica Black ampersand.

Other design elements that could be contrasted include color (using complementary colors, setting color photos on top of grayscale photos, or alternating background tints), illustration techniques (using expressive hand-drawn illustrations as a back-drop for technical illustrations), dimensionality (working with a dynamic interplay between 2D and 3D illusions), or even positive and negative space (providing areas that let the eye rest, lend a Zenlike elegance to your screens, and also help shorten download time).

Contrasting Media Types

When it comes to media types, contrast often arises naturally, as a consequence of choosing the technologies that will achieve the best possible communication for each kind of information you want to present. For instance, it's better to use text where the user may want to quickly scan the information or reread portions for clarity than to use a recorded voice-over. But, for example, using a sound bite for a first-hand commentary on an historical event can add personality and warmth that complements the written word very effectively.

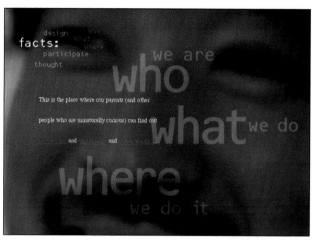

Contrasting small clickable type with large rendered statements creates a dynamic tension that draws the user into the story of the design firm The Designory, Inc. and its site **(designory.com, see page 88)**. To further emphasize this contrast, site designers simulate dimension with a blurred photograph serving as a back-drop for the sharp typography on top.

The retro-style interface of this stock-image CD-ROM, **CSA Archive Sampler (csa-archive.com, see page 190)**, superimposes large semitransparent versions of the featured dingbat on top of mono-chromatic photographs. In this case, the antique typewriter keyboard is actually a navigation tool whose keys can be clicked to display the different dingbats that are available. The size of the circular display window contrasts with the typewriter keys, and the smaller navigation buttons in the lower right corner of the screen.

Within its very first screen this online graphics catalog Web site **(imageclub.com, see page 194)** established a visual style that contrasted regular weight italic type with extra bold sans serif type. The dynamic contrast of the typography was unified by tight letterspacing and the dark halo effect that was consistently used around the section titles.

Visual overload— interactivity's silent killer.

By creating a separate scrollable window for The Edison Group's staff bios and then further dividing The Group into areas of expertise, shown at the top, the design firm's Web site (**theedisongroup.com**) allows for easy access to specific information, without causing users to search needlessly.

In this disk-based portfolio presentation (**Kristine Hwang**) the cursor changes from a default pointer to a text label when it rolls over a navigation element.

Strive To Make It *Uncluttered*

Enough Already!

Interactive presentations, whether delivered over the Internet or disk-based, have built-in potential for both phenomenal success and dismal failure. Success, because large doses of information and experiences can be delivered dynamically and inexpensively to just about any computer worldwide. And failure, because that plethora of information has the potential, if not delivered well conceptually and graphically, to be just another load of visual pollution on the world's growing stockpile of excesses. The designer's job when crafting an interactive presentation is to make the communication easy by offering only the options that help achieve the project's goal.

Power to the Cursor

One approach to uncluttered organization is to empower the cursor—to build into the moving cursor the ability to change its appearance as it passes over important spots in the screen real estate. Changing the pointing finger cursor to a text label, for instance, whenever it rolls over a clickable element can now be accomplished directly within a program such as Macromedia Director. Although cursor changes have so far been used primarily for creating games, or when navigating special elements like QuickTime VR clips, their potential for use in Web sites and other interactive applications is just waiting to be realized.

A Swiss Army Knife Approach

Another way to conserve precious screen space and eliminate elements that aren't needed at the moment is to create a single on-screen navigation tool. When it's needed, such a tool can unfold like a Swiss army knife or slide out like a secret panel, revealing multiple choices.

Leaving a Trail

Besides showing users where they can go, another role for a compact navigation device is to give them continuous feedback about where they are and where they've been—to provide a trail of "bread

The use of frames in Bybee Studios' Web site (**bybee.com**) allows all of the available photographic images to be previewed on the left at the same time that the viewer is looking at the main sample image. This organized access to all options at once (including audio clips and the main section areas shown in text at the bottom of the screen) gives users the feeling of control without cluttering the interface with unnecessary information or forcing users back and forth to a directory.

The menu bar in the *Hybrid CD-i Interactive Television Project* prototype (**see page 96**) is hidden until requested, and rolls up from the bottom of the screen over the live TV program. The roll-up menu brings with it not only the primary navigation icons but also a large panel area for information such as this online shopping catalog.

This self-running promotional, *Pinch* **(see page 178), takes advantage of negative space to lend simplicity to its screens, and to help direct the eye through the concepts being presented.**

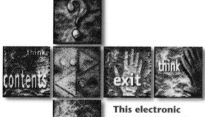

This electronic CD-ROM journal's rotating navigation cube (*Just Think*, see page 158), unfolded here to show all six sides, occupies only a very small area of the screen, but it contains a half-dozen different devices for navigating and interacting with the editorial content.

crumbs" á la Hansel and Gretel. Such a "trail" can be as simple as the standard highlighted hypertext words, abundant on the Web, that change color once clicked. Or it can be more elaborate, like section tabs that change color across the top of a page to give an instant view of where a visitor has been, or a site map with a dotted-line trail that traces a user's journey so far.

Layering Information

Even if you successfully corral the navigation elements of your site, there's still plenty of opportunity for screen clutter to build up in the presentation of the information itself. One method of reducing clutter and visual overload is to keep the length of body copy, or text, to a minimum. The goal here is to distill the information in the main text blocks down to succinct summaries of ideas, then elaborate on them with hypertext links that provide access to extended footnote explanations, definitions, animated demonstrations, or other associated topics.

Filtering and Focusing

Tailoring a Web site's presentation to an individual user is another way to reduce clutter. Reduce the amount of unimportant or inappropriate information on-screen by setting up a Preferences area where the user is questioned about specific needs or interests. Once this information is gathered, the presentation can be set to display only the areas or topics that are important to that viewer, though the entire presentation can still be available through hyperlinked topics. Organizing presentations through this kind of filter that hides unwanted information, or even through agents that personalize the tailored presentation or go out and find requested information, is one of the most exciting communication concepts to come down the cyberhighway.

When Negative Is Positive

The use of negative space, or areas that are intentionally left sparse, not only creates visual interest through contrast, as described on pages 58 and 59, but also helps direct the eye through a layout—showing the connection between certain elements, establishing a progression, and emphasizing areas of importance. Negative space lets the eye rest awhile, giving it time to "chew and swallow" between bits of information. Empty space can be one of the most powerful factors in creating a dynamic and uncluttered on-screen environment.

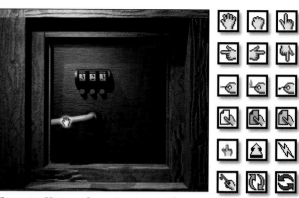

The game *Myst* **employs a transparent interface that has proven to be intuitive to millions. Its secret is that all of its navigational options are embedded in the states of its main cursor. Whatever options are available and appropriate are shown by the changing cursor icon.**

This Web site **(adobe.com, see page 68) leaves a navigation trail of ghosted buttons within narrow horizontal bars that show the current section and all other available areas. This kind of "history" is vital in extensive projects.**

Need a mnemonic for what your Web site should be? Consider engaging, enlightening, entertaining, educational, motivating, and memorable."

Recording artist Amy Grant's Web site **(myrrh.com/amygrant) uses Flash technology, with its extensive animation and sound capabilities, to communicate not only information about the artist, but also the emotion inherent in her music. Users can learn about the artist's passion for social causes in her personal tour journals, which are fully accessible on the site, and her music can play continuously in the background or on demand. Mixing media in this way provides a much more complete picture of the star than could ever be gleaned from a music CD insert.**

Apply *Cinematic Principles* of Storytelling

Gather 'Round the Campfire

Part of the beauty of the Internet, whether we're talking about the Web as a whole or a single site, is the chance for the user to break away from the sequential narrative mode of presentation and leap from link to link. But just like a well-told story, in order to be effective your Web presentation still needs to be structured with a beginning, middle, and end: a beginning to excite or engage the visitor, a middle that delivers the content, and an end that provides a payoff for users, or calls them to action. The more you can apply the time-tested principles of storytelling and movie-making, the more successful your site is likely to be at getting visitors to stop, get the message, and come away as believers.

One way to engage and hold an audience at your Web site is to personalize the interaction. For instance, try to build the kind of drama that goes into telling stories around the fire. But, wherever possible, *show* rather than *tell* the story. To the degree that your target audience is equipped to handle it, animation and video can be used to illustrate and demonstrate, even to give your site a dynamic, almost human personality.

The Sound of Music

Though it can be a touchy subject because of the current bandwidth limitations of the Web, sound is an important part of communication. For a quick take on just how important it is, think about watching a movie or a TV program without sound, relying strictly on the imagery and subtitles or closed captions. Or consider traveling through the Haunted Mansion at Disneyland with earplugs firmly in place.

Sound has become more and more accessible with changes in Web technologies, such as Flash and RealPlayer. For now, add it wherever it's appropriate for the browsers and plug-ins your target audience is equipped with. A very practical way to use sound is in short clicks and beeps that let visitors know that their action—such as pushing a button—has registered. "Yes, we got it," such a sound says. "You're not alone out there. Information *is* coming."

Stumpy knows all. Stumpy tells all. Within the cramped confines of Stumpy's bobbing noggen lie the answers to all questions for those brave enough to approach the jar. Do you have a question for the amazing Stumpy?

Q: *Stumpy, "Elvis & Bonaparte" is a pretty goofy name. Why do they call it that?*

A: Dagnabbit, there ya go agin! Folks 'round here, they're loco er sum such. Always tryin' to do stuff differnt than other folks. They sez thet all them other agencies, they could be ay-ccountants er lawyers er sum such with their big fancy names on their doors. But Elvis & Bonaparte sez "cree-yativity and stratergy" right in the name. Hih-hih-hih! Git it? "Elvis" on accounta thet fancy cree-yative rocken roll feller that keeps poppin' up in convenience stores everywhere and "Bonaparte" on accounta thet little French

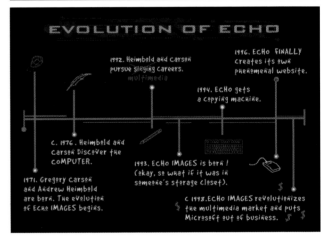

Both the Elvis & Bonaparte Web site, top **(elvisbonaparte.com, see page 187), and the EchoLink site (echoimages.com, see page 170) use humor to tell their story, which helps visitors feel comfortable and enjoy being there.**

Sound can also be used to establish ambience. Both music and environmental sounds can keep the site alive during idle times when nothing seems to be happening—for instance, if the user has to stop and think before making a choice.

You can also use sound in much the same way it's used in the movies or on TV—to enhance the moods of anticipation, conflict, climax, and resolution as the story progresses.

Easter Eggs

Many people use the Web as a source of entertainment. They may enjoy the process of exploring or connecting, or they may just be looking for an engaging diversion. And even visitors who arrive at your site with a specific goal in mind will enjoy being pleasantly surprised or made to laugh, as long as the treat doesn't try their patience by interfering with their getting the information they came for. The *Easter eggs*—hidden bonuses, often in the form of animations—that game developers have added to their programs to reward users for exploring the interface can also be effective on the Web. Forms of Easter eggs that work especially well for the Web and other interactive media include agents that pop up and entertain or explain something, elements that have hidden animations, or even whole unexpected sections of the site that give users the added value that keeps them coming back.

Two-Way Communication

The Web and other interactive electronic media can go a step beyond what even the most engaging cinema can offer, allowing users to provide immediate input. This visitor interaction can be useful in all three phases of the storytelling process—beginning, middle, and end. Matching and trivia games, for instance, can serve not only to engage visitors but also to deliver content or to collect information. And interactive feedback can also provide a way for the visitor to download the payoff or answer the site's call to action—for example, by placing an order, finding the address of a nearby retail outlet, or promoting the site by sending a message to let a friend know of its features.

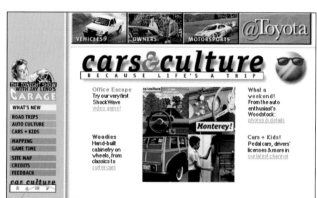

By adding a lifestyle "webzine" with feature articles and interactive games, the creators of Toyota's Web site (toyota.com, see page 86), acknowledge that people are interested in their product for reasons that go beyond the practical. Focusing on the passionate love affair that some people have with their automobiles allows the company to elbow up alongside the user as a compatriot, as a buddy, and say, "Yeah, that's a beauty all right, and did you happen to see the one over here?" Also, providing a way to order specific collateral material online shows users that their interaction with the site, and therefore the company, produces concrete results.

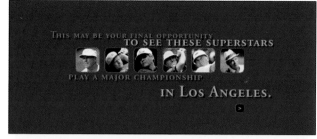

The splash screen (top) of the U.S. Senior Open 1998 site (usenioropen98.com) impresses visitors with the promise to see golf's superstars. Personalized stories about the golfers and the history of the tournament's location paint an appealing picture of the sport and the event.

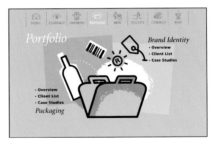

The designers at SBG Partners had two goals in mind when they put together the design firm's Web site (**sbg.com**). First they wanted to market the firm's skills, both in Web design and in more traditional media. And second, they would use the site's development to gain experience—it would be their first Web site design.

SBG's approach was to "make it rich, keep it simple, and keep it direct," says design director Philip Ting, "and hopefully people will find it attractive."

To achieve the richness they wanted for the graphics and still keep download time to a minimum, the designers chose a simple illustration style for the opening pages of the eight sections of the site (right). The line drawings in flat colors on solid backgrounds produced an attractive, unified set of screens that could be compressed very small with the run-length encoding that's employed in the GIF format. The iconography used in the row of navigational buttons that's always present at the top of the screen also employs line drawings, with a change of color indicating which section is currently being visited.

In contrast to the simple line drawings, the company's portfolio section (above) needed to include photos of work done for clients, as part of the site's job of telling "who we are and what we do," says Ting. But in this section, too, the backgrounds are simple, echoing the torn-edge look in the section-opener screens.

Keeping the design of the site clear and elegant helps make it easy to maintain. Although the What's New section is updated quarterly and some other elements may also change, the site's success stems from the implementation of well-established design principles rather than from the use of the latest Web gimicks. So nothing will need to be replaced because its technology goes out of fashion.

The site has been doing very well as a marketing tool for SBG. "Most of our clientele have been on-site and think it's very clean, very clear, easy to navigate," reports Ting.

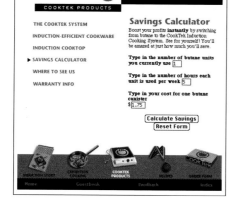

*The World
and other
electronic
unprecede
opportuni
dynamic i
about pro
services, a
personaliz
with the c
provide th*

The CookTek site (**cooktek.com**), developed by Hanson/Dodge Design, is an extension of CookTek's direct sales approach to marketing its induction cooking system, used in exhibition cooking, where the food is prepared right in front of the diners. Two design constraints were important in shaping the site: First, the relatively high-tech product needed to be explained in order to be sold. And second, the budget was small since the company was relatively new.

Hanson/Dodge had developed targeted direct-mail pieces for CookTek. And when the opportunity for a Web site presented itself, the designers found that the grid and layout of the page, the imagery, and even some of the copy from those pieces could be repurposed for the screen. "The clean, sharp look with the photographs and the white space grew out of print collateral," says Thomas Govinski, information designer and production manager.

In what is becoming a norm for Web page design, the designers used a left column for navigational information (and in this case also illustrations) and a right column for the body copy, which was divided into short blocks and limited to small, readable areas. The photographic icons were developed almost entirely from existing CookTek stock. The illustrations were also originally developed for print, but for the Web site they were extended as simple GIF animations like the pan-cooktop-energy field demonstration shown here, to help people understand a little bit more about how the product works.

Because induction cooking is a relatively new technology being offered to an established industry, the site was designed to give visitors a choice of several different ways to learn about the process and the product. "So, for instance," says Govinski, "they can read about the technology behind the induction system. Or they can see how chefs are using the technology through tips and recipes." They can also review the full line of CookTek products, calculate potential supply savings, ask questions—and, of course, place an order.

Holding Everything Together

Overview *The Adobe Systems Web site is organized on a six-column grid. The navigation bar across the top of each page provides easy access to sections, and product information is presented through text, images, animation, video, and PDF (Adobe Acrobat's portable document format).*

"We try to keep most sections of our site to a maximum of four levels and by the third level make sure visitors are involved in something interesting."

–Charles Field, creative director

Supporting the Creative Community

The Adobe Systems Web site, which began as a product support site for Adobe customers, has become a primary resource for creative professionals. Besides promoting and selling Adobe products online, the 13,000-page site showcases creative work, provides helpful tips and techniques, and offers informative feature stories as well as live Webcasts from conferences and trade shows. To keep the site visually interesting and to indicate content changes, the home page is modified weekly.

Providing Structure and Organization

"It's really important with a site this large to make sure that the user has a consistent experience," says creative director Charles Field. "Working with a grid allows us to deal with a vast amount of information in a consistent visual framework." Pages are organized on a six-column grid with a 20-pixel space between columns. The basic grid is evident in the black navigation bar, at the top of the home page shown above, which is equally divided into six buttons. To emphasize specific content and create interesting layouts, columns are often combined to form units of varying widths, as shown above, where the cover illustration occupies four columns. HTML tables are used to define the dimensions of a column. To maintain a line length that's easy to read, the width of any table is limited to a maximum of 400 pixels.

Typography

To relate the site to the corporate identity, Adobe's corporate

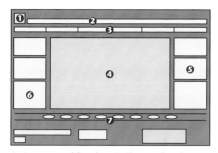

1. Corporate identity 2. Site navigation controls 3. Section buttons 4. Home page cover illustration 5. Weekly callouts 6. Hypertext menu 7. General hyperlinks

On the introductory page of the Type section, a colorful illustration identifies the section title and creates a focal point in the center of the page. The clickable subsections are listed in black type over the illustration. Special features are presented in the two outer columns of the layout.

Clicking on Using Type on the introductory page at left, leads to that subsection. A typographic treatment of the subsection title and the subsection navigation bar identify this level. All of the layout elements in the article are organized on the six-column grid.

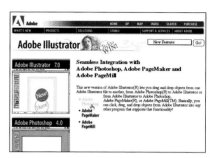

When the cursor rolls over a product name in the product list, the type turns from black to yellow, as shown above, and activates an animation on the left like this one, which demonstrates the drag-and-drop feature of Illustrator.

To emphasize illustrator Louis Fishauf's artwork, which is the focus of this Tips & Techniques section, the colorful images are placed in a wide area on the right, equivalent to four of the grid's six columns. The text that describes the process of creating the work is placed in a narrower two-column space on the left. For interest, the title typography is offset to align with a different grid line.

STATS AND SOFTWARE

The site is maintained by a managing editor, creative director, information designer, multimedia artist, production editor who writes HTML, Web technical manager, developer, and programmer and Web project coordinators who write feature articles. Hardware includes Mac, PC, and Sun Microsystems UNIX workstations. Software includes After Effects, BBEdit, Illustrator, Photoshop, and Premiere. **adobe.com**

typeface Myriad is used throughout. Since Myriad is a Multiple Master font, header banners and display graphics take advantage of Myriad's thousands of possible widths and weights.

Color

The designers chose the color red to identify text that links to other areas, and purple for the areas that had been visited. "A warm color like red works well as the link color," says design production editor Jocelyn Bergen, "because it stands out on the page. It's also a good metaphor because by definition hypertext links are *hot*, meaning that if you click on them something happens. And the red color we chose goes well with Adobe's corporate red."

In the Product section of the site, a GIF animation (part of which is shown at left) demonstrates how Adobe Type Manager Deluxe makes it easy for users to vary the weight and width of Multiple Master fonts without distorting the typeface.

For emphasis or to set a tone, other subtle colors are occasionally used in the typography in combination with illustrations. All colors are selected from the Netscape color palette.

Covering All the Bases

"With the Internet you have to choose the technological level you're going to target," says Charles Field, creative director. "We've chosen a conservative level to make the site accessible to as many people as possible."

"Sometimes we create two versions of the same animation," adds Bergen. "For example, the piece we created to show the drag-and-drop features of Illustrator (shown above right) was done using JavaScript, but we also made a simple GIF animation as a backup that shows the same thing in case you don't have the extension loaded. There's browser detection at the front of the two streams that determines what is enabled, then downloads the appropriate graphic."

"Another thing we try to do," continues Field, "is to create a couple of different sizes of the same file so we have a very small version of it and another size for a T-1 line. If you've got a T-1 line, downloading a 10–15 MB file might be worth your while if it's about an After Effects feature you're trying to learn how to use."

Extending a Brand

Overview *The Grant's Beer Web site takes advantage of a clear color-coding system, an easy-to-use navigation structure, animation, illustration, photography, and streaming video to expand the brand identity of Grant's Beer.*

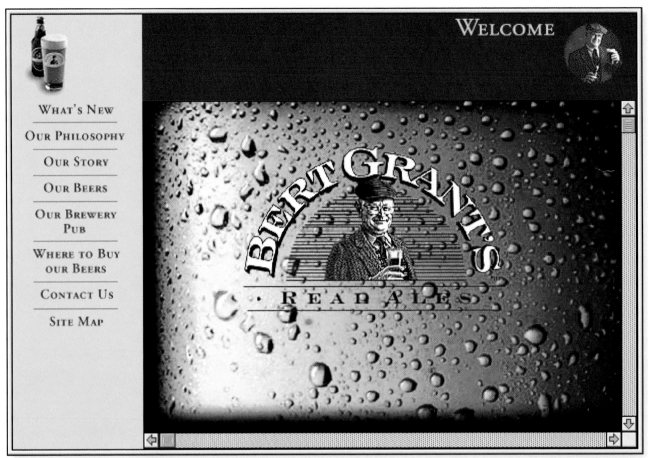

"We designed the site to be informative, as well as entertaining, by including information about the company's heritage, directions on where to buy Grant's specialty ales, and a 'contact us' section so consumers can dialog with the company."

–Colin Riviere, marketing assistant

Building Recognition Online

Faced with increased competition from rival microbreweries, Yakima Brewing & Malting Company hired Landor Associates to develop a comprehensive brand identity for Bert Grant's Real Ales that would include a new packaging system and a Web site designed to enhance and support the brand imagery. Landor took advantage of its wide range of experienced talent by teaming up its Seattle office and the San Francisco headquarters. Copywriting and a selection of visuals were supplied by the brewery, and Incommand Interactive of Yakima, Washington, collaborated with Landor to implement the site.

Relating the Interface

For consistency, the sophistication of the new packaging system (above, upper left) with its rich, natural color palettes and traditional imagery is reflected in the interface. The use of Garamond, a classic serif typeface, set in small caps, and the wood-grain texture over select images build on the hand-crafted theme (See the Our Beers screen, opposite). The texture was created in Photoshop using duplicate images on two layers: The Andromeda Series 3 Screens filter was applied to one copy, which was then layered over the original at 40% opacity. The image was flattened, the number of colors was reduced using DeBabelizer, and then the file was saved in GIF format.

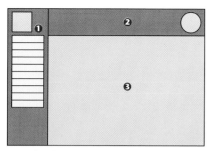

1. Navigation panel with hypertext table of contents 2. Section panel with section title, quote, and graphic 3. Main viewing area

The panel at the top of each screen displays the section title and is color-coded by section. The navigation panel on the left stays the same color but the type changes from brown to black when a selection is made.

On the opening page of the Our Beers section, a faint illustration of an old pub creates an appealing backdrop. The top halves of the bottle labels of the six ales are used as navigation elements. Clicking on a label links to an individual page that describes that particular beer in detail.

You can communicate with the brewing company via email on the Contact Us page by signing the Guest Book, shown above, or by posing a question on the Ask Bert page. Messages from previous visitors, posted on the Guest Book page, are interesting to read.

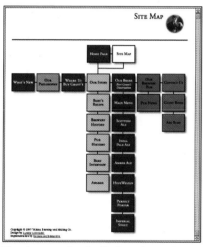

The site map clearly displays the navigation structure and the colors that identify the different sections. Clicking on a page in the site map takes you directly to that page. A vignette of Bert Grant appears in the upper right corner of all the pages.

STATS AND SOFTWARE

A 5-member team worked 9 months to complete the Grant's Beer Web site. Software included BBEdit, DeBabelizer, Illustrator, Photoshop, and Premiere. Macintosh hardware was used.
grants.com

Taking a Personal Approach

The metaphor behind the interface is a personal tour hosted by Bert Grant, founder of Yakima Brewing & Malting Company. Through text, photos, and streaming video, he leads a tour of the brewery and the brewery pub, shares his own philosophy, and even confides his recipes. The first-person point of view of the copywriting reinforces this personal approach, as do the quotes in the top panel and Grant's signature on the home page and in the Our Beers section.

Straightforward Linear Navigation

To create a strong Web site identity and provide continuity, each page is divided into three areas: the main viewing window, the title bar, and the navigation panel.

The site has eight main sections, shown in the table of contents on the navigation panel. A small photo distinct to each section is displayed above the table of contents in the navigation bar. Clicking on a title in the table of contents takes you to that section. To move between pages within a section, click on the hypertext links listed across the top of the main viewing window (see the Contact Us screen, above). A change in type color indicates where you are.

Graphic Concerns

To reduce download time, each page was limited to a total of 25K when possible, which meant that the size of the color images had to be carefully managed. "Image size is determined by file format, the number of colors, the amount of detail, and the actual physical size of an image," explains Pablo Supky of Incommand Interactive. "When saving images in GIF format, we reduce the number of colors in an image as much as possible without sacrificing quality. We convert to Indexed color in Photoshop and use an Adaptive palette. With the JPEG format, we set the quality of the image in Photoshop on Medium, 3. This compresses the image considerably without loss of detail."

Cross-Branding

As part of Landor's branding strategy, the Web site address is included on other Grant's Beer marketing materials, such as banners, flyers, coasters, and the back label of each bottle of Bert Grant's premium beer. Also, links have been established from Landor's Web site, landor.com, as well as from other local microbrewery-specific pages. This visibility adds to the success of the site, which averages over one thousand hits a day.

Bert Grant samples one of his ales in an animated GIF on the home page.

Traveling the Information Superhighway

Overview This Web site created by Digital Facades for the transportation company Interstate Consolidation uses type size and distinctive background shapes to identify location within the site, while photo collages describe what the company does and graphics inspired by industrial materials add visual interest.

"We believe that an interface should reflect the nature of the client's business, so we used photos of daily operations and icons based on industrial elements."

–Oliver Chan, design director

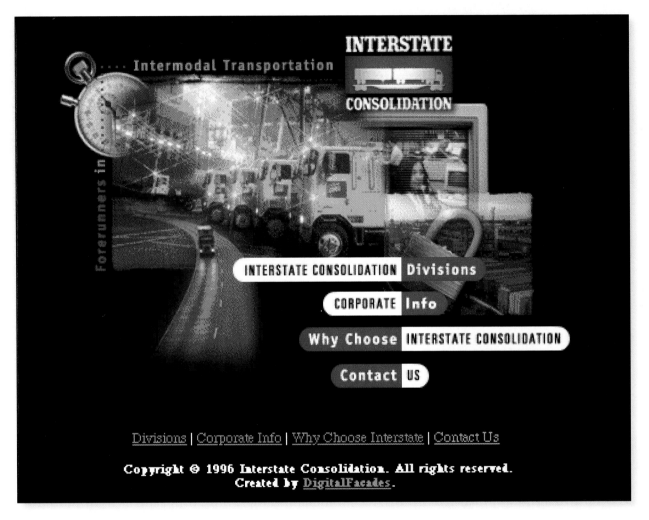

What the Company Does

Interstate Consolidation is an intermodal transportation company that operates throughout North America. The Web site promotes the company's services, provides easy access to their pricing, and allows feedback from customers.

Making Visual Connections

The site's home page, above, features a collage of images that represents the day-to-day operation of the company: The truck driving down a highway symbolizes transportation, a stop watch is used as a metaphor for punctuality, the employee and the computer monitor show the use of state-of-the-art technology, the lineup of trucks bearing the company symbol identifies the service the company provides, and the padlock represents security. The irregular edges of the collage create an interesting shape on the page and the perspective of the highway and the trucks lined up from foreground to background provides depth and a sense of coming and going.

The red and white buttons on the home page identify the four main areas of the site. Here, the design relates the buttons

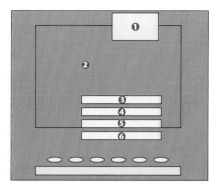

1. Company identity 2. Background photo collage 3. Divisions button 4. Corporate Info button 5. Why Choose button 6. Contact Us button

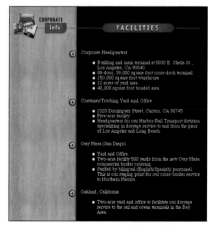

The Info/Facilities page is divided into two panels with a pleasing 1:2 ratio. The screws and the metallic background build on the industrial theme. The screws function as bullets to emphasize the subheads.

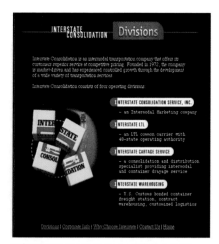

Selecting Interstate Consolidation Divisions on the home page opens the Divisions introductory page. The graphic style of the buttons, above, and the use of the photo collage provide continuity from the home page.

to the company's symbol, shown at the top of the home page—a tractor-trailer rig hooked up to a second trailer. The buttons repeat the red and white colors used in the symbol, and the combination of one red part and one white part is a metaphor for the meaning of the word "consolidation": joining together into one whole.

Typography

The text on the buttons is differentiated by typeface, size, color, and background color. The words that refer to the company (Interstate Consolidation, Corporate, and Us) are typeset in all caps, and are black on a white background. Since the name of the company is very long, a condensed sans serif typeface, Univers 59, was chosen because it takes up less space. The words that identify the topic or content (Divisions, Info, Why Choose, and Contact) are typeset in upper and lowercase Officina Sans white on a red background. The width of the red and white background shapes of the buttons is based on the length of the text.

To add variety to the body text, Times Roman and Courier were used—both are Netscape preselected typefaces. Since it's difficult to read a lot of text on-screen, the designers have broken the text up into short paragraphs or bulleted lists.

Clicking the Corporate Info button on the home page leads to the Info introductory page. For consistency, the heading and background in the heading are the same color as they are on the home page. The shape behind Info shows that it's a main section heading.

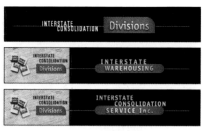

The examples above show the system of placing page headings. Type size, case, and background shape help visitors recognize where they are within the site. After the main page of each section, top, the section heading (Divisions) moves to the upper left area of the screen and the name of the current subsection (Interstate Warehousing, for instance) is displayed at right. To further clarify the hierarchy, the name of the current subsection is typeset larger and the shape behind the subsection name is a rectangle with four rounded corners, whereas the shape behind the name of the current section (Divisions) is a rectangle with only one rounded corner.

Creating the Graphics

The industrial images of the metallic surfaces, screws, and bolts came from royalty-free CD-ROM sources. The colors were altered in Photoshop and the metallic surfaces made tileable.

StudioPro was used to create the embossed effect. First, the type was set in Illustrator and converted to outline so the letterspacing would not change and so the type could be graphically manipulated. The Illustrator file was opened in Photoshop where it was rasterized, creating a texture map file with the white text pasted on a red background. Then a bump map

file was created with the white text on a black background. The Maximum filter was applied to the black-and-white type at 1 pixel to fatten the type, and Gaussian Blur was applied to the entire black-and-white image at 2 pixels. A plane was created in StudioPro and the texture map and the bump map applied to the plane. Then the spotlight was positioned and the final image was rendered.

Worldwide Advertising

Overview *Advertising agency J. Walter Thompson's corporate Web site attracts visitors from around the world with its playful illustrations, hand-drawn titles, clever copywriting, and an entertaining ad game in which visitors play the role of an aspiring ad genius trying to make a name in the business.*

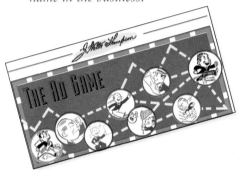

*"When writing a Web site proposal, be specific with regard to scope, number of pages, and how many changes are allowed. Be sure to get everything in **digital format** and **hard copy**, and allow enough time for beta testing—that's really important."*

–Carrell McCarthy, director of digital project management, J. Walter Thompson, San Francisco

Connecting Offices World-Wide

The corporate Web site of J. Walter Thompson, the world's fourth-largest and America's second-largest advertising agency, is designed to showcase the company's multinational focus and its international resources: over 200 offices in 74 countries. The corporate site is the first of the J. Walter Thompson sites to be built. Eventually each office will have its own Web address that links to the corporate site.

Broad Horizons

The site is oriented around the global theme "It's a World," as shown by the welcome message, left, that greets visitors when they arrive. Although the site is presented in English, visitors can choose to read the introduction in French, German, Italian, Portuguese, Spanish, Japanese, or Mandarin. In keeping with the global theme, the home page, shown above, depicts five different parts of the world on a long

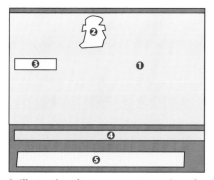

1. Illustration that represents a region of the world 2. Sign that leads to the map 3. Button to go to a section of the site 4. Typographic message 5. Navigation bar with hypertext

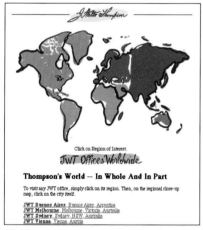

Clicking on an area of the map, above, opens a more detailed regional map, where visitors can select the name of a city to learn more about that regional office. Or clicking on the office name in the list of blue underlined hypertext provides navigation within the section.

STATS AND SOFTWARE

Concept and design were developed by a 5-member creative team from J. Walter Thompson, San Francisco. Production of the site was done by Vivid Studios using Mac and UNIX hardware. Software included Photoshop and CGI scripting. **jwtworld.com**

The Tour page offers an overview of the site, and the large numbers highlight the stops on the tour. Clicking on a number or the name of the stop takes you directly to that page. Clicking on the Tour hat starts the tour and goes directly to the first stop.

Each page is branded at top with the corporate logo, J. Walter Thompson's signature. Each section, like Corporate Profile, here, has its own distinct illustration. Clicking on a book in this illustration takes you to that topic. Click on the Commodore bookend to learn about the real J. Walter Thompson.

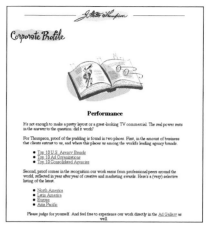

Topic pages within a section have their own identifying illustrations that relate to the section's main image, like the Corporate Profile's Performance page, above. For consistency, pages follow a similar layout: The corporate signature is centered at the top, the section title aligns at the upper left, the illustration and page title are centered below the signature followed by text information, hypertext links to other topics, the navigation bar, and the Home button.

horizontal tableau five screens wide, shown below. Scrolling left and right reveals colorful illustrations that lead to the main sections of the site. Clicking on the section title within each illustration takes you to that section, or you can use the navigation bar below each illustration and select the name of the section you want to visit. The arrow beside the navigation bar, and the long text message above it, are cues that let users know they can scroll horizontally.

The part of the world you're in when you enter the site determines what part of the world is displayed on the globe on the welcome page and in the tableau on the home page—a nice way to orient visitors and to extend a warm welcome.

Creating Distinction

To give the site its own distinct look, illustrator Steven Salerno was chosen to create ink-and-watercolor illustrations, and to hand-letter a complete alphabet. The agency's in-house design studio later converted the alphabet into a digital font to be used for future alterations to the site. Salerno's whimsical and light-hearted style provided just what the agency was looking for: a fresh contrast to the high-tech surroundings of the Web.

A Route for Everyone

There are two versions of the site: the graphics-rich version and the graphics-lite version. On the welcome page, visitors can choose the one that best suits their connection capabilities.

A Global Presence

Overview *The Landor Associates Web site includes a listing of worldwide career opportunities with the company, a downloadable brochure in PDF format, and a slide show of projects.*

"When designing Web sites, keep visual metaphors and navigation elements consistent from page to page so people understand where they are. You've got to remember that your users range from someone who has never signed on to someone who is very experienced on the Internet."

–Dean Wilcox, design director

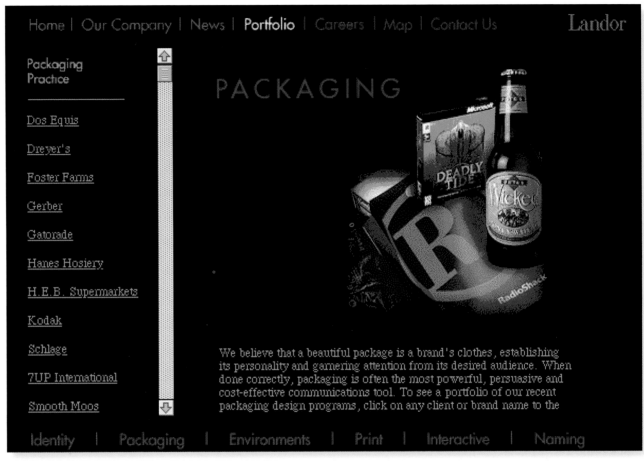

Taking Aim

With offices in North and South America, Asia, and Europe, Landor develops corporate identity and packaging systems, and product and environmental branding for clients throughout the world. Aimed at communication and marketing executives, the Web site provides information about the company and showcases projects done for clients.

Presenting Their Capabilities

The site, which contains approximately 200 pages, is organized into six main areas. The largest section is the portfolio, above. The pages in the portfolio section are differentiated by a black background, which creates a dramatic backdrop for the work.

Like the printed promotional materials, left, the Web site shows examples of Landor's broad range of interrelated services: Identity, Packaging, Environments, Print, Interactive, and Naming.

Screen Layout

The screen layout is based on a grid structure composed of up to four HTML frames. A horizontal frame across the top contains the overall site navigation elements and is visible from every page. When needed, a second horizontal frame at the bottom provides section navigation, as shown in the Portfolio section above. The scrollable vertical frame on the left offers clickable section contents, and the wider frame on the right presents information and images—the section's content. Frames help

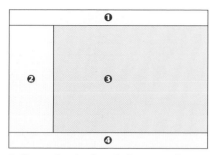

1. Site navigation bar 2. Contents of selected Portfolio section 3. Content area with project images and descriptions 4. Portfolio section categories

On the home page, the typography and graphic elements, well organized within a lot of white space, set the design tone of the site. The sans serif Futura typeface, which is used for headings, subheads, and body text, is very readable on-screen, and complements the thick-and-thin contrast of the Landor wordmark.

Clicking on the paint palette on the home page, left, opens the Our Company section, which has its own photographic icons that represent the section's content areas. To identify the section, the words "Our Company" change to black in the navigation bar at the top and a large screened-back palette appears in the background.

Clicking on the picture frame on the Our Company introductory page, left, opens the History section, where visitors can read about founder Walter Landor and key events in the company's history. In the navigation bar at the top, when the mouse rolls over the type, the words change color to show they are hot.

After a 5-second delay on the first portfolio page, a series of 20 images present an overview of the portfolio in a slide show format. To view specific portfolio categories, click on the categories at the bottom of the page.

organize the page and make it easier to update specific content without affecting other frames on the page.

Career Opportunities

To take advantage of the telecommunications potential of the Internet, the Landor site includes a job search feature in the Our Company section. Interested applicants can review career opportunities in any of Landor's offices around the world. To apply for a position online, you can email a resumé via the Landor Web site as a Microsoft Word, Adobe Acrobat, or Text file.

The Career Opportunities page links to a database that is maintained and updated by Landor's Human Resources department. "The employees don't have to track down the Webmaster or an HTML programmer, they just input the information directly into the database in their office. It really empowers them to use the Web," says Chris Jones, Webmaster.

Tracking Hits to the Site

In designing this version of the Web site, Landor designers followed the same working process that they apply to all of their client projects: audit and analysis, planning, creative development, and implementation. As part of the audit and analysis phase, they reviewed email that they had received from visitors to the previous version of the site and analyzed the Web log that tracked which pages were being hit most often, what path users took through the site, how many pages they requested, and how long they stayed on each page. This helped the design team make decisions about where to focus their energy. For example, the Web log indicated that the Portfolio section was visited the most, but based on user feedback it took too many steps to get there, so they made it easier to get to. They also found that people were spending an average of 8 minutes on the History page, which indicated that they were actually reading it, so the designers left it in.

Adapting the Wordmark

The elegant Landor wordmark is reminiscent of the Bodoni typeface, which is characterized by condensed letterforms with hairline serifs, extreme contrast between thick and thin strokes, and an emphasis on the vertical. Since the serifs and thin strokes are so thin in the original design, which is used primarily for printed materials, a second version was created for use on-screen. Serifs and thinner strokes were thickened for better legibility.

Landor created a 280K Adobe Acrobat version of a brochure, which can be downloaded from the site as a PDF (portable document format) file and accessed with the free Acrobat Reader by virtually any type of computer operating system.

Over the Net and Under Par

Overview In this Web site developed for Lynx Golf, multiple frames provide direct access to related information, the typeface and color selection expand on existing promotional materials, a Lynx Golf product inspires the background pattern, and photographic icons represent the sections of the site.

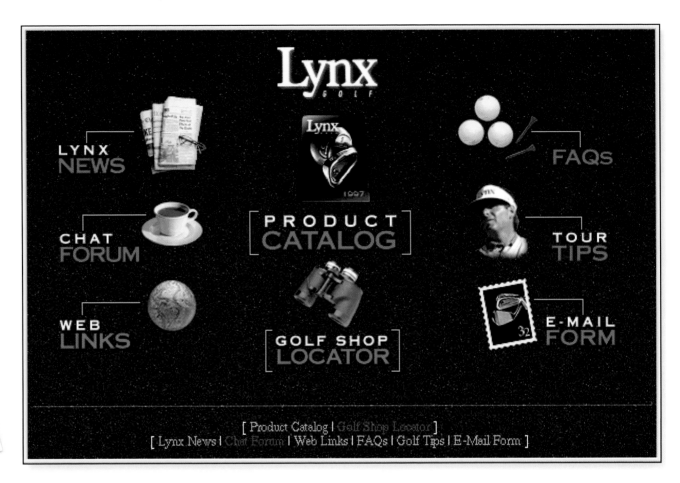

"The interface design takes three things into consideration: brand personality, technology, and the user."

–Jay Baker, designer, DigitalFacades

A Golfer's Site

Buying golf equipment involves a big decision, not only because golf clubs are expensive, but because consumers are investing in their ability to play the game well, so they tend to do a lot of research and take shopping very seriously. Lynx Golf, one of the leading U.S. manufacturers of golf clubs and golf-related merchandise, offers immediate and direct access to in-depth information through its Web site. Customers can browse the online product catalog for Lynx Golf merchandise and equipment, locate a nearby golf shop, get tips from professional golfers who use Lynx products, confer with other golfers in the Chat Forum, and send questions directly to Lynx via email.

Designing the Interface

To achieve a look consistent with other marketing materials, developed by advertising agency DDB Needham Los Angeles, the same typeface and color palette—predominantly black with red and yellow highlights—are used in the Web site's interface. Product shots and photos of tour players are also similar to those found in the company's advertising and print materials.

Photographic icons, accompanied by descriptive titles, are used to represent the different sections of the site, as shown above on the home page. To call attention to the two main areas of the site—the Product Catalog and the Golf Shop Locator—their icons and titles are placed in the center of the home page

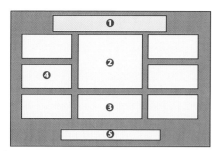

1. Company logo 2. Product catalog button 3. Golf Shop Locator button 4. Buttons to other sections 5. Hypertext index

On the Product Catalog introductory page, clicking on the picture of a product leads to more information. For consistency, the typographic treatment on the home page is used throughout the site, as shown here: White type is used to identify the name of the line of golf clubs and yellow to identify the specific type of club.

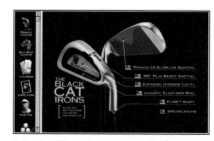

Selecting Black Cat Irons on the Product Catalog introductory page, left, displays a color photo of the product with key features indicated. Clicking on a feature leads to another page that provides more information. The type was set in Illustrator, combined with the photo in Photoshop, then saved in GIF format.

In the Tour Tips section, pro golfers share their expertise. The "tip of the month" is displayed when the section first opens, but other tips can be selected from the Tips Archive listed in the upper-right frame. Once a tip is selected, the text changes from yellow to red. This layout uses four frames, two of which are scrollable.

The opening page of the site, or splash screen, presents different Lynx Golf promotions, such as this special certificate offering for customers who purchase Black Cat irons and metal woods. White, red, and yellow are used strategically to emphasize key words and to visually activate the page. The cursor changes when rolled over hot spots: "The hottest clubs," the photo of the clubs, and the Lynx symbol, at upper right, all link to the home page. Clicking on the binoculars or the hypertext, at lower right, leads directly to the Golf Shop Locator.

and the titles are enclosed in white brackets. The white right-angle leader lines that connect the other icons and titles relate visually to the white brackets. The type was set in Illustrator using Copperplate all caps, then placed in Photoshop, where it was combined with the prepared stock photos. The complete layout was then saved in GIF format.

The background was created by scanning the black texture of the head of a Lynx Black Cat metal woods golf club. A tile of the texture, manipulated in

Photoshop to a 3-bit color depth, repeats in the background until it fills the whole page.

Marketing the Site

To promote the Web site, all of the Lynx Golf advertising and printed collateral materials display the site's address. The Web site is also registered with search engines, such as Webcrawler, Lycos, and Yahoo, so when a user searches the Web for golf-related sites, the Lynx Golf site shows up as a resource.

STATS AND SOFTWARE

An 8-member development team that included representatives from Lynx Golf, DigitalFacades, and DDB Needham Los Angeles worked 9 months to plan, develop content, and design and produce the Lynx Golf Web site. Software included BBEdit, Illustrator, and Photoshop running on Macs. **lynxgolf.com**

Clicking on the Chat Forum icon in the navigation frame at the left of the screen opens the Chat Forum introductory page where visitors sign in to participate in a discussion. An animated GIF in the upper left corner takes you back to the home page.

Managed by XPound!, with custom software developed by Digital Facades, the Chat Forum interface is made up of five frames: the section title, top, the index of messages, left, the selected message, right, the forum controls, bottom left, and the posting tools, lower right.

Clicking on Lynx News on the home page or on the Lynx News icon in the navigation frame opens the section's main page, where press releases are listed by date and topic. Clicking on a title takes you to that press release.

An Interactive Showroom

Overview *Aimed at car enthusiasts and potential buyers, this floppy disk direct-mail marketing piece, developed by Xronos of San Francisco, uses subtle navigation controls, a space-saving grid, and an interactive driving game to promote Nissan's Altima.*

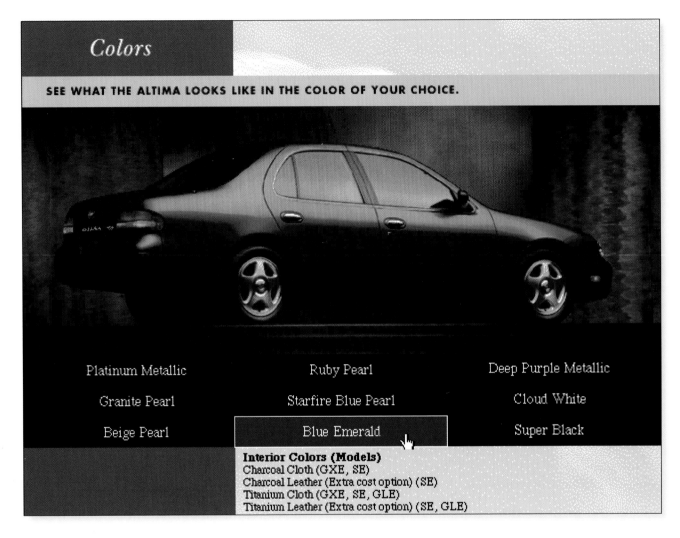

"We had a lot of flexibility as far as screen layout was concerned. So we chose not to give up screen real estate to controls that we'd have to work around the entire time."

– Kris Wainscott, visual art director

Straightforward Navigation

To complement the sophisticated design style of Altima's existing printed promotionals and TV advertising produced by Chiat Day, Xronos kept the layout of *Nissan Interactive* clean and simple. To maintain the aesthetic balance between photographs, typography, and background images, navigation controls are intentionally hidden.

Navigation procedure is clearly explained early in the presentation, but if the mouse sits idle for up to a minute, a helpful border with descriptive text appears along the left, right, and top edges of the screen as a reminder of how to get around: Click on the right edge to continue the presentation to the next screen; on the left edge to move back to the previous screen; or on the top edge to return to the main menu from any screen. When the cursor is moved to the right, top, or left edge of the screen, it changes to a small triangular-shaped arrow pointing you in the right direction.

Budgeting Disk Space

Space was a big issue from the outset. The presentation designers

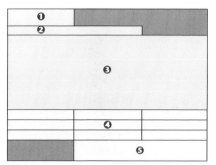

1. Screen title 2. Subtitle 3. Photo of Altima 4. Color choices 5. Interior colors and models

In the opening screen, words and phrases that identify Altima's unique features were typeset in New Baskerville Italic and antialiased to retain design detail. Small type emerges from the background and gets progressively larger until it covers the entire screen.

This interactive table compares features, availability, and pricing of different Altima models. The screen title is set in New Baskerville Italic, and the table headings in Futura Bold, all antialiased. The live text is set in Times since that font is available on most computers.

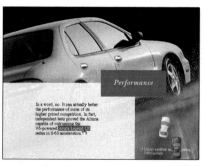

Hypertext is displayed as white type on a black background. On rollover the cursor changes to a pointing hand and the background turns blue. A mouse click opens a hypertext information screen. In anticipation of the virtual test drive, two small animated cars drive across the screen.

From the main menu, shown here, go directly to one of the three contents sections, or choose Exit or Help. When the cursor rolls over an active interface element, the arrow changes to the pointing hand and the background behind the type shifts to its assigned color.

STATS AND SOFTWARE

A full-time 4-member team, including a producer, a writer, a programmer, and a graphic designer, and 1 part-time sound designer worked 9 weeks to complete *Nissan Interactive*. Software included Director, FileMaker, Illustrator, and Photoshop. A Mac and a Windows version were produced. The program shipped on 2 HD floppy disks packaged in a unique wrapper (see opposite).

decided to use two high-density floppy disks for delivery, because one disk didn't provide enough space, and more than two was just too cumbersome. Early calculations showed that, after compression, the two disks could accommodate only fourteen 8-bit images, so Xronos devised a system of combining 8-bit and 1-bit versions of the same image. For every 8-bit image, a corresponding 1-bit image was created. The two versions were cut into pieces, then reassembled based on a grid (below). This approach, in combination with repeating some of the color images, gives the illusion that there are more photographs in the presentation than there actually are. Transitions between 1-bit images are well paced and add a sense of motion and drama.

Shifting Color Palettes

The Colors screen, on the opposite page, displays a series of car color choices. When one is selected, the car in the photograph changes to that color. To accomplish this transition effectively

and to economize on disk space, Xronos created nine individual custom color palettes just for the car. The System palette, applied to the rest of the screen, stays constant.

Interactive Test Drive

Miniature animated cars cross the screen at various points in the presentation, leading up to the Accessories screen, where the key to the virtual Altima is found. The test drive is both a game and an alternate navigation device to maneuver through the 45 presentation screens. Players race against the stopwatch, ac-

cumulating penalties when they crash into barriers or knock over cones. Sound effects, like squealing tires, a revving engine, and cheering at the finish line, add to the excitement of this dynamic feature.

In this series of screens, a grid is used to create variety while maintaining a unified layout. A combination of 8-bit and 1-bit images keep file size small. The "gray" 1-bit portions move sequentially from the top to the right and then to the left side of the screen. Text is positioned on the light areas to ensure good readability.

Plug-In to San Diego Gas and Electric

Overview In the San Diego Gas and Electric Company (SDG&E) Web site, visitors can roam around a virtual power plant created with QuickTime VR, tour a virtual greenhouse built with ShockWave, watch an animation of a turbine at work, participate in scenarios that help children understand the dangers of electricity, and buy energy-saving light bulbs.

"**To create an interface that appeals to a diverse audience—in this case business and residential customers—we chose not to develop icons to identify the sections; instead, words provide the clarity and directness we need.**"

– Gregory Carson, president, EchoLink

Hi. I'm Dave, a San Diego Gas and Electric Lineman. You'll find lots of information here on how to save energy and money, both at home and at work (click Residential or Business). In the process, you'll have the opportunity to request service, ask questions or request free brochures by e-mail (click on Customer Service). Of course, you can also reach us by phone, 24-hours a day, at 1-800-411-SDGE (7343).

Come visit our Electric Industry Compet site.

You can also click on the Business section. That department is very straightforward and efficient and won't take up too much of your time. But maybe you can come back after you get off work and have some fun with other features on our home page.

The Residential section has a lot of good information that can help you save energy and money. I bet

Listening to Customers

One of the early objectives of the SDG&E Web site was to expand communication between the public utility company and the community. To better understand community needs and expectations, a lot of time was spent with focus groups whose participants represented a broad cross-section of the company's customer base, including residential and commercial customers, among them both frequent and infrequent users of the Internet. These informative sessions helped the company establish goals that guided the site's organizational structure and interface design.

Responding to Customer Needs

The focus groups indicated not only that business and residential customers need different kinds of information but that commercial customers prefer a more direct approach that allows them to take care of business quickly. The design team responded with a well-organized site that divides business and residential information into separate sections clearly identified by labeled buttons on a navigation panel, shown above. The navigation panel provides an overview of the site's main areas and makes it easy to go directly to a specific location.

1. SDG&E logotype 2. Navigation buttons
3. Home page illustration 4. Dave, the
lineman, illustration 5. Introductory text

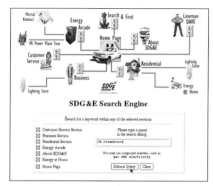

On the Search and Find page, a diagram
maps out the site using electrical outlets
to designate key areas and illustrations
and text to identify sections. Clicking on
an illustration takes you to that section.
Or you can search the site by typing keywords into the space provided.

The Energy Arcade is an educational center
that includes a virtual power plant tour
and Mortal Kontact, an activity
designed to teach children how to avoid
the dangers of electricity. You can also
learn about SDG&E's commitment to the
environment, how to prevent carbon
monoxide poisoning, and the dangers of
digging near underground service lines, or
read the online version of the SDG&E
customer newsletter, *Energy Notes*. Clicking
on the titles or images opens the activities.

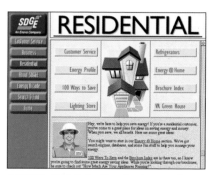

The interface of the power plant tour
has an industrial theme. The diamond-
shaped yellow signs posted on the pipes
are navigation buttons, and the icons
on the buttons represent the different
areas of the power plant. The steel-gray
metal panel displays photographs, illustrations, and animations.

A warm, cheerful yellow background
identifies the Residential section. Like
the other illustrations in the site, the
house, above, was created in Illustrator
and uses a strong perspective that
reaches out to the viewer in a
welcoming gesture.

Defining the Interface

When presented different interface options, focus group participants reacted more positively to designs that were personable
and friendly. As a result, on-screen personalities were created:
Dave, the lineman, and Marie, the customer service representative. Dave's friendly smile greets visitors on the home page,
opposite, and he and Marie appear throughout the site ready to
provide information and offer assistance. Customers also wanted
the site to feel familiar, so on the home page the city's recognizable skyline is shown in the background, and the sky blue and
turquoise palette chosen from the Netscape palette reflects
colors common to the local environment.

Enhancing Site Tours

The site offers a virtual tour of one of the SDG&E power plants
created using QuickTime VR and photographs that form a 360-
degree view of the plant. Since most requests for power plant tours
come from schools, the virtual tour is designed primarily for
classroom use, where the connection speed of ISDN lines can easily
handle the memory-intensive graphics. The virtual tour provides
students with more information than they would get by actually
going to a power plant. For example, they can't see how a turbine
works in a real plant but they can see a descriptive animation of a
turbine at work on the Web site tour.

Programming for Efficiency

SDG&E worked with two San Diego firms to develop the site:
EchoLink and Bien Logic. EchoLink designed the interface and
created the visual content, including illustrations, QuickTime
VR files, and 2D and 3D animations, and Bien Logic programmed the site using custom CGI (common gateway interface)
scripts that assemble each page on-the-fly. This approach reduced
the amount of time needed for programming, made it possible
to efficiently incorporate interactivity, different media, and a
search feature, and allows future changes to be made easily. For
example, if SDG&E were to change the company logo, the new
logo would only need to replace the old one in the pool of
artwork. Rather than have to recode every page on which the logo
appears, the updated version of the logo would be called up on all
pages where the older version had been as the pages were individually created on the spot. With a site like this one with over 600
pages, it's easy to see how this approach saves time and money.

Staying in Contact

"A unique feature of the Internet is interactivity," says Ed
van Herik of SDG&E, "and we wanted to make use of this in our
Web site, so we created plenty of opportunities throughout the
site for customers to email us with individual questions and
comments, and most are answered in one business day."

www.lights. camera.action

Overview The Sundance Channel's online Webzine uses 2D animation, audio, video, and hypertext to present information about the world of independent and foreign films.

"I do my best to give each section a different look, styling each group of pages so people can tell where they are in the site."

–Barry Deck, art director

The Mission

The Sundance Web site was designed to promote the Sundance cable channel, whose mission is to develop new filmmaking talent and to preserve the voice of independent film. An online monthly magazine, the site publishes feature stories, a column written by filmmakers, live Webcast coverage from film festivals, programming schedules, and an archive of previous articles.

The Interface Metaphor

Like the dark theaters in which films are viewed, the solid black background of the interface sets an appropriate tone and provides a dramatic contrast for the colorful graphics and display typography. Many of the interface elements suggest projection: glowing shapes, rays of light, soft shadows, blurred images, and angled shapes and typography that give the illusion of protruding off the surface.

The glowing red circle, shown above on the home page, symbolizes both the sun of "Sundance" and the light source of a film projector. The glowing light concept is repeated in the Channel button, shaped like a TV screen. The spotlights radiat-

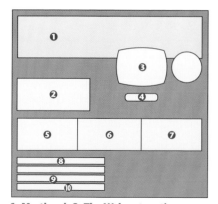

1. Masthead 2. The Webcast section
3. Sundance cable channel section
4. Sundance cable channel schedule 5. In
Profile 6. Rant 7. Filmmaker Focus 8. Fall
Festival Files 9. Archives 10. In The Mail

The masthead designs of the Sundance
Channel Screening Room, Independent
Feature Film Market, and Archives, above,
show how the projection metaphor spills
over onto the home pages of different
sections of the site. The soft shadows
behind the type and out-of-focus typography reinforce the concept. Each masthead
is styled to represent the content of its
individual section.

Clicking on the In Profile title on the home
page leads to feature articles on current
independent and foreign films. This article
is tightly organized in a magazine-style
layout that uses a four-column grid as a
basis for delicately balancing headlines,
photos, text blocks, negative space, and
accents of color. The section name, title,
byline, and even the introductory paragraph were converted to graphics. Clicking
on the glowing red button, shaped like a
TV screen, starts a QuickTime video clip of
the film under discussion. The Next button
leads to the following page of the article.

This layout for Filmmaker Focus shows
designer Barry Deck's effective combination of typography and graphics to reinforce content. The red color draws attention directly to the filmmaker's picture,
and leads up to the title, then over into
the HTML-based text type. To build on the
meaning of the title, the two o's in *looking*
are set larger to imply a pair of eyes, and
each of the circular photos is cropped so
that an eye is right in the center.

In the filmmaker's column Rant, an animated title reinforces the meaning of the
word, takes advantage of the expressive
possibilities of multimedia, and adds
dynamic interest to the page. Title and
subtitle, "Filmmakers Tell It Like It Is,"
emerge from the bright warm colors of
the ranting animation. Meanwhile, the
strip of photos and the type below fade
in and out of focus giving the impression
that you're looking through a camera lens.

ing from the light source build on the projection metaphor and
direct attention to the Webcast heading and to the changing
film images, upper left, that appear to be projected onto a
screen. When the cursor rolls over interactive graphics, it
changes to a pointing hand to show that they're clickable.

Typographic Potpourri

Each section of the site has its own unique look. On the home
page, for example, arrows connect related elements and direct
eye movement. Fine lines anchor and frame information and
subtly imply buttons and hypertext. Different type styles, sizes,
weights, and colors distinguish the section titles, emphasize key
words, and preview the look of each section.

To preserve the integrity of the layout, the typography is
created in Illustrator, converted to outline, then placed in

Photoshop for coloring and creating special effects. Converting
the type to graphics wherever possible maintains a consistent
look across platforms and among browsers. The Photoshop
document is submitted to the programmers with an indication
of where the HTML-based text type goes and often what size and
color that text should be. To further control the look of the pages,
the column width of the HTML-based text is designed so that it
does not rewrap when a page is adjusted by the viewer.

Designing On-the-Fly

Since content changes every three weeks, and in some sections
daily, articles must be designed quickly—often in a day, including
HTML programming. Page grids designed for each section help
designer Barry Deck keep up with the pace, though he often takes
creative license: "You know, the grid is there to be violated."

Everything but the New Car Smell

Overview *The Web site for Toyota Motor Sales, USA, Inc. makes good use of masthead navigation, icons, and hypertext links for getting around the site, while 2D animation, QuickTime VR, and PhotoBubbles show off the full line of Toyota models.*

> **"We wanted the site to be a destination in and of itself, so we developed a unique name and logotype to give it its own identity."**
>
> –Alan Segal, associate creative director, Saatchi & Saatchi Pacific

Launching the Web Site

@Toyota, Web headquarters for the world's fourth largest auto manufacturer, was developed to provide owners and prospective buyers with 24-hour access to dealers, product information, general Toyota news, and electronic lifestyle magazines.

Cruising the Site

To move from the home page, shown above in an early version of the site, to any of the site's eight sections, the visitor can click on any part of the masthead (the top portion of the screen) or any of the round buttons at the bottom of the page. Each section is identified by the icon on the button and the title just below it.

The masthead at the top of each subsequent page, shown opposite, contains key navigation elements: the @Toyota Web site logotype, a section button, and the name of the section. The logotype is a clickable graphic and returns visitors to the home page. The section button links to the opening page within that particular section. The section name becomes hot once the user goes more than one page deep into the section. Clicking on the section name on the masthead takes visitors back to the section's

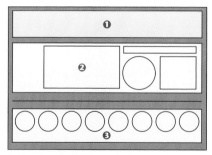

1. Masthead with hyperlinks 2. Information area with hypertext links 3. Navigation buttons that link to eight sections

The Hub, shown opposite on the masthead and in the row of buttons at the bottom of the home page, contains four on-line lifestyle magazines: *Car Culture*, *Living Home*, *A Man's Life*, and *SportZine*. The issue of *A Man's Life* shown above displays a photo of celebrity Tim Allen in a magazine-style layout surrounded by headlines, spot color, and text with hyperlinks to additional articles.

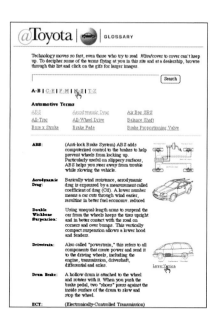

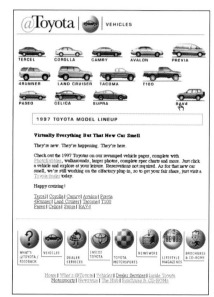

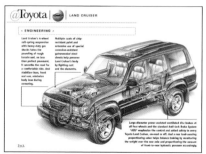

The glossary, far left, offers a search feature, definitions of automotive terms, and illustrations created in Illustrator and saved in GIF format, many with a "larger version" option. Center, on the introduction page of the Vehicles section, clicking on any of the Toyota models links to vehicle pages that include larger JPEG or GIF images (like the one above) complete specification charts, 360-degree Quick-Time VR walkarounds, and PhotoBubbles.

introduction page. Hypertext in body copy and in tables of contents also link to other pages within the site.

Accomplishing Consistency

Coordinating colors, type styles, and photography throughout all of Toyota's corporate communications accomplishes a unified effect that associate creative director Alan Segal calls "brand synergy." Achieving a consistent look and feel is important for a large company like Toyota that has more than a dozen models for sale in the United States and over a thousand dealers nationwide. To encourage visitors to the site, the Web address appears on all corporate communications.

Photography

Each year Toyota produces over 800 photographs of current models for use in brochures and advertising. Most are shot with large-format cameras on high-resolution film to obtain the best quality. To convert them to digital format, the original film is scanned at high resolution and the images are retouched as needed. After being approved by the client, images are stored in a central Web-based image bank that provides immediate access for advertising agency Saatchi & Saatchi. Since image resolution is lower for the Web than for print media, when images are downloaded from the image bank for use on the Web, the resolution is adjusted and the file size reduced, sometimes to less than 1 percent, since some of the originals can be over 15MB.

PhotoBubbles

With spherical photographs called PhotoBubbles, visitors can move around inside a vehicle, zoom in on details, and look out of the windows and sunroof by simply moving the mouse. To create Photo-Bubbles two cameras with 180-degree fish-eye lenses facing in opposite directions were mounted inside the Toyota vehicles on a rotator provided by Omniview, developer of the PhotoBubble technology. The film was processed at Omniview Studios and electronically scanned to create a digital file; then the two images were seamed together to provide a total 360-degree view of the interior.

When the 28-year-old design firm, The Designory, decided to establish a presence on the Web **(designory.com)**, they wanted the opening pages of the site (far left, top) to express their design philosophy: "When people actively participate in a communication, they create their own meaning. So they're more likely to recall and even value that meaning than if someone else gave it to them, or if they just participate passively," says principal and executive creative director Lannon Tanchum. "The goal of these pages, which are based on the juvalamu principle of perception, is to illicit an intuitive response to three nonsense words, resulting in immediate user interaction." The interlacing and layering of type and image, as seen on the juvalamu page and the opening pages of the Facts and Design sections, create a visual-verbal message, which is designed to feel rich, download quickly, and introduce the typographic approach to the site's general navigation.

In addition to the typography used to move through the main sections, navigation within deeper sections of the site is done with pictures. In the Brochures & Catalogs section within the Portfolio Archive (left) a picture matrix presents available options. Clicking on one of the 12 images opens that project's page, the picture matrix moves to the upper right corner of the screen, and all of the photographs lighten except the one representing the active page. "The picture matrix gives you an overview of the whole section, shows where you are within that section, and allows you to flip through the pages in any order you choose," says designer David Glaze.

In the spirit of interaction, the Participate area (above) is an open forum where a topic is posted to inspire dialog on issues related to design. The software Web Crossings was used by programmers at Genex Interactive to program the threaded discussion.

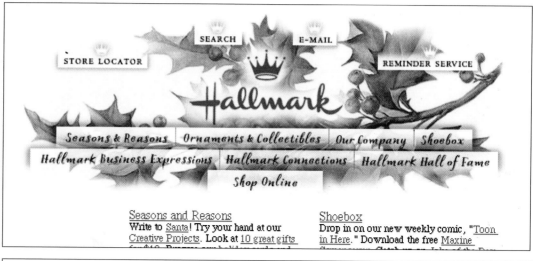

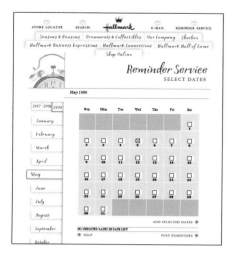

Reminder Service
SELECT DATES

When Melisa Vázquez and Tim Irvine of Giant Step were working on the design of the Hallmark Web site **(hallmark.com),** the marketing strategy was to create an online experience that matches the good, warm feeling that people get from Hallmark cards, stores, and commercials—and to keep visitors coming back for more. Among the features that add value to the site and draw visitors to return are the store locator (typing in an address and Zip code prompts a list of nearby Hallmark stores) and a reminder service (above), which sends an email reminder in advance of important dates marked on the calendar by the visitor.

Another objective was to strengthen the bond between site visitors and Hallmark. One way to do that was to develop a sense of community and interaction among Hallmark enthusiasts. For instance, a bulletin board for ornament collectors allows hobbyists to post messages to find or sell ornaments from the Hallmark collection, or just to chat about ornaments.

The section of the site that presents creative gift-wrapping projects also strengthens the tie between visitors and

Hallmark by encouraging creativity and promoting Hallmark products as a way to make projects successful.

Changing the Hallmark site frequently is one of the techniques used to encourage return visits. Since Hallmark's greeting card and ornament business is highly seasonal, it makes sense for the Web site to change to fit the current holidays. "The site is given a major overhaul every couple of months," says Vázquez. "We change all the content in the Seasons and Reasons section, and some, but not all, content elsewhere on the site."

With so much change, the designers find that it's helpful to have strict standards for the look and feel of the various categories of information presented on the site, for the sake of organization and visitor comfort. For example, three different sections of the site include artist profiles, and in all three sections the format is the same. The artist's photo is always in the lower left corner of the layout, and always has the artist's name under it, always in the same font. The same consistent approach is used for the What's New sections that appear in three

different locations. Another place the designers wanted site visitors to have a consistent, predictable experience was with navigation. "We worked really hard," says Vázquez, "to make sure that you always know where you are in the Hallmark site, and you can always find your way to wherever you need to go and back."

5 Entertainment

Whether adventuring through time, discovering nature, or singing along to a musical beat, interactive media provides imaginative new ways for us to entertain ourselves.

SOME INTERACTIVE MEDIA PRODUCTS AND WEB SITES aim to teach while they entertain us and others are designed just to be pure fun. While some are entirely fictional and others are grounded in reality, mystery and suspense are common themes in the virtual world of adventure, where tales are brought to life through animation, sound effects, video, music, and text—and with interactivity, you're in control of what happens next. Several of the case studies in this chapter are CD-ROM titles, since entertainment products have typically depended on the speed and higher quality of graphics and sound that CD-ROM technology offers.

The nature of the content is reflected in the interface and in the navigation structure, both of which can add value to the entertainment experience. The dark color palettes and high-tech interfaces of the *Buried in Time* CD-ROM (page 92) and its interactive TV prequel *Pegasus Prime* (page 98) reinforce the mystery themes of these science fiction adventure games. A map is an appropriate interface metaphor for the quirky enhanced music CD *Quattro Formaggi* (page 100), which takes you to six cool collages on a road trip with the rock band Dogstar. The roll-up menu of *Hybrid CD-i* (page 96) is an efficient use of TV screen space that's shared by a live cablecast and the overlying interactive interface. Nonfiction stories featured in the Discovery Channel Online Web site (page 94) are easy to find with the help of a clearly organized interface and a palette of six colors that differentiate the feature sections.

A BioSuit, a Few BioChips, and Arthur

Overview Using the 3D controls of the BioSuit, plug-in BioChips, and an artificial intelligence agent to maneuver through photorealistic environments is almost like being there in Presto Studios' The Journeyman Project 2: Buried in Time, *an interactive science fiction adventure game full of challenging mysteries, which has been translated into several languages, including Korean, shown below.*

"We learned from previous projects that it's important to have all the critical controls on the screen at one time so players can get instantaneous response."

–Phil Saunders, creative director

Going Back

Agent 5 has been framed for tampering with the past, which he has sworn to protect as a Temporal Security agent. Wearing his BioSuit, a self-contained time machine, he travels through time to investigate who framed him and why.

Inside the BioSuit

The *Buried in Time* interface, shown above, is the environment inside the helmet of the BioSuit. Necessary tools and navigation controls have been carefully conceptualized and meticulously rendered from the perspective of the player, who has assumed the role of Agent 5. Details, like the slight curvature of the border elements, define the dimensionality of the helmet and support the 3D illusion. To further enhance the feeling of being inside the BioSuit looking out, a dark color scheme is used in the surrounding area to contrast with the lighter, brighter colors seen through the main view window.

Deciding What's Most Important

Interface elements were prioritized to determine where they

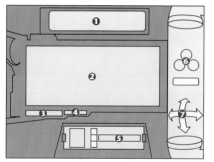

1. Message window 2. Main view window
3. Date indicator 4. Power indicator
5. Inventory window 6. BioChip holographic display 7. Navigation control

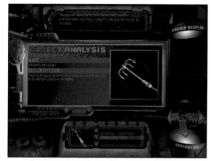

Use the up and down arrows to scroll
through the inventory. Select an object
from the list by clicking its name. The
object appears in the small display area
to the left. Click the magnifying glass
icon to open the information screen.

STATS AND SOFTWARE

It took 16 team members 22 months to
complete *The Journeyman Project 2: Buried
in Time*, a 3 CD-ROM set. Planning and
design took 18 months, asset production
16 months, programming and testing 14
months. Photoshop and Illustrator were
used for 2D graphic design and creating
texture maps, FormZ and VIDI for 2D
modeling, Electric Image for 3D animation and rendering, After Effects and
Premiere for video compositing and
rotoscoping, and Director for the Mac
programming. The PC version is entirely
coded in C++. Learn more at **presto.com**

should be positioned on-screen. Since players interact most
with the navigation control, it's conveniently placed in the
lower right corner and all the other interface elements are
positioned in relation to this corner. The inventory window,
where objects important to the mission are stored, is the second
most used device and is placed at bottom center just left of the
navigation control. Next in importance is the BioChip display
that's positioned above the navigation control. All are easily
reached with only a slight movement of the mouse.

These three elements form a right angle that anchors the
main view window, where all action is seen as players jump
between time zones and explore exotic locales. This window is
positioned at eye level in the center of the interface. Above it is
the message window, where warnings of danger appear.

Right, Left, Up, Down, and Forward

The 3D arrow cluster of the navigation control allows players to
turn a full 360 degrees right or left, look up or down, and move
forward when the corresponding navigation arrows are highlighted. Using five arrows in a spherical form makes it easier for
players to understand how to move.

BioChips

BioChips are high-tech program modules, acquired during the
adventure and stored compactly in the inventory, that add
value to game play. For example, the Cloak BioChip renders
the BioSuit invisible, and the Translate BioChip can decipher
both the written and spoken forms of
every known language, which comes in
handy when a player is trying to decode
clues such as a letter found at Chateau
Gaillard written in Middle English or an
inscription on the Mayan temple Chichén
Itzá. When a BioChip is being used, its
holographic image is shown in the
BioChip Display.

Arthur, at Your Service

Feedback received from players of the
original *Journeyman Project* and focus-
group testing led to modifications in the
sequel, such as the addition of a unique

Leonardo da Vinci's workshop was modeled from detailed concept
sketches based on extensive historical research. The 3D models
were then texture-mapped and animated in Electric Image. The
horizontal letterbox format was chosen to optimize image size
and playback.

Artificial Intelligence Agent named Arthur, whose persona was
downloaded into a BioChip, and who helps players through
difficult puzzles. Depending on how a user plays the game,
audio clips of this empathic sidekick respond either with subtle
hints or with obvious clues, usually seasoned with a touch of
humor and often with bold sarcasm.

Finishing Touches

Flowing movement is achieved by a combination of computer-
generated animations and full-motion video. In some scenes
players encounter live actors intermixed with computer graphics. To achieve this, actors were shot against a blue screen. The
blue was later removed and the live foot-
age matted onto 3D environments. After
extensive testing to optimize playback on
low-end PCs, 12 frames per second was
chosen for the computer-generated animations shown in the main view window,
and 15 frames-per-second for smaller live
video segments.

Full-color graphics were reduced to a
16-bit custom color palette, and the master sound file was down-sampled from
16-bit to 8-bit to deliver smaller file sizes.
All the different moving assets were
converted to QuickTime movies using
Cinepak compression.

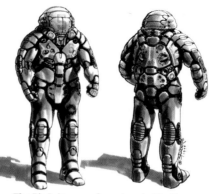

The BioSuit, worn by actors in the live
footage, was produced by All Effects in
Hollywood from Presto Studios' detailed
sketches, shown here.

Guided by Experience

Overview *This redesign of Discovery Online features original interactive nonfiction stories with photographs, illustrations, audio, video, and 2D animation.*

"It's really important that designers have a strong design foundation, no matter what medium they're working in. I would much rather hire an outstanding designer who needs to learn the tools than a Photoshop whiz who has no sense of design—and I've worked with both."

–Lisa Waltuch, art director

Complementing the TV Channel

Discovery Online features original nonfiction interactive stories devoted to history, technology, nature, exploration, and science. The Web site complements the programming of cable television's Discovery Channel and shares its mission: "to help people explore their world."

Setting Goals

The design and production were guided by what had and hadn't worked in the earlier version of the Web site. The goals were to simplify navigation so users would always have a sense of orientation; to provide more direct access from the home page to everything else; to create content—text, graphics, forums, audio, and video—that would download more quickly while still offering a rich experience; to develop a clearer and more immediate interface that would invite a nearly automatic response; and to build a structure that would be flexible enough to grow and adapt to changing technology and to content that changes daily.

Simplifying Navigation

"In the original site you had to go through four screens before you could select a story," explains art director Lisa Waltuch. "We realized that this was confusing and too time consuming, so we

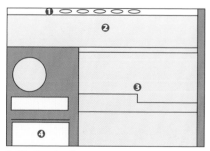

1. Navigation bar 2. Feature story head-line 3. Story lead-in 4. Contents

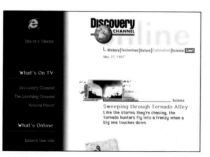

The first level of the site uses a two-panel vertical grid. The black panel leads to the general areas and cable TV programming and the white panel leads to the feature sections of Discovery Online. An animated GIF calls attention to the navigation bar at the top.

A three-panel vertical grid identifies each section's introduction page. The title typography, set in Interstate Black Condensed and Regular, uses type style, size, and color value to show hierarchy: This is the Nature section, which is one level away from the Online home page.

Each story, found on the third level of the site, has its own unique layout. For good readability text is set in an HTML font size of 3 in a 300-pixel column width. The colored box on the navigation bar, top, shows where you are. Clicking on the globe or Discovery Online goes to the home page.

Subtleties in the layout create visual distinctions between the different areas of the site. When you select an item from the black panel on the home page, the subsequent layout retains the two-column grid but the title typography is positioned flush left, shown above, instead of centered, to distinguish these pages from Discovery Online areas, lower right. To return to the home page, the hub of the site, click on the globe.

STATS AND SOFTWARE

A typical feature story takes a 5-member core team 3 months to complete. Software includes Director, Illustrator, and Photoshop. Macs are used for design and graphics, PCs for HTML coding, and Silicon Graphics workstations for proprietary software and special programming, like Java. **discovery.com**

changed the deep navigation to a shallower and wider structure that provides more direct access. Now you can go directly into one of the highlighted stories, or anywhere else in the site, from the home page." Straightforward rather than metaphorical terminology also helps eliminate confusion—for example, world was used before as a metaphor for stories. "Now we just say what we mean," adds Waltuch.

Designing Efficiently

The first version of the site used complex tables with large graphics, including graphics-based headline type, and took too long to download. "We've learned to utilize HTML code more for design purposes, by creating tables and borders and using horizontal rules, for example. That has helped cut the 150K page size in half, so now pages load quickly," says Waltuch. "There's a delicate balance between dazzling users with wonderful graphics and frustrating them by making them wait too long for the graphics to download."

Six colors, selected from the 216-color Web-safe palette, are used to differentiate the feature sections of Discovery Online, as shown here in the introduction pages of each section. The color of the section title and tiled background pattern corresponds to the color that identifies each section in the navigation bar.

Flexible Structure

Using a modular structure based on HTML tables allows changes to be made easily and efficiently—and that's important in a site like this one that changes every day. For example, the story on tornadoes, whose introductory page is shown opposite, is given top billing on the home page, shown above left, but another story may take its place on the following day. The items in the contents list are interchangeable.

Teamwork

History, technology, nature, exploration, and science—each has its own production team, which includes an editor, a writer, a designer, an HTML developer, and the Discovery Online media editor. The art director and

This series of still images makes up the animated GIF on the home page.

the production manager monitor and approve all stories. Depending on the demands of the project, a programmer, who specializes in Java and proprietary software, and a digital producer, who digitizes and edits video and audio, work with the team as needed.

Interactivity Adds Value to TV Programming

Overview *GTE Entertainment's* Hybrid CD-i Interactive Television Project *superimposes interactive data from a CD-ROM disk—2D and 3D animation, audio, video, and hypertext—over real-time cable TV programming on the Discovery Channel.*

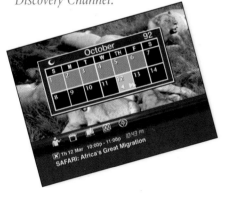

"We took the Discovery Channel and made it interactive for 18 hours a day. Users couldn't do anything to the TV programming, but what they could do was get a lot of additional information."

–Steve Lomas, designer/director

The Concept

The Hybrid CD-i Interactive Television Project was a pilot study conducted in Cerritos, California, by GTE Entertainment in collaboration with the Discovery Channel. For a year-and-a-half live television programming was supplemented with articles and information stored on a CD-i (compact disc-interactive), as well as with real-time data, which was being accessed from six different databases around the country. The data was embedded into the active video signal and synchronized on-the-fly with the TV programs, using TCP/IP (transmission control protocol/internet protocol).

The Interface

Since TV screen space was shared between the live cablecast and the interactive overlay, the CD-i interface was designed so the viewer could make it appear and disappear quickly and easily by pressing a button on the hand-held remote control device. The interface solution, above, was a roll-up menu that unfurled from the bottom of the screen to display the main navigation icons and provided a gray background on which other interactive elements and information could be presented. Closing and then reopening the menu opened it at the same point where you left it.

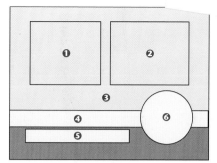

1. Content window 2. Text area 3. Live TV program in the background 4. Roll-up menu with primary navigation 5. TV program icon bar 6. Navigation atlas globe

Hybrid Shopping Mall

Select a storefront from the Hybrid Shopping Mall options displayed below the navigation icons. Every time a new selection is made, the name in the Title Area at the bottom of the interactive interface changes to identify where you are.

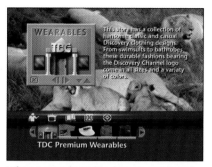

TDC Premium Wearables

When a storefront is selected, a video of the chosen shop plays in the video window that overlays the live TV program. Descriptive text appears to the right of the window, and a selection of merchandise, in this case clothing, is displayed at the bottom.

Discovery Sport Shirt

When the viewer chooses one of the articles of clothing, the bar beneath it changes color to show that the item is selected, and the selected item appears larger in the video window with descriptive text on the right.

Icons on the navigation bar represent, from left to right: Agent Help/Preferences, Tell Me Now (to display current show information), Browse, Calendar of Programming, and Atlas Globe. Below the navigation bar the title of the current program and the date, program time, and current time are displayed. At bottom right the Help Agent explains how the interface works.

Spinning the Atlas Globe

When a geographic location was mentioned in the current TV program, the Atlas Globe, opposite, rotated and a blinking red dot identified the specific location being discussed. Clicking on the hot spot linked to other information about that location. The globe could also be rotated using the four arrows that appeared when the cursor rolled close to the globe. Clicking on the arrows on the left and right of the globe rotated it on its axis. The arrows on the top and bottom tilted the globe up and down.

Getting Help

Using a videotaped actor as a Help Agent related well to the videotaped programming. The agent's sense of humor also provided a personal touch as he led viewers on a complete tour of the interface and unexpectedly popped up from time to time to say that a holiday or special event was currently being celebrated in a particular part of the world.

NATURE	GEO	SCI/TECH	PEOPLE	OTHER
R = 75	R = 57	R = 116	R = 164	R = 173
G = 165	G = 107	G = 80	G = 61	G = 99
B = 63	B = 165	B = 145	B = 70	B = 57

Current / Future Timecon Examples

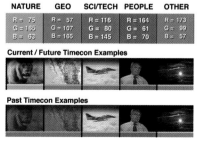

Past Timecon Examples

Timecons, photographic icons that represent TV programs, were positioned in the order in which the programs were broadcast. Colored bars beneath the timecons identified the topic of the program. When a program had already been broadcast, the bar turned gray.

Alignment and Sharpness

"Our tests showed that when we videotaped the Help Agent walking around in a staged area that correlated with the viewer's TV screen, he was so small on the video that the resolution of the resulting image in the interface was too low," explains designer Steve Lomas. "To compensate, we shot the actor as large as possible in the video frame and then reduced his image to the appropriate size once the video was digitized. This resulted in a much sharper image." To position the actor in the interface, he was videotaped in front of a large seamless piece of blue paper that had the interface drawn roughly on it and a ruler drawn across the top. The same ruler was superimposed over the actual interface, then frame-by-frame the digitized video was aligned to the on-screen interface.

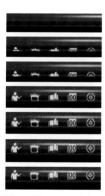

The roll-up menu is a 1-second animation displayed at 10 frames per second. Each frame was cropped manually to create the illusion that the video was rolling up.

Integrating Diverse Databases

Data was accessed from different databases around the country. So a proprietary tool, nicknamed "Data Cop," was created with C and C++ programming language to detect and correct formatting inconsistencies in the data.

Venturing Onto TV

Overview Presto Studios' The Journeyman Project: Pegasus Prime *incorporates 2D and 3D animation, audio, and digital video in this interactive time-travel adventure designed for Sony's Playstation, a TV set-top game system.*

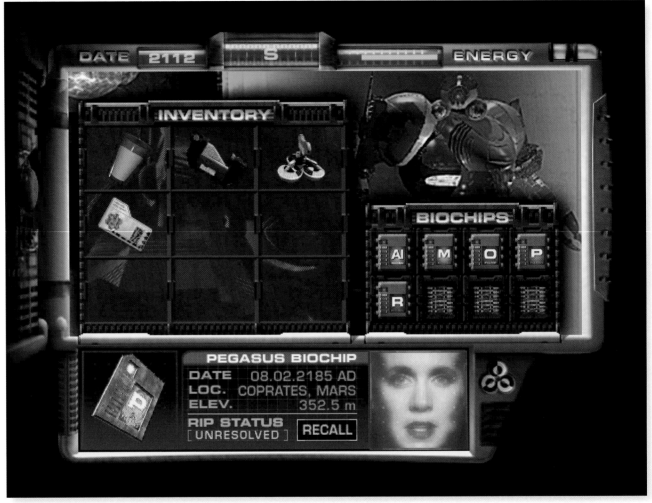

"**One of the main differences between designing for television and designing for the computer is TV's low screen resolution.**"

–Tommy Yune, lead conceptual designer and special effects

Computer Screen to TV Screen

Presto Studios re-created its award-winning computer game *The Journeyman Project* as *Pegasus Prime* for use on Sony's Playstation, a TV set-top game system. Advancements in game consoles made it possible to expand the game play and graphics of *The Journeyman Project* to allow for fully animated 3D walkthroughs, but the interface had to be completely redesigned to adapt to the low resolution of TV screens, NTSC (National Television Systems Committee) color standards, and the use of a remote hand-held direction pad instead of a mouse to control play.

The Challenges of Low Screen Resolution

The Sony Playstation displays 320 x 240 pixels—or one-fourth the number of pixels of a typical computer monitor. Like television viewers, players of set-top game systems usually sit 10 to 15 feet from the television set. Coupled with the low resolution, this makes on-screen text difficult to read. To compensate for low resolution, viewing distance, and limited screen space, text was kept to a minimum and supplemented with audio and video. To optimize readability when text was necessary, designer Tommy Yune created a custom bitmapped font.

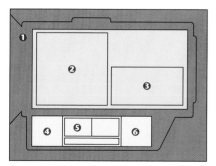

1. Main interface frame 2. Inventory panel 3. Biochips panel 4. BioChip display 5. Information panel 6. Artificial-Intelligence agent display

Players venture through different environments, like the one on Mars, shown here. The position of the Artificial Intelligence agent on the right side of the information panel at the bottom reminds the player that the selected Access Card was taken from the Inventory panel, which, if open, would appear directly above the agent.

STATS AND SOFTWARE

A 15-member team worked 2 years to complete *Pegasus Prime*: Planning and design took 6 months, asset production, 18 months, and programming and testing, 12 months. Software included After Effects, PowerAnimator, ElectricImage, Form Z, CodeWarrior, Photoshop, Premiere, and Tree Pro. Hardware included 10 Macs, 2 PCs, and 2 Silicon Graphics workstations. Learn more at **presto.com**.

Game play not only includes the ability to wander around elaborately rendered virtual 3D environments, but also offers players animated puzzles, like the one above that challenges the player to deactivate a bomb. Beginning players get up to three hints, or they can ask the Artificial Intelligence agent to solve the puzzle for them.

These details show some of the variety of the interfaces that were created to be displayed within the main interface frame. Looking up at a computer monitor, the player can control two video clips to gain information about game characters.

A wounded player chooses a self-diagnosis. The second of these sequential images shows an animated detail of the body with a red dot indicating the location of the wound. The color and weight of the border around the word "yes" indicates that it's selected.

Using Artificial Intelligence

Since a lot of text couldn't be used, other means had to be developed to communicate important game information. Audio alone wouldn't work because of the possibility of distracting ambient noise, so Presto decided to use audio and video in the form of an artificial intelligence (AI) agent who offers general help, provides information, and guides players through difficult situations. Testing showed that using the AI agent improved comprehension dramatically.

The AI agent appears in the information panel at the bottom of the primary interface, shown on the facing page, directly below the open Biochips panel about which the AI agent is talking. When inventory is referred to, the video appears on the opposite side of the information panel directly below the Inventory panel. This change in positioning adds to successful communication and better understanding.

Interface Within Interface

When selected, the Inventory and BioChips panels slide up out of the main interface frame to display objects that assist in playing the game. Both the panels, shown open on the opposite page, share design features with the main interface: rounded corners and modeled edges, hinged articulation to the main

interface frame, and type style. These common features visually reinforce that all three panels are part of one mechanism—an ocular neuro-prosthesis worn by Agent 5, whose identity the player assumes in the adventure.

NTSC-Safe Colors

Certain colors, such as white, which can be displayed without problem on a computer monitor, don't fare well on a regular television screen, so the artwork for *Pegasus Prime* was adjusted with a Photoshop filter to NTSC-legal colors. This helped retain detail and avoid a vibrating glow, known as *bleeding*. To compensate for the different color gamuts of television screens, color saturation was reduced, especially in the reds, greens, and blues, as well as the black and white extremes.

Navigation Controls

Players move around the interface and make selections using a device that they control with both hands. To make game play intuitive the designers coordinated the controller buttons for the Inventory and BioChips panels with where these panels appear on-screen: For example, the Inventory panel appears on the left side of the screen so the button that controls it is located on the upper left side of the device.

On the Road With Dogstar

Overview *The enhanced music CD Quattro Formaggi uses surrealistic photo collages, humorous 2D and 3D animations with sound effects, candid video footage, and four new audio tracks from the rock band Dogstar to promote the band's full-length CD.*

"**The livelihood of the enhanced CD is definitely in question—there are many skeptics of the format who dismiss its place in the market. However, there are more titles being produced than ever, and the quality is improving everyday.**"

–E. J. Dixon III, producer and creative director

Enhancing a Music CD

Record company Zoo Entertainment chose nu.millennialstudios to create an enhanced CD to introduce four new songs from the rock band Dogstar with Bret Domrose, guitar and vocal, Rob Mailhouse, drums, and Keanu Reeves, bass. The music tracks on *Quattro Formaggi* (Italian for "four cheeses") can be played on a standard audio CD player or on a computer, as users join the band on an interactive multimedia road trip to six destinations, each represented by an elaborate surrealistic collage full of unexpected audio, video, and animation that invite exploring.

Creating the Interface

To provide fans, who range in age from 12 to 25, with a cheesy, off-the-wall experience, the production team, under the direction of E.J. Dixon, created a lighthearted and impromptu interface that includes familiar icons from well-known destinations, many of which the band visited on tour. The images in the six collages were selected from the Corel Stock Photo Library, a collection of digital stock photo CDs. Then in Photoshop the images were sized, cropped, masked, manipulated as necessary, and assembled into fantasy environments.

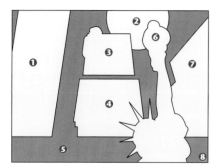

1. Animated windows of the Chrysler Building 2. Moon leading to music video 3. Animated billboard 4. Animated billboard 5. City street leading to next destination 6. Torch microphone leading to a candid video 7. Billboard that plays a video 8. Dogstar identity that leads to main menu

The main menu is displayed on a map above the dashboard of a car. Rolling the cursor over the name of a destination on the map shows a picture of the destination collage as simulated above. Clicking on the rearview mirror opens the Fan Club screen.

Clicking on a destination on the map starts a QuickTime movie: The car veers off the road and drives through the billboard as the screen transitions into the destination collage. The sequences were rendered in SoftImage, compressed, then pixel doubled for playback at 640 x 480.

Like all the collages, the Los Angeles screen is a composite of separate images: the sky, the mountains, the beach, the palm tree, the freeway with individual cars added, the sign, and City Hall. Dogstar's identity, the paw print and star, lower right, connects back to the map.

When the mouse rolls over an object in a destination collage, the object turns into a big piece of cheese and plays a sound bite from one of the band's songs. Clicking on the object takes you to a music video screen that presents one of the featured songs. Typeset lyrics are shown next to a video of the band performing that particular song, such as "Honesty Anyway," above. In keeping with the theme, a yellow road sign in the lower right corner returns you to the destination collage.

STATS AND SOFTWARE

A 5-member team worked 120 hours over a 3-week period to produce this enhanced CD. Software included Director, Photoshop, Premiere, and SoftImage. Mac, PC, and Silicon Graphics workstations were used.

Everything in the collages is designed to respond to the rollover of the mouse. For example, in the New York scene, opposite, when the mouse rolls over the Chrysler Building the windows flash and change colors to the sound of car horns honking in traffic. When the mouse rolls over the billboard on the right, a video of the band plays.

Creating Cues

The objects in the collages that link to other screens change their appearance as the cursor rolls over them. For example, as the mouse rolls over the torch held by the Statue of Liberty, on the facing page, the torch switches to a microphone accompanied by a piercing high-pitched squeal. Clicking on the microphone leads to another screen with a candid video of the band doing a sound check before a performance in New York. Whenever the mouse rolls over the road, an interface element common to all of the collages, the main cursor becomes a piece of cheese and clicking with the cheese takes you to the next stop on the tour.

Long Days, Sleepless Nights

Following three months of concept development and extensive planning that included detailed flow charts and explicit storyboards, production was completed in just three weeks. "The flow charts mapped out the links from one screen to another, and the storyboards visually represented what would happen when you rolled over or clicked on different parts of the screen. These guided the designers, the programmers, and the beta testers, and allowed production to go a lot more smoothly," says Dixon.

Using Premiere, images were captured from video, then opened in Photoshop where textures and layering effects were applied to create the backgrounds of the video screens.

Tucson, Arizona

Mount Rushmore

Australia

Seattle, Washington

Experience Peter Gabriel's Secret World

Overview Xplora 1, Peter Gabriel's Secret World *is an imaginative interactive CD-ROM, which presents four distinct realms of musician and entertainer Peter Gabriel's life using photographs, animation, graphics, and extensive video and audio.*

"Designing an interface is about creating a mood and an experience. If you focus on creating a great experience for people, rather than on using technology, your product is much more likely to succeed."

–Steve Nelson, creative director and producer, Brilliant Media

Setting Goals

Produced by the San Francisco-based Brilliant Media and Real World Multimedia in Box, England, *Xplora 1* invites fans to explore and discover the secret world of Peter Gabriel. "Our goal in creating Xplora 1, one of the first interactive music CD-ROMs, was to produce a very creative interactive experience—and to communicate the feeling of Peter Gabriel's music and other music from around the world that he supports through his record label Real World," says Steve Nelson, founder of Brilliant Media.

Organizing the Content

The extensive content is divided into four main sections with a hide-and-seek game woven throughout. The Us section features music, videos, and artwork from Gabriel's *Us* album. World Music presents samples from 40 albums, instruments users can play, and coverage of the World of Music and Dance festival. Personal World showcases Gabriel's earlier records, an interactive photo album, and human rights projects he supports. Behind the Scenes provides an interactive tour of Real World studios where you can join in a jam session and remix a hit song.

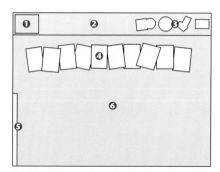

1. Video agent 2. Navigation bar 3. Main section icons 4. Subsection icons 5. General controls bar 6. Main content area

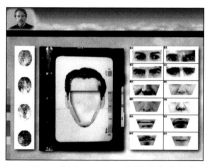

In a video window, upper left, Gabriel gives instructions on how to complete this interactive puzzle of the features of his face. Clicking on a puzzle piece on the right moves it into the appropriate position on the face. When you complete the puzzle, the pieces change color and move to the locations shown in the screen at right.

On the main menu screen, the features of the face become active buttons that you can click to enter the four sections. To avoid interrupting the process of exploration and discovery, this is the one screen where text identifies an interface element when the mouse rolls over the buttons on the bottom of the color strip.

Clicking on the ear, left, opens the introductory screen of the World Music section. The four icons in the navigation bar, top right, represent the four sections of *Xplora 1*. The four icons in the main content area of the screen represent the four World Music subsections.

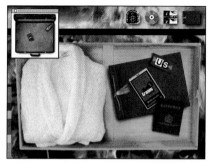

Throughout *Xplora 1* there are items to be discovered and stored in the suitcase provided at startup, such as the pass to the Grammy rehearsal. Clicking on the green button at the top of the vertical color strip, left, opens the suitcase window, upper left. After certain items have been collected, players win a backstage pass, a screensaver, and other surprises.

STATS AND SOFTWARE

A 20-member design and production team that included creative professionals from Brilliant Media in San Francisco and Real World Multimedia in England, spent 3 months on design and prototyping, and 7 months on asset production and programming over the period of a year. The authoring software, running on Macs, included HyperCard and Digital Montage, a proprietary authoring tool developed by Steve Nelson of Brilliant Media. Other software used included After Effects, Photoshop, and Premiere.

Organizing the Screen

The screen is organized into three main areas: a navigation bar at the top, a main content area, and a strip of colored rollover buttons on the left side, where general controls such as Return to Main Menu and Quit are found. The color strip echoes a similar color bar used on the cover of the *Us* album, which was released at the same time as *Xplora 1*.

Since the concept of *Xplora 1* is to get people to feel like they're exploring and discovering, photographic icons, instead of text, are used to identify the interface elements and to tie in with the photographic look that characterizes Gabriel's album covers. Color photographs are used as background textures to represent each of the main areas and to build on the world theme by focusing on the four physical elements—earth, wind, fire, and water.

Enhancing the Experience

Using Peter Gabriel as the video agent personalizes the experience. He actually responds to what you're doing. If you try to sneak backstage at the World Music festival without a pass in your suitcase, he'll pop-up and say, "You can't do that," and if you try again he responds with, "nah, come on."

Fire represents the Personal File section of *Xplora 1*. Clicking on the CD-ROM icon on in the main image area of the introductory page, above, leads to a selection of Gabriel's earlier albums, at right.

Beyond the introductory page, the fire background also appears in the navigation bar. Clicking on the fire in the navigation bar leads back to the section's introductory page, at left.

Clicking on an album on the preceding screen, left, leads to the screen for that particular album, like *Shaking the Tree*, above, where a sample song plays and information about the album is displayed.

Caption This is part of The Dominion a promotional Web site (**scifi.com**) for television's Sci-Fi channel. It's associated with What's On Air Now, which presents a new frame-grab every 30 seconds, a current still uploaded to show site visitors what's on the Sci-Fi Channel. Since the pictures are sometimes fairly funny out of context, designers decided to let people respond, producing running commentaries much like the sometimes sarcastic feedback that adds flavor to the Sci-Fi Channel's *Mystery Science Theatre 3000*. "We rolled that functionality into the site," says Smith, "and it's been a huge success. People love it."

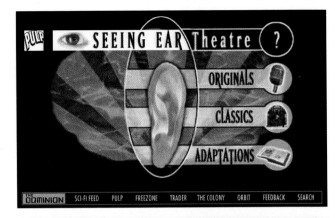

Free Zone and Orbit were parts of The Dominion from the very beginning in 1995. Web cruisers love finding "stuff out there," says Smith, "a gold mine of shareware and freeware." So these areas provide downloadable sound bites and audio clips, such as The Bionic Man's "boing" or The Hulk's roar. "We don't necessarily see it as a way of increasing traffic, but just giving our dedicated fans what they love."

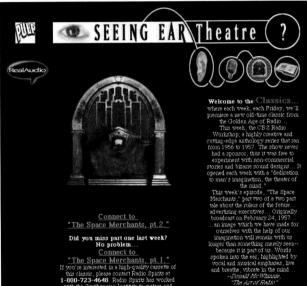

When the Seeing Ear Theatre section of The Dominion was created, its designers knew they wanted it to be more than just radio online. "This was a new medium," says creative director Sharleen Smith, "with possibilities of its own."

Not only does Real Audio technology make streaming sound possible, but it also allows the site's creators to integrate multimedia—using an audio clip to trigger an associated Web page to come up. Using these multimedia capabilities to enhance its programming, the site presents three kinds of material: classic radio dramas; audio narratives adapted from the works of Poe, Kafka, and others; and new dramas based on original scripts written especially for presentation on the site.

The Golf Channel Online supports the actual cable television channel in several ways **(thegolfchannel.com)**. "In the early days of the channel," says Philip Hurst, "it provided a program guide for channel subscribers whose local newspapers and *TV Guide* didn't yet carry its program listings." More recently, the site's weekly updates provide Golf Channel program information in more depth than print listings can accommodate, with program highlights and special events. Not only does the Web site deliver this additional information to current Golf Channel subscribers, but it also lets nonsubscribers know about the channel so they can subscribe or request that their local cable company carry it.

Successful use of an underlying grid helps make the site's information easy to get to. Modular organization of information is supported by the site's page design to make navigation easy. In the top right corner of each page, a list of clickable headings provides access to all areas of the site, and a blue arrowhead indicates the current location within it.

6 Tools and Applications

The Program
A CD-ROM, a Brochure, and a Web Site **108**

Bryce 2
Reshaping an Interface **110**

Art Dabbler
Drop-Down Drawers **112**

CyberMom
Plan Your future with Help from CyberMom **114**

On-Screen Television Program Guide
A 500-Channel Program Guide **116**

Making It Macintosh
Look and Feel Like a Mac **118**

Gallery **120**

Like a well-balanced hammer or a sharp kitchen knife, software applications and other tools assist us in completing a task, or in creating and producing our own work. We've come to rely on these products and to expect a lot out of them.

WHETHER YOU'RE DEVELOPING AN INTERFACE for graphics software, a business application, or an entertainment tool, users expect efficiency. No story, no plot, no mystery, no time for wandering or exploring—these tools are workhorses whose clarity, responsiveness, and accessibility are critical.

In recent years there has been an increase in the number of creative design solutions within this group. With increased RAM, better color capabilities, and video cards, and improved processing speed becoming the norm, "disk space" can be set aside for more sophisticated and complex interface elements. Where we used to see only flat 2-bit black-and-white icons and bitmapped type, we now see color, 2D and 3D illustration, sound, and animation integrated into the tools and controls of the user interface. These additions can make programs more appealing, more engaging, and clearer.

The case studies in this chapter inspire us to push the boundaries of interface design for software applications and other screen-based tools. The interface for the rendering program Bryce 2 (page 110) makes use of the software itself to create the dramatic 3D tools. The paint program Dabbler 2 (page 112) uses a unique system of drawers to present the electronic tools of the trade. The whimsical animation sequences of *Making It Macintosh*, Apple Computer's guide to Macintosh interface design standards (page 118), illustrate the principles behind the Macintosh interface and use interactive media to effectively explain interactive concepts.

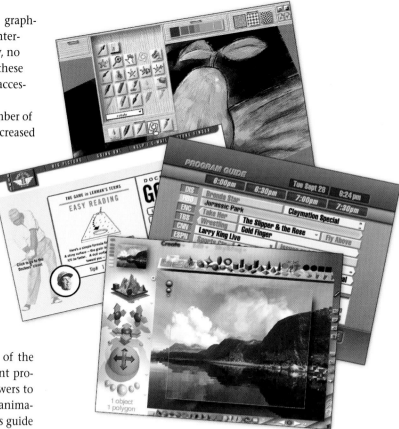

A CD-ROM, a Brochure, and a Web Site

Overview *The CD-ROM component of Potlatch Corporation's The Program uses photography, video, audio, and animation to provide customers with information about Potlatch's commercial printing papers.*

"The Program software on the CD-ROM allows customers to do their jobs better and at the same time serves as a marketing tool for Potlatch by keeping the Potlatch name in front of customers while they work."

–Kevin Kuester, creative director

Complementary Media

The Program, designed and produced by Kuester Partners for Potlatch Corporation, is a set of three integrated tools that helps graphic designers, print specifiers, and corporate communicators select appropriate papers from Potlatch's full line of coated printing papers based on the goals and needs of their projects. The Program includes a brochure, a CD-ROM, and a Web site.

The brochure presents printed examples that demonstrate the unique attributes of Potlatch's line of papers. The CD-ROM contains a project management software tool called The Plan-

ner, which conveniently resides on the computer's desktop and is designed to help customers efficiently plan, track, and specify their print projects. Also on the CD-ROM are The Paper, an interactive multimedia paper resource, and a bookmark to The Paper Site, which offers online updates to The Program and access to a directory of Potlatch paper distributors.

The Interface

The interface of The Paper, above, uses human models as visual metaphors for the customers who specify paper. To represent the

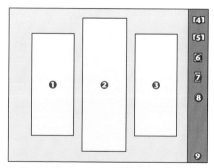

1. Paper Catalog button 2. Select by
Needs button 3. Merchant listing button
and title 4. Contents icon
5. Sound icon 6. Print icon 7. Information
icon 8. Quit icon 9. Company logotype
and credits button

To show which section is currently
selected, when you click on one of the
models on the Contents page of The
Paper, the other two go out of focus and
fade into the background. The navigation
bar, right, is available from all pages.

Clicking on the model with the flat sheet
of paper presents the Select by Needs
information. When an item is selected in
the contents, upper right, the color of the
type changes, the sheet of paper spins and
becomes the video window, and a video
tells about the selected item.

Each item in the list of paper attributes,
upper right, has a horizontal slider. When
you click and drag the sliders, the names
of the papers that have the specified
attributes appear in the best, better, and
good lists. Different type sizes are used
to prioritize the titles of the three lists.

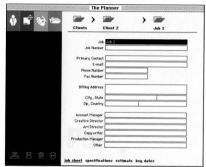

The Planner can be downloaded to a hard
drive and linked to The Paper, which runs
off the CD-ROM. Using The Planner you
can easily maintain databases on your
own organization, clients, printing companies, and vendors. The layout is well
organized and user-friendly. The database
icons, top left, and the tool icons, lower
left, are available from anywhere within
The Planner. The contents list at the bottom shows the sections of The Planner.
The underlined text shows where you are.

STATS AND SOFTWARE

An 8-member team worked about 9
months to complete the CD-ROM portion of The Program. Software included
Access, After Effects, CodeWarrior, Director, Photoshop, Premiere, SoundEdit 16,
and Visual Basic. Mac and PC computers
were used. **thepapersite.com**

three different sections of The Paper, each of the models is
holding a different example of paper use—a bound booklet, a
small flat sheet, and a large rolled-up sheet.

Subdued and Nonintrusive

Since The Planner and The Paper are support tools that customers use while working on their own design projects, color in the
interface is kept to a minimum. A neutral color palette and
black-and-white photographs are used so the tool doesn't compete with the customer's own work.

The type on The Paper contents screen, opposite, is rotated
so the section titles read upward and relate to the vertical
emphasis of the models. The key word in each title is empha-
sized using a larger type size. The change in size and the slight
overlapping of the words create depth and visual interest. The
contemporary sans serif typeface, Univers Condensed, was
selected to tie in The Program with other Potlatch materials. The
condensed version of Univers reads well on-screen and allows
letterspacing to be used as a design element without the words
taking up too much screen space.

The Paper Catalog section of The Paper
provides descriptions of each of the
Potlatch papers listed at the left. You can
select a name from the list to learn more
about that specific paper. The heavily
leaded text on the right lends a feeling of
spaciousness and makes it easy to follow
along as a voice-over recites the text.

In addition to selecting paper by name
from the list, shown at left, you can also
click on the brochure held by the model
to actually turn the pages. As the pages
turn, the specifications of each paper are
shown in the center of the screen.

To get an overview of The Program, play
The Tour, a multimedia tutorial. The contents page of The Tour, above, uses photographs to identify the three components
of The Program and the original soundtrack. You can click on a photograph to
learn more about that component.

Reshaping an Interface

Overview *Bryce 2, by MetaCreations, is a software application for designing and rendering natural and surreal 3D landscapes and terrains. It introduces 300 new features in this version and a unique interface with 3D tools and controls that are intuitive and responsive.*

"A decision we made early was to keep the front end of Bryce 2 really friendly, but behind that front end to provide a lot of functionality for more advanced users."

–Phil Clevinger, MetaCreations, Inc.

Look and Feel

The innovative buttons and controls of Bryce 2 glow in virtual spotlights, dramatically casting digital shadows and producing the illusion that they could actually be picked up. Created in Bryce 2, and mapped in Bryce's terracotta and turquoise flat color, the controls are a testimonial to the application's 3D capabilities.

Hiding Complexity

Surrounding the work space, above, are six primary palettes full of inviting objects and icons designed to show what they do, to encourage exploration, and to respond quickly to a mouse click. The control palette, found on the left side of the work space, is used most often. Its importance is demonstrated by the amount of space devoted to it in the interface, the size of the controls, and the fact that it's always visible.

The three main tool palettes found at the top of the screen—Create, Edit, and Sky & Fog—are needed often and therefore allotted the second largest amount of space. To make all the tools accessible without overwhelming users by the sheer number of them, only one of the tool palettes can be opened at a time.

The least used palettes, the Selection palette below the work

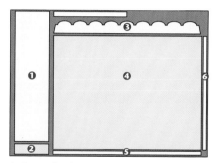

1. Control palette 2. Help text 3. Create, Edit, and Sky & Fog palettes 4. Work space 5. Selection palette (normally hidden) 6. Display palette (normally hidden)

The challenge of designing the Edit palette tools, shown open above the work space, was how to visually express in a uniform manner the notions of resizing, rotating, repositioning, aligning, and randomly redistributing objects.

The Edit palette's Materials Editor "plop-up" menu, a combination of the standard dialog box and the click-and-drag pop-up, follows through with the 3D design theme as it floats above the screen and casts a shadow on the work space.

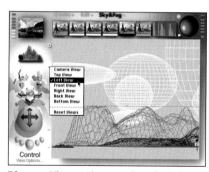

Diorama View options can be selected from a pop-up menu or by clicking the 3D control. Small gray arrows throughout the interface show locations of other option menus. Note that the Camera Controls are white here, meaning they're unavailable.

Bryce 2 tools are quick to respond. Click on the Create palette's circular spotlight tool and it casts a beam of light onto the dark round shape to show what it does. Below, click and drag along the appropriate X, Y, or Z axis of the Edit palette's resize control to reshape a selected wireframe in the work space. The tool extrudes in the direction the cursor is pulled. When selected, the tool pulses back and forth between the static and extruded states.

PRODUCTION STATS

After a year of research and development, a team of 6 worked 3–4 months to design and produce the program. Macintosh was the primary hardware used. Software included a development version of Bryce 2, Photoshop, and the programming language C.

space, and the Display palette along the right edge, are hidden, like the menu bar, until needed. Rolling the cursor over the areas where they hide on the screen makes them visible. When the contrasting style of the desktop menu bar is hidden, the consistent design quality of the Bryce 2 interface can be better appreciated.

Guiding the Process
The order in which the typographic buttons for the Create, Edit, and Sky & Fog palettes are positioned across the top of the screen represents the order in which they are typically used. First, objects are created, then edited, and last, environmental effects are added around them.

Fun and Full of Functionality
The vignetted light gray type identifying the Create, Edit, and Sky & Fog palettes blends into the background to avoid interfering with the overall balance of the interface elements. Moving the cursor over the type changes the letters to a darker gray value to indicate that the words are clickable. Clicking once on the palette's name—for instance, on Create, shown opposite—turns the type a still darker shade of gray and opens the selected palette.

In the Create palette, which displays the objects available for building a Bryce scene, rolling over an object changes it to its wireframe highlight state, which then pulses gently between states to show that it's active. The Edit palette, see above, and the Sky & Fog palette, shown at right, also respond in unique and dynamic ways.

Under Control
Not only are the objects in the Control palette attractive and enticing, they are also efficient. The "nano preview," a small preview screen, at the top of the Control palette, shows a fully rendered update of work in progress, which means a shorter wait time than if it were to be previewed larger in the work space and which lets the operator quickly make creative decisions based on the preview. The "memory dots," to the left of the preview screen, allow up to eight variations of the current scene, including settings, to be saved for later comparison. The "aerial preview" button below the screen preview, gives a rotating look at the wireframe—a quick way to track down hidden objects that are taking up unnecessary file space.

Help Text
Help text, at the bottom of the control palette, uses large, easy-to-read Helvetica sans serif gray type to identify the palette and name the tool or control at which the cursor is pointing. When the cursor is within the work space, the number of polygons in the scene is displayed at the bottom of the control palette, which is helpful for anticipating render times.

The Sky & Fog palette is the control center for atmospheric conditions that permeate an entire scene. The illustrations in the palette are interactive: When you click and drag on an illustration to change a scene, a built-in animation shows the results.

Drop-Down Drawers

Overview *In Art Dabbler, a beginner's painting and drawing program developed by MetaCreations, art tools, color swatches, and paper textures are stored in unique pull-down drawers, animated tutorials introduce basic art techniques, and a handy on-line user manual offers help at any time.*

"Interface objects are designed to give clues about how they work. For example, the handles on the drawer fronts clue users that the drawers can be opened."

–John Derry, vice president of creative design

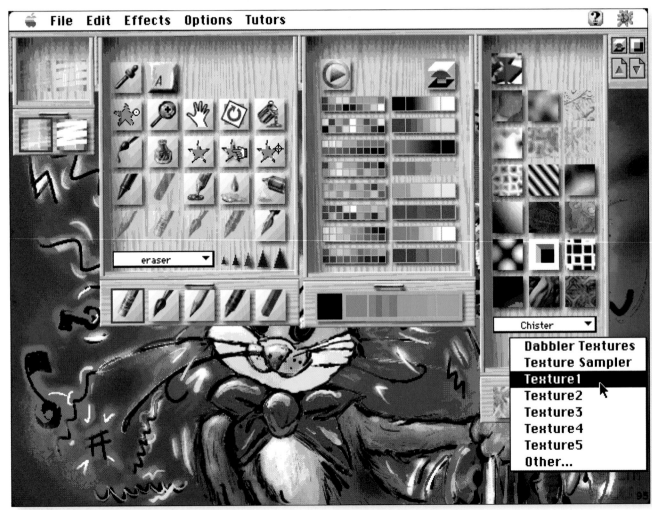

Making It Easy To Understand

The goal was to make Art Dabbler a drawing and painting program that would be visually easy for all ages to understand. To achieve this, MetaCreations used an approach to product design that they call "natural media"—emulating the look and response of traditional art tools and materials.

Grouping in Drawers

The interface tools and controls were created in MetaCreation's Painter, a more sophisticated painting and image-editing pro-

gram. They are grouped by function and neatly organized in four main drawers until needed: an extras drawer, a tools drawer, a colors drawer, and a paper textures drawer, shown above. Clicking the handle of any drawer opens or closes it. Added sound effects help reinforce the action and make the experience seem more real.

Selecting Tools

When a drawer is open, the user selects a tool, color palette, or paper texture by clicking on it. The selected item moves to

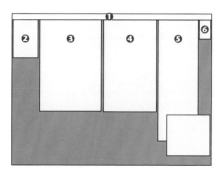

1. Menu bar 2. Extras drawer 3. Tools drawer 4. Color drawer 5. Papers drawer 6. Controls to turn sketchbook pages and select tracing paper 7. Pop-up menu

The rotate tool was designed with real-world work habits in mind. The page can be turned to an angle that's comfortable for drawing and painting. This option is especially handy when using an electronic drawing tablet and stylus.

The electronic user guide is available at all times by choosing How To Use Dabbler from the Tutors menu. It describes the interface, explains how tools work, and offers lessons. Click on underlined green hypertext for more detailed information.

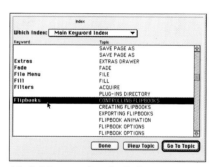

A helpful comprehensive index offers direct access to specific topics in the electronic user guide. To open, click on the index icon—the file folder covered with text—at the bottom of the How To Use Dabbler window, shown at left.

To change a color, click on a swatch. A black outline shows that it's selected. Then click anywhere on the color spectrum ring in the open drawer, or drag the small black circle to choose a color. To vary the saturation and value of a selected color, click anywhere on the color triangle, or drag the small white circle.

its respective drawer front. A bold outline shows up around the item, and the corresponding object inside the drawer dims. Five tools, one color palette, and three paper textures can be on the drawer front at one time. The program keeps track of the number of times each tool or paper swatch is used. When an additional tool or swatch is chosen, it replaces the one on the drawer front that has been used the least.

Layering Information

The drawers are organized efficiently at the top of the screen in close proximity to the menu bar. They are compact and, when closed, leave plenty of space for working.

There are three primary information layers: the main screen with all the drawers closed; the open drawers that present all the tools, color palettes, and paper textures; and the secondary drawers, such as the color wheel drawer, at left, which opens when its icon in the color drawer is double-clicked. There are also alternate pop-up menus for selecting tools and papers, and for choosing a paper library, shown open on the opposite page.

Unifying Diverse Imagery

A visual system was developed to organize and display the many tools and

swatches available in Art Dabbler. All are based on a square, selected because of its neutral shape. After testing various sizes, the designer determined 32 x 32 pixels to be the minimum size at which the images of the tools could still be clearly recognized. For consistency, the background is light gray, and color is used to show similar types of tools. Some tools are centered within the square and others are positioned at a 60-degree angle from upper right to lower left—a right-handed orientation that reflects how most people would hold the tool.

The form of the cursor changes depending on its location. When over the drawer handle, it changes to a clasping hand that, on a mouse click, opens or closes the drawer. When rolled over a tool, it changes to a pointing hand that, on a mouse click, selects the tool.

A "tutor" is a digital book that floats over the Dabbler desktop. This one by Disney animator Preston Blair uses animation, graphics, text, and video to teach the anima-tion process, from developing a character to making it move.

Cool Features

Used with a pressure-sensitive tablet, many of the tools interact with the paper textures—the more pressure that's applied, the more visible the grain of the paper. And step-by-step progress of individual drawing sessions can be recorded for later playback.

Plan Your Future With Help From CyberMom

Overview CyberMom, *an electronic personal organizer designed for young adults, uses video, audio, colorful graphics, animation, and an attentive maternal character to help you plan, schedule, and organize.*

"The Web site is intended to be a complementary product to the CD-ROM and to extend the personality and character of the CyberMom brand. Her future is probably going to be more Web-oriented than CD-ROM-oriented, but exactly what will happen next is yet to be seen."

–Kevin Kuester, creative director

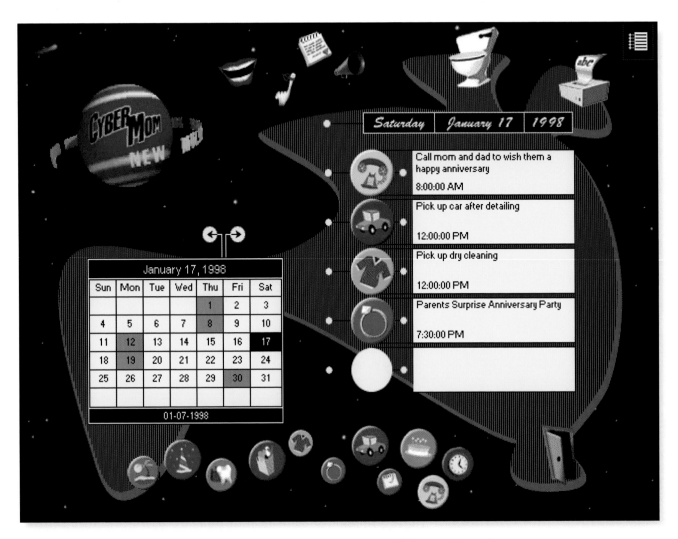

CD-ROM and Companion Web Site

Developed by the Minneapolis-based Kuester Partners, a marketing and interactive media development firm, the CD-ROM *CyberMom* is a colorful and humorous approach to the personal organizer and planner. Designed for high school and college-age computer users, *CyberMom* revolves around a warm and wacky mother figure who helps plan your life, offers domestic tips, and reminds you to clean your room and brush your teeth. The companion Web site promotes the CD-ROM, and offers related information, fun games, and other giveaways.

Personifying a Metaphor

The product was originally conceived as *CD-MOM,* a play on the acronym CD-ROM, but was changed to *CyberMom* so the product brand could easily be expanded to other formats and media, such as the Internet. For variety and practicality, the CyberMom character is represented on-screen in different ways: at startup in the installation video sequence, a live actress introduces the CyberMom personality; to create smaller files for the downloadable screensavers, she was drawn in Illustrator as flat 2D art; and for the adjustable Nag-o-Meter and Tip of the Day

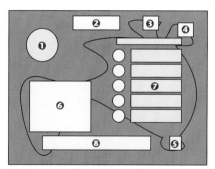

1. CyberMom identity 2. Utility and navigation icons 3. Trash icon 4. Print icon 5. Quit icon 6. Monthly calendar 7. Daily calendar 8. Event buttons

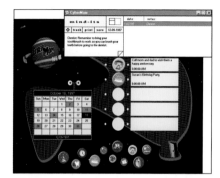

Clicking on the notepad icon on the main screen opens the Mind-Its window, above, where you can jot down notes and ideas. The main screen stays in view in the background, and the CyberMom sphere in the upper left corner is a QuickTime movie that continues to play even when other windows and dialog boxes are open.

A 5-member development team worked 11 months to complete *CyberMom*: 4 months for planning and design, 3 months for asset production, and 4 months for programming and testing. Software included After Effects, Director, Illustrator, InfiniD, Photoshop, Premiere, SoundEdit 16, and Visual Basic. Macs were used for graphics and PCs for programming. **cybermom.com**

The game show format of the install sequence introduces the offbeat personality of *CyberMom* in a video that plays on the screen of a retro-style TV. The sequence also demonstrates that *CyberMom* is not only a functional software application, but that it's entertaining, as well.

For consistency, the home page of the CyberMom Web site builds on the bright colors and visual elements found in the interface of the CD-ROM and on the packaging, shown opposite.

On the Top 10 page, the Web site offers additional household tips written in the irreverent style of CyberMom. The navigation elements of the site, above left, relate to the event buttons on the main screen of the CD-ROM.

Dragging an event icon onto either calendar on the main screen opens the brightly colored event dialog box where the selected icon is displayed at upper right and the event type (Birthday) is identified in the text box.

In the text box, right, you can enter information about a specific event. Using the square buttons on the Nag-o-Meter, left, you can set when and how many times you would like to be reminded of the event.

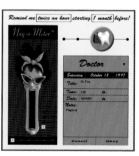

The Nag-o-Meter's version of CyberMom was created from a scanned photograph of actress Phyllis Wright, who plays CyberMom in the install video. The mouth stretches to show how many reminders have been selected.

dialog boxes, she takes on a softer, modeled appearance thanks to Photoshop's airbrush tool. Where CyberMom's image is not shown, voice-overs bring her to life, such as on the main screen of the CD-ROM, on the opposite page.

The Interface Style

Looking back to the look of the future, the designers were inspired by the shapes, color, and fashion in the futuristic imagery of the '50s and '60s—CyberMom's heyday. In keeping with the retro/techno appeal, the primary interface, shown opposite, uses an irregularly shaped space-age element to anchor the main screen components: a monthly calendar, left, a personalized daily list of things to do, right, and three commonly used

utility icons designed to show what they do—a toilet to dispose of unwanted information, a printer to print schedules and reminders, and a door to leave, or quit, the program.

Four additional icons float conveniently in cyberspace at the top of the screen: the lips open the Tip of the Day window, the spiral-bound notepad leads to the Mind-Its window, the finger with string tied around it provides a view of all current reminders, and the megaphone adjusts the volume. Rolling the cursor over any of these icons, or any of the 11 event buttons at the bottom, prompts CyberMom to explain the button's function. All of the interface elements were drawn in Illustrator and finalized in Photoshop.

Tip of the Day

"When you have the ability to develop this kind of product—from concept to programming to packaging—within your own organization, like we do," says creative director Kevin Kuester, "it takes discipline and restraint to balance the energy and effort required to create the product with what you anticipate your payback will be. At the same time, because everything is at your fingertips, you have the ability to make decisions faster and make better use of time."

At startup, CyberMom offers a tip to get your day off on the right track.

A 500-Channel Program Guide

Overview *This On-Screen TV Program Guide prototype accommodates 500 channels and options for viewing, searching, recording, and locking out programs–all selected with a hand-held remote control.*

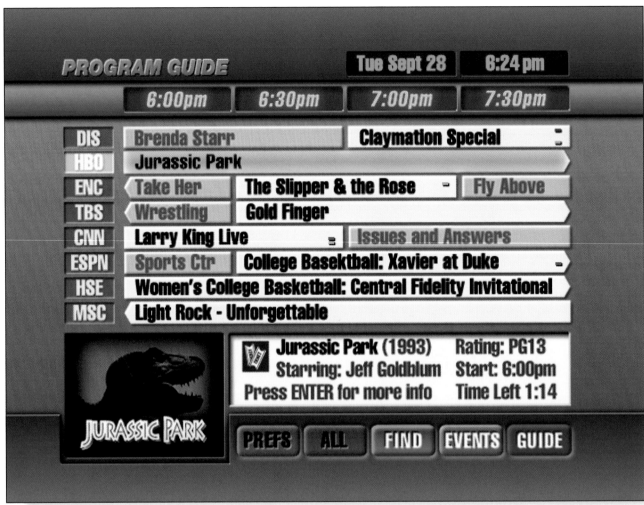

"The navigation structure had to be very shallow so users could get to any section of the guide with only one click of the remote."

–Jack Davis, art director

Meeting the Challenge

The on-screen program guide prototype shown here was designed by Jack Davis of JHDavis Design with Elena Morris of VideoCypher, a division of General Instrument. It was designed to determine how the guide would look on a TV screen and how it would work using custom, low-cost set-top hardware and a remote that could only tab around selectable areas on the screen.

Since the potential user of an on-screen program guide is anyone who watches television, the audience would be very broad. The biggest challenge was how to present a lot of information and a range of options in a format that almost anyone could understand and use.

Facing Technical Constraints

Designing for a television screen dictates low screen resolution, viewing from a distance, user interaction by means of a remote control, and analog rather than digital display technology, which affects color and image clarity. Type and pictures need to be larger, bolder, and less detailed than those designed for a computer screen.

1. Main section heading 2. Current date and time windows 3. Program start times 4. Television channels 5. Program titles 6. Program preview window 7. Information about the selected program 8. Navigation buttons: Prefs, All, Find, Events, and Guide

These three screens demonstrate the way a well-designed grid can adapt to changing content needs. The color of the border at top and bottom changes to identify the section.

In the Program Info screen, unit 7 (see schematic at left) expands to accommodate more information, and units 4 and 5 merge with the left and right borders to provide a larger viewing area.

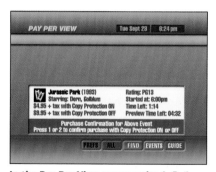

In the Pay Per View screen units 4, 5, 6, and 7 merge to provide space for an expandable list of personal programming preferences. The navigation buttons in unit 8, and the date and time windows in unit 2 remain active.

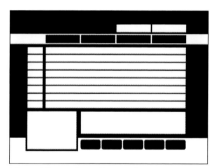

The grid template shown above was created in Illustrator and placed in Photoshop, where the final buttons and other artwork were produced.

STATS AND SOFTWARE

The 500-channel electronic program guide prototype took 5 designers and programmers 3 months to complete. Illustrator and Photoshop were the main programs used. Custom code was written for all functions.

Designing a Familiar Layout

As shown in the Program Guide screen, the information is presented in a familiar way. As in a printed TV guide, show times are listed across the top, channels are identified on the left, and program titles are organized in a table by time and channel.

Making Information Clear

The layout clearly shows the relationship between program title, viewing time, and channel. The arrow at the left or right end of a program title bar indicates that the program began earlier or continues beyond the displayed time. When a program title is selected, a representational graphic and program information are presented.

Screen information is grouped appropriately and shown in small amounts (8 channels and 2 hours at a time) so the user doesn't feel overwhelmed.

Adding Structure With a Grid

An underlying grid helps organize information and maintain visual consistency from screen to screen so the viewer doesn't get disoriented when navigating. But the grid also has to be flexible since the amounts and types of information vary.

Color-Coding

Color-coding the five main section buttons in the lower right corner of the screen to match the backgrounds of the five sections helps users know where they are within the guide. For example, the Guide button is blue and coordinates with the blue background of the Program Guide screens.

Using Appropriate Visual Metaphors

Clickable buttons appear raised, suggesting to the viewer that they will respond to a click of the remote. Inactive areas of information are recessed and suggest the opposite.

It's important that feedback to the user is immediate. In this case, the available buttons change to a highlight color when selected, to let the user know that the selection is active.

Choosing Type

Balancing readability with aesthetics and technical limitations, Helvetica Bold Condensed type was chosen for its sans serif design and its ability to accommodate large amounts of text. To distinguish between categories of information, uppercase italics are used for section titles and lowercase italics for show times.

The previous product interface displayed limited content in an unappealing format.

Look and Feel Like a Mac

Overview *The interactive training tool,* Making It Macintosh, *uses well-thought-out design standards, a consistent system of color-coding, and more than 100 animated examples to illustrate the principles behind the Macintosh interface.*

"Design involves thinking about all the issues connected with the structure of the content, the way the interface looks, how it functions, how people use it, and the message it sends about the organization."

–Jim Faris, principal, Alben+Faris

Macintosh Human Interface Guidelines Companion Contents Index ←·· ··→

Making It Macintosh

Going Beyond the Book

Making It Macintosh, the companion CD-ROM to Apple Computer's *Macintosh Human Interface Guidelines*, uses interactivity and more than 100 graphic animations to teach software developers how to incorporate the Macintosh look and feel into the products they develop for this computer platform. The animations are accompanied by written descriptions and suggestions for adapting to the Macintosh interface standards.

A team of as many as 15 experts were involved over a 2-year period in developing *Making It Macintosh*, but Harry Saddler, user experience designer at Apple, worked most closely with designers Lauralee Alben and Jim Faris of Alben+Faris to develop the product identity, define the interactive experience, and design the interface. "It was exciting to be able to use interactive media to explain something that's interactive," adds Alben.

Setting Standards

An underlying grid guided the placement of elements on the screen and provided a framework for writing, designing, animating, and building the individual examples. Graphic standards established a consistent look and behavior of the elements. For example, the background is always standard gray, graphics depicting a portion of the desktop always use a torn edge and shadow, and thought balloons always touch

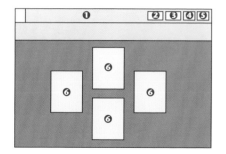

1. Header bar 2. Table of contents button
3. Index button 4. Previous screen button
5. Next screen button 6. Identity icons

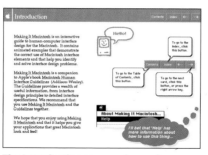

The **Introduction** screen, above, shows
how to use the main navigation controls.
Throughout the program, the different
expressions on the computer character's
face, the character's animated antics,
and the message inside the oval balloon
provide clues and instructional feedback.
The cloud-shaped balloons contain likely
user reactions and are a unique way to
offer tips and give directions.

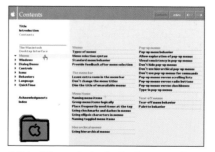

A list of the main topics is shown on the
white background on the left side of the
Contents screen. Clicking on the arrow to
the left of a topic shows the contents of
that topic in the light gray area on the
right. The gray background extends
behind the selected title to visually
connect it to the Contents. Blue is used
to identify the title of this particular
section, its icon, and the selected topic
within the section.

The header bar at the top of the example
screens is color-coded blue to identify the
Examples section. Clicking on the See Also
button, located in the lower left corner of
the screen, opens the See Also window,
which references related information in
the interactive program as well as in the
companion book. Clicking on a topic in
the See Also window opens that screen.

On the example screens, clicking on an
arrow to the left of the text changes the
arrow and text to blue to show that
they're selected, and plays an accompanying animation on the right side of the
screen. Animations were created in
Director, exported as QuickTime movies,
then optimized with Apple's MovieShop.
To achieve good readability, the text is
typeset in 12- point Palatino, flush left,
ragged right, and colored black.

STATS AND SOFTWARE

As many as 15 people worked for 2 years
to complete *Making It Macintosh* in 1993.
Software included Director, MovieShop,
QuickTime, Studio 8, and SuperCard.
The hardware was Macintosh. The book
and CD-ROM are published by Addison
Wesley Longman.

a right or bottom edge of the screen. To achieve good legibility on-screen, Palatino, Helvetica Heavy, and Espy sans serif
typefaces were chosen.

Communicating with Color

To represent the four parts of *Making It Macintosh*, Alben+Faris
selected four colors from Apple's standard 256-color palette
after an extensive analysis that focused on how visible the
colors were against different colored backgrounds, how well
the colors worked together as a set, and whether they were
distinct enough from each other to clearly differentiate the
parts of the program.

Establishing an Identity

Alben+Faris created a spirited personality for the product
using the well-known Macintosh icons. "They're a cross
between the fatbits of the actual icons and a hand-drawn style

that adds a human touch," says Alben. The humorous illustrations counterbalance the technical information and provide
an enjoyable experience. For continuity, the illustrations are
used on packaging, in promotional materials, and throughout the interface. *Waw*

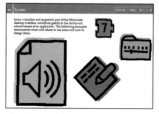 

The hand-drawn style of the icons and the repeated use of four bold
colors establish a memorable identity. They also provide continuity
from the program title screen, opposite, to the various section title
screens, such as the Icons and the Behaviors title screens shown here.
The icons on the title screens represent the content found in that
particular section. Clicking on a title screen plays an animation.

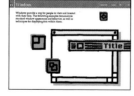 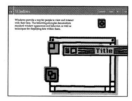  

A series of still frames
shows the animation
sequence designed
for the title screen of
the Windows section
that describes how
Macintosh windows
look and behave.

The Surf Check site is a subscription-based tool (**surfcheck.com**) for folks who surf the ocean as well as the Web. "The Internet has such a wealth of inform-ation about upcoming swells, general weather, storms, and hurricane and cyclone tracking, all of which is vitally important to surfers," says site originator Ted Deits. "We designed Surf Check to bring all the information together, so surfers could come to one place to find out what would be happening in the next day, two days, three days, week, or 10 days."

In addition, "since a picture is worth a thousand words," says Deits, "we put together a staff of photographers, who videotape the surf conditions every morning on about 100 beaches in Hawaii, California, Mexico, and Costa Rica." This allows surfer-subscribers from around the world to get an idea what the surf is like before spending the time, energy, and gas to make the 10-minute, half-hour, or hour-long trip to the beach.

Originally the site was loaded with graph-ics and animations, and subscribers found it fun for the first hour, but then the long download times became annoying. "So now we've stripped it down to the bare essen-tials," reports Deits of the work that he and designer Tim Chandler have done. "The pages are fairly stark." But it down-loads quickly and delivers the information subscribers want: "Here's the surf in pic-tures. Here's a text description of the surf. Here's the tide schedule. Here's the wind. Now go surfing."

In addition to registering with every search engine he could find, Deits has made good use of traditional advertising media to promote the Web site. As the Cyber Kahuna, he does the surf report three times each morning for a Los Angeles radio station. At the end of the report he gives the Web address for the Surf Check site, thereby reaching about a million potential subscrib-ers each day.

South H.B. Pier
Huntington Beach, California

NOV. 16 1997   NOV. 16 1997

Click the images for beach information and larger pictures

Today's Surf Report
Sunday, November 16, 1997

Time of Report: Sunday 8:00 AM
Wave Size: Shoulder to Head High
Wave Direction: Westnorthwest
Water Temperature: 64-67
Wind Speed: 0-5 MPH
Wind Direction: Off Shore
Today's Hot Spot: Cliffs,Cliffs,Cliffs

Area Details
Sunday update....It's firing at the Cliffs, the Pier, Bolsa Chica, just about everywhere in north Orange County. Smaller than yesterday, at least today you won't die paddling out. Sets are a few feet overhead with fast hollow peaky sections, with some slight off shore breeze to clean up the face. It's a surf day today!! Forget the lawn.

This beach
updated M-Fr

Send mail to the local spotter

Surf Valet At Dawn

Surf Tours

Off Da Lip Chat

Surf's Up E-mail

**Live Local
46025 buoy data,
updated all day**

Buoy ID: 46026

Updated: 19:00

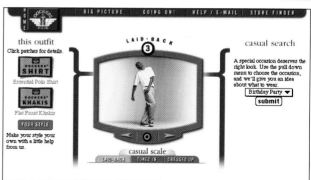

"The Dockers site is not for entertainment," says Kevin McSpadden in Dockers® Brand Consumer Marketing. "The focus is on product, positioning the Dockers® Brand as the ultimate khaki resource for all of your social and business wear needs, and providing a shopping guide." Men come to the Web site (dockers.com) to find out what kinds of products Dockers® Brand has, where to buy them, and how to put them together to arrive at just the right look on a "casualness continuum" from laid-back to dressed-up.

The site was designed to make its shopping tools available to people with 28.8-baud modems, small screens, not a lot of patience for reading directions about how to operate the site, and not many plug-ins for their browsers. So technologies such as streaming audio and virtual reality weren't included in the design. And an earlier version of the "dress-o'matic," which helps men pick clothing by the type of occasion and their own sense of style, was replaced with a lower-tech version because it was

frustrating visitors who didn't have the plug-in it required.

The designers have employed framing technology, however, so that a site visitor doesn't have to leave the clothing he's looking at in the main window to get additional information. And they are continually on the lookout for ways to make site navigation more intuitive.

Once a visitor has chosen the clothes he's interested in, the site provides an easy way to get hold of the product. He can enter his physical address and the site will find the stores that are closest, usually recommending two or three locations that have received the chosen product within the past 30 days.

The Dockers® Brand really stands for genuine effortless khaki," says McSpadden. "So we want the site to come across as sincere." Everything about the site is designed to support the brand's personality of casual sophistication. Instead of loud colors or flashing, animated graphics, the site's added value comes from subjects that the dockers.com audience is interested in. One example

was a sweepstakes built around an independent film festival that was touring the country. Another is The Game in Lehman's Terms, above, a series of golfing tips from Tom Lehman, provided for the many Dockers customers who are interested in the sport.

7 Education and Training

We learn from experience, and the quality of that experience determines how much we learn.

To enhance learning, many educational and training programs on CD-ROM and the World Wide Web combine multiple media with hands-on self-paced activities designed to appeal to a variety of learning styles. Communication is heightened when colorful photographs and illustrations support text, when music provides ambience, when sound effects offer feedback, and when virtual reality creates an illusion of space and time. Depending on your audience, add a challenging activity, a fun game, or an interesting story and the participant is more likely to become involved and remember more of the information that was presented.

CD-ROM technology offers a closed environment, permanence, speed, and good image and sound quality. The Internet provides an open environment with links to related resources, up-to-date information, and the possibility to interact with experts around the world. Some programs offer the best of both worlds by presenting permanent data on a CD-ROM disk with access to a companion Web site where information is updated on a regular basis.

The colorful objects and bold graphic icons of the *Lost & Found* interface (page 140) provide the framework of a matching game for children. In *The Cartoon History of the Universe* (page 128) a 3D console, influenced by principles of industrial design, displays the navigation controls. Simplicity and clarity speak to an international audience in the interface of the tutorial *Adobe Photoshop 3.0 Deluxe CD-ROM* (page 124). And a virtual living room complete with TV and telephone provides the interface metaphor for the tutorial *Leave It to SEEMIS* (page 138).

Tips and Techniques

Overview *This interactive tutorial on the* Adobe Photoshop 3.0 Deluxe CD-ROM *combines straightforward navigation buttons with video and self-running demonstrations to explain the features of the program.*

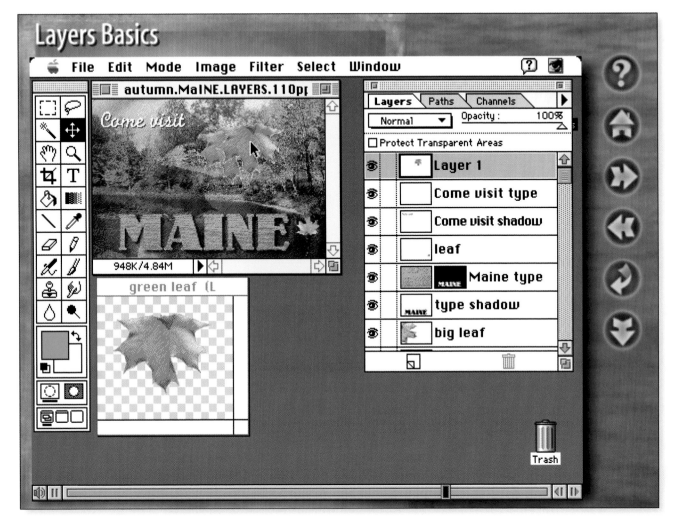

"Take the time to improve and perfect audio recording and processing—it's well worth it."

–George Jardine, digital video evangelist

The Format

There are three main sections to the interactive portion of the *Adobe Photoshop 3.0 Deluxe CD-ROM*: Digital Art Show, Adobe Products, and the Photoshop tutorial, above, which uses Quick-Time movies to describe new features, to review fundamentals of Photoshop, and to offer tips and techniques.

Interface Influences

The concept behind the interface was to illustrate the layering capability of Photoshop. The use of layers is demonstrated in the start-up animation sequence, and on the main menu screen by the overlapping images, typography, and information panels.

The Bare Necessities

Simplicity and clarity are especially important when designing an interface for a product that's used throughout the world. Interface elements, such as the set of six navigation buttons, above right, must be easy to understand. All six are based on universal icons—the question mark represents "help" and directional arrows indicate movement through the program. A

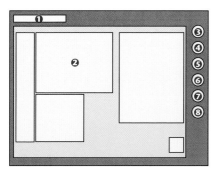

1. Screen title 2. Tutorial area 3. Help button 4. Main menu button 5. Forward to next screen button 6. Back to previous screen button 7. Return to main menu button 8. Quit

The main menu lists the five primary sections of the presentation. When the cursor rolls over a section title, the dove-in-the-circle icon appears on the left, indicating that the title can be selected. Click on a title to go to that section.

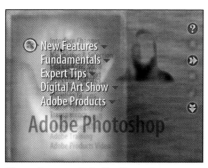

On the main menu, click on a small arrow to the right of each section title to open a pop-up menu to see the contents of that section. Clicking on any of the choices in the pop-up menu takes you directly to that subsection.

The Digital Art Show features professional work created in Photoshop. Choose the self-running version or the interactive show. Clicking on an image enlarges it to full-screen. Clicking on the enlargement returns to the artist's screen, above.

The startup screen features an animated collage, accompanied by music, of work created in Photoshop. The color palette and visual theme used throughout the presentation are introduced here: the dove used in the round pointer icon, the hand on the left side of the main menu screen that appears faintly in the background, and the concept of layers. The position of the words "Adobe Photoshop" on this screen is repeated on subsequent screens for continuity.

STATS AND SOFTWARE

A team of 1 full-time and 5 part-time members completed the *Adobe Photoshop 3.0 Deluxe CD-ROM* in 9 months on Macintosh hardware. Software included Director and Photoshop.

modified upward-facing arrow is used to represent "home" and a downward-facing arrow is used for "quit."

Using a consistent design style for the six buttons, applying the same color palette, and placing each icon in a circle achieves visual unity. Grouping them together on the right side of the screen provides easy access. When buttons are not available they are ghosted back, which results in an interesting unexpected group of the six buttons.

Tutorial Movies

Self-running tutorials, such as Layers Basics, on the opposite page, demonstrate key features of the program and offer tips and techniques. Voice-overs by presenters Laura Dower, Luanne Cohen, and Russell Brown describe the action taking place on-screen. The slider at the bottom of the Quick-Time window represents the duration of the particular tutorial movie. An indicator glides along the track to show where the speaker is within the presentation. All the standard QuickTime controls are available, including pause, continue, rewind, fast-forward, and volume, which can be adjusted using the control to the left of the slider.

In order for the navigation buttons to be on-screen at all times, the tutorial movies don't fill the entire screen. They were created as large as possible within the remaining space. This also allows space above the tutorial movie for that tutorial's title.

Each movie was carefully scripted, then recorded in one session to provide a coherent lesson that could easily be digested in one viewing. For maximum quality a good microphone, a good mixer, and high-quality DAT tape were used to record sound meticulously at 16-bit/44 kHz. It was then down-sampled to 8-bit/22 kHz for maximum quality. Data rates were kept below 90 Kbps for delivery on any CD-ROM player.

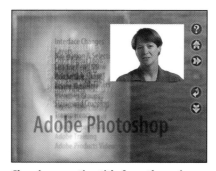

Choosing a section title from the main menu leads to an introductory video in which an expert describes the content of that section. To bypass this introduction, select a destination from the pop-up menu on the main menu screen.

When the introductory video is finished, the color image in the video window fades into a black-and-white still photo, and then into the background, as the menu for that subsection emerges on a plane that appears to float above the surface.

A Museum Without Walls

Overview Waypoint 1—*two CD-ROMs and a World Wide Web site—uses audio, 2D and 3D animation, video, and QuickTime VR to bring Australia's Museum of Victoria to the desktop.*

"**Large-scale CD-ROM and Web site projects require time and energy to develop. Client expectations often run ahead of what is achievable, so educating your client early in the process helps avoid disappointment.**"

–Wayne Rankin, principal designer

A Virtual Museum

Waypoint 1, aimed primarily at 10- to 20-year-olds, is a pair of integrated CD-ROMs and a Web site developed for the Museum of Victoria in Melbourne, Australia, by Gyro Interactive, an Australian multimedia communications firm. Due to the lack of exhibition space, much of the material held by the Museum is in storage. The Internet and other electronic media, which transcend traditional boundaries, provide unique opportunities for the Museum to extend its walls and reach the public through interactive virtual scenarios.

The Program's Structure

The CD-ROM contains 12 sections that represent waypoints— or stopping places—along the journey through the Museum's three departments: Natural Sciences, Social History, and Indigenous Studies. In keeping with this theme, principal designer Wayne Rankin created an overall visual style based on light and movement. Each waypoint has its own unique feeling, which relates to the content of that particular section. For example, Digging for Dinosaurs, above, is an adventure game that deals with an historical reconstruction of what the world might have

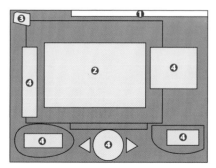

1. Main navigation bar 2. QuickTime VR window 3. Audio icon 4. Status information

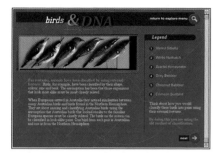

The Web site introduces material that supplements the CD-ROM, such as this section on how scientists classify birds using DNA, rather than by external features. The birds are from the Museum's collection. For consistency, the Web site's interface uses the same blue background on all pages, and employs round clickable buttons and hypertext to navigate. The color red shows when a button is active.

STATS AND SOFTWARE

A 20-person team spent 12 months developing *Waypoint 1*: 3 months for planning and design, 6 months for asset production, and 3 months for programming and testing. Both Macs and PCs were used. Software included 3D Studio Max, Bryce, Director, HyperCard, Illustrator, Photoshop, and SoundEdit, as well as World Builder, a proprietary authoring tool. **waypoint1.aone.net.au**

Users learn the basics of scuba diving in the interactive Scuba Dive section. The large window plays video of underwater creatures found in the depths of Australia's Port Phillip Bay, and photographs are shown in the smaller window. Text identifies and describes the species.

In The Dig section, a streetscape in Melbourne, which was destroyed in the 1950's, is re-created from old photographs and maps using 3D Studio Max. The navigation bar, at the bottom, leads to areas where users collect evidence to help prove or disprove an archeological hypothesis.

The 12 introductory screens leading to the waypoints display collages that relate to the content of that section. The Swinging Sixties screen showcases the life and work of fashion designer Prue Acton. The general navigation bar, top, is available from all of the section screens.

been like during the age of the dinosaurs. The ancient scene was created in Bryce, then brought into Photoshop, where it was inserted into the activity's high-tech interface.

Design Development

Although the final interactivity was implemented in Director, Gyro Interactive used Dreamtime, a proprietary media integration tool, to design and prototype the product. Developed using HyperCard by Gyro Interactive's John Swales, Dreamtime allows designers to explore different design directions quickly and at low cost. "With Dreamtime, media designers and content developers don't need to interact with programmers in order to see the outcome of their design ideas," says Swales. "Easy-to-use editing tools let them direct the development process longer than is usually the case, before it gets taken out of their hands and given to the technologists who have to beat it into shape for delivery on the PC or Mac."

Final Touches

Since *Waypoint 1* is intended mainly for schools, the CD-ROMs were designed for delivery on PC Intel 486–based machines. Images were reduced to 8-bit color and 640 x 480 resolution and sound was down-sampled to 8-bit/22kHz, in order to achieve smooth playback on the lower-end machines.

Future Plans

Waypoint 1 can be used as a conventional information product, or its content and how information is organized and accessed can be modified with World Builder, a built-in authoring tool based on Dreamtime. Internet connectivity enables users to interact with the Web site, which provides additional content, a chat area, and downloadable information and projects for teachers. The Museum plans that, over time, the collaborative work of students and teachers will be assembled on the site, in the form of curriculum materials, resources, and examples.

The colored buttons at the bottom of the Explore Menu page on the Waypoint 1 Web site, far left, represent the 12 waypoints featured on the CD-ROM. Clicking on the Digging for Dinosaurs button takes you to that page, left, where a preview of a computer-simulated rift valley fly-through can be downloaded. Clicking on the round red button, top right, takes you back to the Explore Menu, or clicking on another colored button at the bottom of the page takes you directly to a different waypoint.

Transforming a 350-Page Comic Book

Overview *Human Code's CD-ROM adaptation of Larry Gonick's* The Cartoon History of the Universe *features 13 billion years of history, 2000 animations, 17 challenging interactive games and puzzles, and over 5 hours of original audio.*

"For this project we developed what we call an infospace—a blending of interface, virtual environment, and interactive experience into something that users can understand."

–Lindsay Gupton, project director

Expanding on Existing Text and Art

When Chipp Walters, president of Human Code, was asked to transform Larry Gonick's *The Cartoon History of the Universe* into an interactive CD-ROM title, he was handed a 350-page black-and-white comic book that covered 13 billion years of history. The challenge was to create an entertaining educational experience that expanded on the book's text and art.

The art was scanned, colorized, and animated, and the text supplemented with voice-overs, sound effects, and original music. Historically accurate games, puzzles, and 3D renderings of historical sites were added to the original content. All were merged into an intuitive and user-friendly environment.

Meet the Professor

An animated character called the Professor personalizes the experience, guides you through the vast amount of information, and offers help along the way. The Professor's time machine and the artifacts he collected on his own adventures through history are found in his study. The time machine is the gateway to *Cartoon History,* and the artifacts that sparkle when the cursor

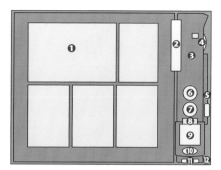

1. Page 2. Bookmarks 3. WhizBack console and navigation controls 4. Volume dial 5. Time slider for scrolling 6. Pause/play button 7. Forward/backward button 8. Page number indicator 9. Preview screen 10. Bookmark controls 11. Exit button to the Professor's study 12. Help button

The Professor appears in his study on the monitor of his flying machine as he introduces himself and explains how the interface works.

To select the index or one of the volumes from the bookshelf inside the time machine, click on it. Or drag the WayBack Slider, at the bottom, to a specific time and topic.

Click the Acropolis artifact in the study to follow the Professor on an animated tour where an interactive puzzle challenges the user to rebuild the Acropolis from ruins.

Digital audio editor Mike DeLeon says the hardest part about doing the voice of the Professor was trying to maintain consistency over the multiple recording sessions. He cleverly solved the problem of inconsistent volume levels by rigging a microphone to a pair of glasses so the distance from mike to mouth stayed constant.

STATS AND SOFTWARE

A team of 26, including full-time employees and outside talent and consultants, completed planning, design, asset production, programming, and testing in 10 months. AfterEffects, Cameraman, DeBabelizer, Director, ElectricImage, FormZ, Photoshop, and SoundEdit 16 were used in addition to C++. The content fills two CD-ROM disks.

is rolled over them lead to games and adventures.

Once inside the time machine, the user can view a page from history by reaching up and pulling down a volume, or can adjust the slider to choose a time period. A magical transition reveals an animated page and the WhizBack console with navigation controls.

Applying Product Design Concepts

The detailed lighting and texture effects applied to the console, opposite, are good examples of the product design expertise at Human Code. The controls are thoughtfully placed and each is represented by a different visual metaphor to add clarity to its function: The volume dial turns, the time slider moves up and down, and the buttons can be pushed.

The small screen at the bottom of the console shows a preview of the page you'll go to if you click on the screen. To preview other pages, click the forward or backward arrow above the preview screen. A proprietary feature called *Blit PICT*, or *off-screen blitter compositor*, a dynamic link library (DLL) custom-coded in C++, allows many images to be kept ready in memory at one time, making it possible to quickly flip through the preview images.

Marking a Page

Below the preview screen are the bookmark controls. Click the bookmark icon to show marked pages. To place a bookmark, click in the margin of any page. Personal bookmarks are saved in the log-in file and appear the next time the time machine is used. Some historically significant events have already been marked and color-coded by the Professor.

Color Palettes

Colors in the seven volumes of *Cartoon History* are suggestive of the colors found in printed comic books and were selected for aesthetic balance within the constraints of a full spectrum 8-bit System palette. To create appropriate moods in other areas of the CD-ROM, such as in the Professor's study, the time machine, and the game sections, individual custom palettes were carefully assembled, then down-sampled from 24-bit to 8-bit. In-between sections the screen becomes black to prevent color flashing that happens when changing images that use different palettes.

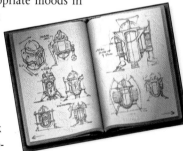

Drawings of the time machine can be found in the Professor's scrapbook in his desk.

The Role of Audio

Audio plays a big part in this program—from the Professor's voice to sound effects that provide user feedback to background music that sets mood, adds depth to transitions, and smooths the flow from one page to the next. Most of the music was created with MIDI sequencing, but guitar, bass, drums, and vocals are also used.

Exploring Forest Habitats

Overview *In the Fantastic Forest section of The National Geographic Society's Web site, designed for children in grades K–12, a map and QuickTime VR allow students to explore colorful 3D illustrations of different forest habitats.*

"Making Fantastic Forest was like making a movie: National Geographic was the studio, and they provided the producers, the script, and the assets, and we directed it. After a tremendous amount of teamwork and time pressure, we all had created a fantastic world for people to explore on-screen."

—Brad Johnson, designer, Second Story

Building Awareness

Fantastic Forest, a feature activity on The National Geographic Society's Web site, was developed for students in grades K–12 in conjunction with the Society's annual Geography Awareness Week. Building on the designated theme "exploring a world of habitats, seeing a world of difference," Fantastic Forest provides students with an entertaining way to learn about the forest and the flora and fauna that live there.

Creating a Mood

The natural mood of Fantastic Forest is portrayed by a palette of earth tones, thematic copywriting, and sounds of the forest—chirping birds, crickets, a gurgling stream. The interface elements effectively reinforce the mood and set the stage for interactivity: Colorful 3D illustrations invite exploration, a map with clickable buttons suggests an adventure, and clues below a tally of leaves imply a guessing game.

Softening the Interface Elements

The screen is divided into three content areas: the forest scene, the map, and the information area, each of which is built with a borderless HTML frame colored green. To achieve an organic feeling and a unified look, highlights and shadows created in Photoshop and saved in GIF format soften the edges.

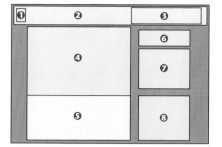

1. The National Geographic Society symbol
2. Title bar 3. Ad banner 4. Forest scenes
5. Navigation controls 6. Forest Finds tally
7. Detail image 8. Related information

On the first page encountered after entering the site, instructions explain the activity and describe how the interface works. Clicking on the number 1 on the map, shown above, leads to the first scene in the forest. To quit, click the Q button on the right side under the map.

A clue, at right, hints where to click on the forest scene to find a hidden creature or a forest feature. You can see a different perspective of the scene by clicking on Left View, Center View, or Right View. Take a 360-degree QuickTime VR tour by clicking Panoramic View.

The cursor changes to a pointing hand when rolled over a hot spot in the illustration that relates to the clue. If the student's response to the clue is correct, a photograph and additional information are shown, and a leaf icon is added to the Forest Finds tally, upper right.

Clicking on the stream brings students to the end of the journey, where a mystery question quizzes them on what they have learned along the way. If the student answers correctly, the reward is an interactive game, above, where the student can assemble his or her own fantastic forest using individual elements painted by illustrator Bud Peen. Peen also created the *Fantastic Forest* logotype used in the title bar. The typeface Comic Book is used to identify the locations on the map and the other navigation controls. Its hand-drawn style relates well to the illustrations and the hand-drawn logotype.

STATS AND SOFTWARE

A 6-member production team worked 5 weeks to plan, design, produce the interface elements, program, and test. Software included BBEdit, Illustrator, Photoshop, SoundEdit 16, and StudioPro with HTML and JavaScript programming on Macs. **nationalgeographic.com**

Mapping Out the Site

Since the scenes are key to the user experience, they appear at the top of the screen on the left with the map just below. The scrolled information frame is placed on the right, so its scroll bar runs along the outer edge, instead of in the middle of the screen.

The forest map doubles as a navigation tool and a table of contents by presenting an overview of the forest path and providing active buttons that lead to all of the stops along the way. Students can visit the different habitats in numerical order or choose them randomly. When selected, the numbered button changes color to clearly show where you are.

Controlling Window Parameters

To control the placement of all of the frames and artwork of Fantastic Forest within the proportions of a 14-inch monitor, JavaScript was used to open a completely separate window from the browser window. This provides consistent screen space without the interference of browser tool bars, location bars, or navigation buttons, and avoids the conflict when a browser is set to text only. "With a JavaScript window, we know everyone will be able to see everything as we designed it," says project manager Julie Beeler of Second Story. "It also achieved the CD-ROM-like environment we were after."

Painting the Picture

Using quill pen and watercolor, illustrator Bud Peen painted individual forest elements, such as rocks, shrubs, and trees, then scanned them, duplicated and manipulated them in Photoshop, and saved them in PICT format before emailing the files to designer Brad Johnson of Second Story. Johnson made outline silhouettes of each object in Illustrator, which he saved in EPS format. The outlines were imported into StudioPro where they were used to create 3D shapes, and then the PICT files were used as texture maps that were applied to the 3D shapes to create the illusion of a dimensional forest. This made it easy to build many scenes without having to create original artwork for each of them and provided a realistic-looking image with depth of field and soft atmospheric patterns of light and shadows. Three different views were rendered for each of the five environments, in addition to the forest entrance and the stream scenes.

At the end of the activity, student explorers receive a certificate of completion.

Adding a Realistic Touch

Photographs from The National Geographic Society's extensive archives, along with sound files from their audio library, provide a realistic complement to the illustrations. And the accompanying text offers valuable information from which students learn more about the environment.

Lifelike Laboratory

Overview *Animation, video, hypertext, sound effects, and original music complement the environmental interface of* How Your Body Works, *a CD-ROM based on the best-selling book of the same name.*

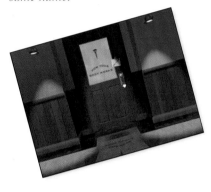

"We developed a realistic metaphor for the main interface to relate to the realistic content of the program."

–Barc Holmes, producer/director

Searching and Exploring

An inviting interface and clear organization add to the success of *How Your Body Works,* an interactive reference tool designed for use at home and at school. The program uses audio, video, 2D and 3D animation, hypertext, and dramatic animated fly-throughs to present anatomical tours of 12 systems of the human body, plus related material on health and wellness.

Wander through the main interface—the 3D environment of the pathology laboratory, shown above—or use the Browser, a comprehensive directory of the program's contents, to search and go directly to any topic, including scripts from audio and video segments. A glossary of medical terms, a health directory of over 200 healthcare associations, and 98 related articles offer additional information.

A Well-Staged Interface

The door in the dramatically lit hallway, left, leads to the laboratory, where a virtual environment draws the viewer in. Realistic-looking objects and curious gadgets, which represent different topics, are hard to resist. But wait—the telephone is ringing.

1. Anatomy chart 2. Anatomy button
3. Body Tours button   4. Medicine Cabinet
button 5. Reference button 6. Nurse's
Notebook button 7. Browser button
8. Help button 9. Disorders button
10. Wellness button 11. Exit button

When you enter the lab, a familiar ring
cues you to click on the telephone, where
the table of contents is found. Select a
topic, click its number at left, or press the
corresponding number on the keypad.
Offering different ways to make a selection assures user interaction.

The top shelf of the Medicine Cabinet
leads to information about prescription
drugs and the second to information
about over-the-counter drugs. The third
presents medical instruments, and the
bottom shelf leads to the first-aid manual.

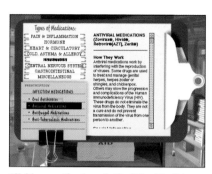

Clicking on the top shelf of the Medicine
Cabinet presents a clipboard with category
labels, a prescription pad, and a text window. Select a category to see a list of medi-
cations on the prescription pad. Select a
medication to show text that describes it.

The Wellness interface relies on the user's
familiarity with a VCR and videotapes.
The tapes offer health tips from medical
experts and are categorized according to
the 12 body systems featured throughout
the program. Clicking on a videotape
moves it into the VCR. A recognizable
control panel allows users to rewind,
play, and stop.

The cursor changes to a skeleton
hand when it rolls over an active
object that makes a funny sound
or plays a short animation.

STATS AND SOFTWARE

A 24-member team worked 10 months
to complete *How Your Body Works*.
Software included C++, 3D Studio,
Photoshop, SoftImage, and Word. Both
PC and Mac hardware were used. The
product ships on one CD-ROM.

Clicking on the telephone, which represents the Help feature, fills the screen, and a friendly voice offers instructions on
how to use the program—a clever and comfortable way to
introduce how the interface works. Select a topic listed on the
telephone for directions on finding that section, or just explore
the laboratory on your own by rolling the cursor around the
screen. When the cursor rolls over a hot spot, like the model of
the human body in the case on the opposite page, a pop-up label
shows what the object represents. Clicking on the model in the
case, as on other labeled objects, enlarges it and displays that
topic's unique interface. The colorful laboratory turns gray to
indicate that it's inactive, until the user clicks on it again.

Using Media Effectively

Different media present different types of information. This
adds depth and diversity to the program and allows content to

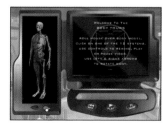 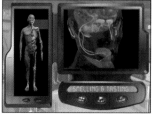

The high-tech Body Tours interface displays a 3D model of the human body that can be rotated using the arrows below the display
screen, left. Selecting a body part on the 3D model, right, opens
the animated Body Tour identified in yellow above the controls.

be presented in the most accessible and appropriate manner.
For example, the voice of nurs-
ing expert and radio personality
Pat Caroll is most effectively presented as a radio-style consumer
health program, and interviews
with leading medical experts are
best presented using video. Video
adds credibility, and the combination of voice and moving
images helps distinguish one
expert from another. Fly-through
3D animation allows travel inside
the body, an experience that
would not be possible with
printed media.

All Work and No Play?

No way. A note pinned to the lab door describes details of a
scavenger hunt designed to challenge young scientists. To play, find
notes hidden throughout the lab for directions on what to hunt for.
The reward for successfully completing a scavenger hunt is interaction with a fascinating 3D model, such as a head that can be
examined in five different layers. Just for fun, the lab is also full of
objects, like a brain in a jar, beakers, and equipment that produces
sound effects or plays a short animation when selected.

The Nurse's Notebook fea-
tures 25 audio segments
that offer consumer health
advice. The radio interface
displays the segment title
and four controls. The number identifies the segment
and when clicked advances
to the next presentation.
Clicking the knob stops a
presentation, and the two
arrows move ahead to the
next presentation or back
to the preceding one.

As Big As Life

Overview *The King Cobra module featured on The National Geographic Society's Web site uses an illustration key and a life-size image map of a king cobra to link to 11 different topic segments within the site.*

"We used a traditional storytelling tool called an 'illustration key' that shows an overview of the site's contents, identifies where you are, and keeps track of where you've been."

–Julie Beeler, designer, Second Story

A TV Companion

The King Cobra module of The National Geographic Society's Web site was developed in conjunction with a *National Geographic Explorer* television program of the same name. The goal was to create an interactive experience to educate users of all ages about the king cobra—the largest poisonous snake known.

Fitting It All In

Impressed by the size of the snake, Laura Carter of National Geographic Online asked the designers of the module, Brad Johnson and Julie Beeler of Second Story, to feature a life-size illustration of the king cobra, a portion of which is shown above. The original artwork of the snake measures roughly 3½ feet and

was painted by illustrator Paul Kratter according to detailed source information provided by The National Geographic Society and leading king cobra experts, such as Rom Whitaker in India.

After tightly drawn pencil sketches were approved, the realistic artwork was completed, and then an 8 x 10-inch color transparency was made. The transparency was scanned and opened in Photoshop, where it was segmented into 11 parts, to represent one of the 11 different topics presented on the site. The snake's head, above, represents The King's Armory section.

Setting the Stage

Thematic copywriting, background patterns, and architectural

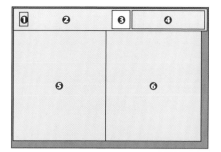

1. The National Geographic Society symbol
2. Title 3. Snake Key button 4. Ad banner
5. Contents frame 6. Enlarged illustration

To distinguish between the different topic segments, the background pattern and color of the contents area on the left side of the screen vary from segment to segment. For good readability, the color and value of the type contrasts with the background.

The pose of the snake is both horizontal and vertical to show that king cobras can strike while moving forward. Scrolling the frame on the right, which displays the large portions of the illustration, gives the impression that the snake is slithering across the screen and preparing to strike.

The informative text is supported by color photographs, animation, sound, and graphics, such as the map shown above. To move between pages in the content area, click on the colored arrows below the text. To return to the snake key, click on the Snake Key text in the title bar.

The Snake Key on the left side of the page is divided into 11 parts, each identified by a roman numeral. When the cursor rolls over one of the segments on the snake key, the outlined segment fills with colored texture to show that it's active, the title appears above the snake key, as well as on the enlarged segment on the right, and the cursor changes to a pointing hand. To go to a particular section, click on a segment of the snake key or on the life-size outline drawing of the segment on the right. The snake key segment and the corresponding life-size portion remain filled to show that you've been there.

STATS AND SOFTWARE

The development team, which included 2 designers, an illustrator, a producer, and a programmer, completed the site in 6 weeks: about 2 weeks for planning and design, about 3 weeks for asset production, and 2 weeks for programming and testing. Software included AfterEffects, BBEdit, GIFBuilder, Illustrator, Photoshop, Premiere, and StudioPro running on Macs.

nationalgeographic.com

design elements set the stage. To further the mood of the site and reinforce the content, the Sanskrit for *naja raja*, the Indian name for king cobra, is incorporated into the title behind the English "King Cobra" at the top of each page, and is displayed at the back of the arched niche that contains the Snake Key. Background patterns and architectural design elements, inspired by Medieval Indian court paintings of kings and their families, are used to create a royal setting for this king of reptiles. The colors used in the background patterns were selected based on the subject matter in each segment. The background images, that range in size from 1 to 3 K, were all created in Photoshop.

Adhering to Guidelines

The National Geographic Society requires that the organization's symbol and an ad banner be displayed on every page at specific sizes. To keep download time to a minimum, each page must be under 30K. Like most Web sites, modules for The National Geographic site need to work on 14-inch monitors with both Mac and Windows operating systems and different versions of the Internet Explorer and Netscape browsers. To adhere to these guidelines, two versions of the site were created: one for low-end and one for high-end browsers. Users choose one of two paths based on the browser they're running.

Simulating Action

Using GIF animations allows viewers to see some of the action shown in the TV program without having to download plug-ins or memory-intensive video clips. Frames from the original video file were captured using Premiere, then imported into AfterEffects, individually tweaked, and exported as a series of PICT files into GIFBuilder where the animations were created. "An added benefit of the GIF animations," says Julie Beeler of Second Story, "is that as they come on-screen you can see the action in slow motion."

GIF animations call attention to clickable objects. In this animated GIF, the flicking tongue of the cobra points to the message "Enter, if you dare."

Simulating a Panel Discussion

Overview *GTE Entertainment's* Interactive Roundtable *CD-ROM, a remake of the* Verbum Interactive Roundtable, *uses text, audio, video, and 2D and 3D animation to present a virtual panel discussion with six multimedia experts.*

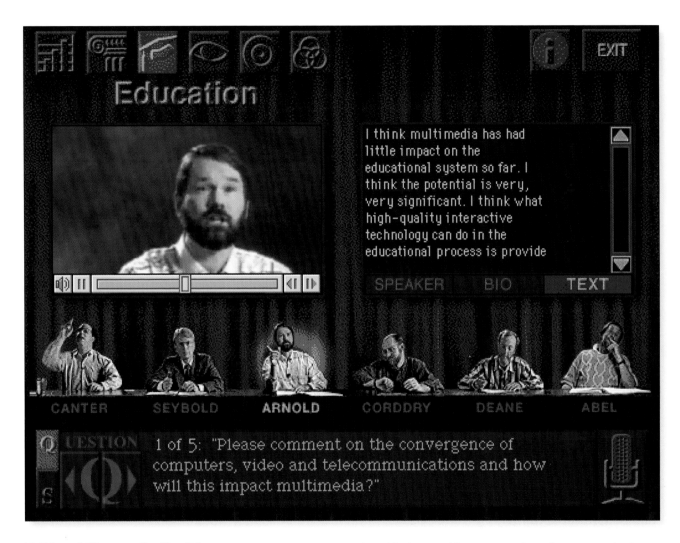

"The idea was to create a stellar panel that could go into much more depth than typical conferences, where time constraints apply."

–Steve Lomas, designer/director

Taking Off on an Earlier Idea

Interactive Roundtable assembles a panel of multimedia experts in a simulated conference setting—six panelists, seated behind a table in front of an audience, prepared to answer questions about the state of the industry. This stand-alone version of *Interactive Roundtable* is a redesign of the original roundtable discussion that was first published as one of the sections on the *Verbum Interactive* CD-ROM (see page 164). The goals of the remake were to produce a cross-platform CD-ROM, incorporate full-motion QuickTime, extend the length of the video from 1½ to 2½ hours, add an integrated search engine, and enhance comprehension by displaying the questions and answers in writing while they are being spoken.

How It Works

There are basically two ways to use *Interactive Roundtable*. You can choose a topic represented by the six buttons in the upper left corner, as shown above, then select a question from the options that appear in the Question window at the bottom, then click on a particular panelist to answer the question. Or you can search for

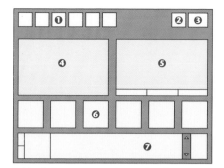

1. Topic buttons 2. Information button
3. Exit button 4. Answer window
5. Question/Text window 6. Panelists
7. Question and Search window

Clicking on the Information button, upper right, allows users to choose a self-running video tour, shown above, in which designer/director Steve Lomas explains how to use the interface. Clicking on the History button offers background information about the project.

To hear the selected question, click on the microphone icon, at bottom right, and a participant from the audience, above right, asks the question while the written question is displayed below. Numbering the question "1 of 5" provides feedback. To read other questions click on the arrows.

To search by keyword, click on the "S" button, at lower left, then enter a word in the text entry field, such as "Education" shown here. All of the instances where "education" occurs are listed at right. Scroll the list of options and click one to hear the videotaped response.

When Credits is selected, the credits roll in the video window on the right side of the screen. The video clips of the design and production team, shown here, are full-motion QuickTime.

STATS AND SOFTWARE

A 12-member team worked 8 months to complete the redesign of *Interactive Roundtable*. Software included AVID, DeBabelizer, Director, Electric Image, Photoshop, Premiere, SoundDesigner, SoundEdit, and various proprietary video processors. Mac hardware was used.

a subject of interest by entering a keyword in the Search window at the bottom, which activates a search string that looks through all of the transcripts and displays every instance where that particular word appears. In both cases, the panelist's videotaped response plays in the window on the left and the written answer may be shown in the window on the right.

Videotaping

Prior to videotaping, the six panelists were sent a list of 36 questions and asked to prepare their answers ahead of time. The experts were also encouraged to pose their own questions to the other panelists.

A video crew went on location to videotape each of the panelists individually while they responded to the questions. The videotaping was done in three different locations over a 2-week period. Since it was important for all of the panelists to look like they were in the same place at the same time, detailed notes ensured consistency: The focal length of the lens was documented and the height of the lens, the distance of the lens to the speaker, the height of the table and chair, the angle of the light,

Each panelist was captured in several different active poses, which are randomly displayed when the mouse rolls over them.

and the intensity of the light. "We plotted the entire room and re-created the environment in each location," says designer/director Steve Lomas.

All of the experts were taped on Hi-8 video that was transferred to betacam SP, edited on an AVID editing system, and digitized. The images of the panelists at the table were placed in Photoshop where they were masked, cleaned up, reduced, then composited over the background—a dark green curtain that was created in Photoshop.

Icons

Designer Stephen King created the series of icons in Illustrator that represent the topic categories: State of the Industry, Standards, Education, Vision, Markets, and Strategic Alliances. When the mouse rolls over a button, the name of the topic appears below. When a topic is selected, the icon and the name are highlighted in an aqua color, such as Education, opposite.

Spotlight on the Panelists

How to highlight the panelists when they were selected posed an interesting design challenge. "There's a real-world model for that," said Lomas. "We highlight people by shining a spotlight on them." So, when you click on a panelist, the spotlight turns on to show which panelist is selected and stays on until you click on another panelist.

All the Comforts of Home

Overview *The goal of this training program was to keep oil rig workers up-to-date on the most effective methods of reporting potential environmental hazards.*

"The challenge of design is to know your audience so you can get them excited and keep them involved."

–Jack Davis, designer

Developing the Concept

Understanding your audience is often the key to developing an effective design solution, and *Leave it to SEEMIS* is a good example. The goal of this training program was to improve reporting methods on oil rigs to avoid potential environmental hazards. The material was important but a bit dry, so designers Jack Davis and Ed Codere set out to develop an interface that would be fun and engaging for workers who spent a lot of time away from home, offshore. After 3 months of planning and concept development with the main design firm, Internal & External Communication, everyone agreed that the virtual space depicted above was perfect.

Making It Intuitive

In the comfort of this virtual living room, perched in front of the television set, the trainee begins the tutorial. Sit back and relax, there are no high-tech buttons to push, no menus to consult. Familiar household objects, such as the telephone, beverage glass, television set, and *TV Guide* become friendly controls in this intuitive interface.

1. Telephone for testing and input
2. Television display for movies and information 3. *TV Guide* directory 4. Beverage showing time remaining in session
5. Television dial to show current chapter
6. Forward and Back buttons
7. Escape/Quit button

The first training session begins in this early morning setting, while the user is wearing pajamas, watching cartoons, and drinking a glass of orange juice.

In Session Two the glass of juice is replaced by a bottle of Coke, a Western movie is on television, and pajamas have been replaced with jeans.

In Session Three the curtains are drawn, the lamp is on, a glass of milk has replaced the Coke, and a variety show is running on the TV.

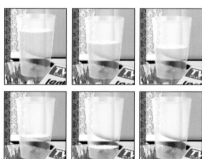

As instruction progresses the liquid in the glass slowly goes down to show where the trainee is within the scope of the session. The rough outline of these animation sprites was rendered in a 3D program and the progression was completed in Photoshop.

Organizing the Content

The content is divided into three distinct training sessions. To differentiate one from another, three different times of day are represented—morning, afternoon, and evening—as shown above. The lighting, clothing, beverage, time on the clock, and TV programs change accordingly.

Each one of the scenes serves as a section opener and as the section's home base. When a section is first opened, a teaser movie clip plays on the television—cartoons, nostalgic movies, or a variety show. Many assets needed to be produced for the set: A model was constructed in Swivel 3D, objects and textures were drawn with Illustrator and Photoshop, and animations and text areas were created and programmed in Director.

Navigating

Familiar objects serve as navigation elements. Clicking on the *TV Guide* opens and displays the tutorial selections. It's fun, and an appropriate metaphor for presenting the software program directory. Clicking on a topic in the directory enlarges the television set, and the TV screen becomes the delivery area for the tutorial content (see below left).

When the telephone rings and shakes, who can resist picking up the receiver? Clicking on the telephone brings another appropriate metaphor

to the screen—a mock Nielsen Rating questionnaire that is actually a test to determine what the user has learned during that particular session. Custom XCmds (extension-commands) were written so the test forms could be filled out and graded from within Director.

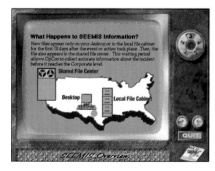

The television set fills the 640 x 480-pixel screen to present instructional content and tests. The dial shows the current chapter within the tutorial section. Once back to the main screen, clicking on the animated telephone (far right) stops the ringing and opens an interactive test form.

Interactive Games for Learning

Overview *GTE Entertainment's*
Lost & Found *is designed to
enhance vocabulary development,
comprehension, and deductive
reasoning of children aged
4 through 9.*

*"Off-the-shelf
software offers many
advantages over custom
programming, but the
trade-off is that you're
at the mercy of the
authoring tool and its
built-in priorities."*

–Steve Lomas, design director

Making It Fun and Easy To Use

If your target audience is too young to read, images and sound become very important interface elements. In GTE Entertainment's *Lost & Found,* cute buttons and colorful tools, whimsical sound effects, sing-along jingles, rhyming clues, and video responses create a fun and understandable environment for children.

Getting Around Is Easy, Too

Twelve games branch from a main screen that's divided up into 12 puzzle pieces, as shown at the top of the next page. Click on a puzzle piece to go to a game, such as Land of Pins, shown above. To go back to the main screen, click on the puzzle icon on the right side of the menu bar at the top of the screen. Now you can choose a new game from the main screen, or click on the hand beside the word Quit to wave good-bye.

The Object of the Game

Each puzzle screen displays an array of familiar objects separated into thematic categories: art tools, pins, refrigerator magnets, birthday party favors, vegetables, fish, animals, letters,

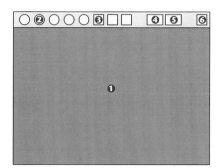

1. Photographic puzzle screen 2. Happy face icons 3. Mouth icons 4. Flashlight tool 5. Magnifying glass 6. Puzzle piece icon to return to main screen

Puzzle pieces on the main screen represent 12 different games. Roll the mouse over the pieces to preview the puzzle screens. Click one to play. Happy faces show that different levels of some games have been completed.

Puzzle screens, like Number Jumble above, are divided into a menu bar with interactive buttons and tools at the top of the screen, and a game area full of objects to be found.

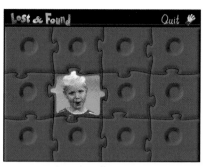

After you complete a game, Zachary, the five-year-old host, congratulates you. He also explains the rules at startup and offers hints and words of encouragement while playing.

The single happy face indicates that one out of eight objects has been found in Keychain Kraze. The blue glow around the open mouth shows that the audio clue for object 7 is being given. The spotlight shows that the flashlight is in use.

numbers, musical instruments, or key chains. The goal of each game is to find the eight objects described in the rhyming clues spoken by the mouth icons on the menu bar.

When the object is found, click on it. To reinforce a correct answer, the object flashes, a sound is heard, and the mouth is replaced by a yellow happy face. Choosing an incorrect object prompts hints and encouragement from host Zachary until the correct object has been discovered.

Increasing Play Value

When all eight items have been found, a happy face appears on the game's puzzle piece on the main screen (see above). This indicates successful completion of the first level of the game.

To increase play value, players can revisit completed games up to four times and hear a new set of clues for eight different objects. A successful second visit to the game adds a silver ribbon to the happy face, a successful third visit adds a red stripe, a fourth, a blue stripe, and a fifth, a rainbow stripe.

Creating the Puzzle Screens

To create the 12 puzzle screens, objects were collected, arranged, and photographed using a 2¼-inch (medium-format) camera and color transparency film. The transparencies were drum-scanned to maintain quality and detail. The scans were saved as full-color images, then opened in Photoshop, where cropping, composition changes, and color manipulation were done. The final images were indexed into an 8-bit System palette.

Assembling the Pieces

The scanned photographs, button and tool art, video, and sound files were assembled in Director. To accomplish special effects like the flashlight hot spot and the WYSIWYG magnifier, proprietary programming tools, XObjects, and DLLs (dynamic-link libraries) were used to extend the basic capabilities of Director.

STATS AND SOFTWARE

A 10-member team worked 10 months to complete *Lost & Found*. Software included AfterEffects, DeBabelizer, Director, Excel, MovieShop, Photoshop, Premiere, SoundDesigner, and Word, as well as XObjects, DLLs, and proprietary programming tools.

Colorful icons are used as interaction tools. The different states of the mouth, flashlight, and magnifying glass were created in Photoshop and sequenced in Director. Click the closed mouth to hear a clue.

 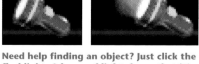

Need help finding an object? Just click the flashlight. A beam of light shows that it's on, and a spotlight highlights an area of the screen (see opposite page). Click the flashlight again to turn it off.

To activate the magnifying glass, click on its icon. The funny face enlarges to demonstrate the tool's function and show that it's on. Then drag the cursor onto the puzzle screen. The glass appears over the photograph, magnifying the objects beneath.

Meetum! Matchum! Morfum!

Overview *GTE Entertainment's* MegaMorf Monster Lab *is designed to enhance comprehension, memory, and pattern recognition in children aged 5 through 9.*

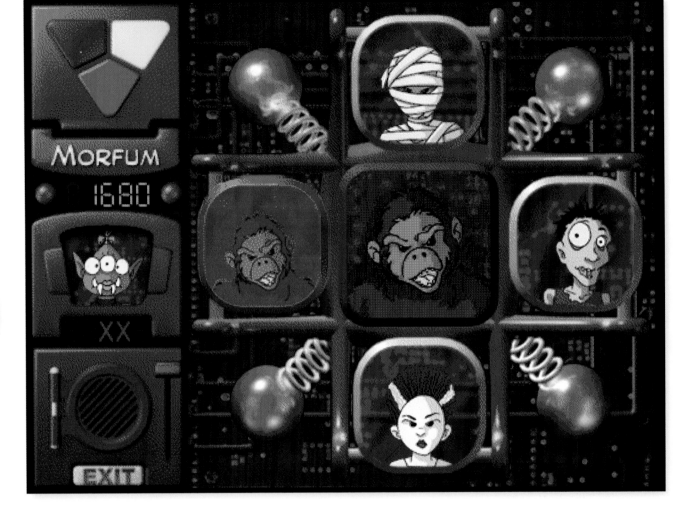

"**One of the big breakthroughs in this game was successfully communicating to children when it was their turn to play.**"

–Steve Lomas, executive producer

Fiendish Fun

"What we set out to accomplish with *Monster Lab* was a set of simple games that would be fun to play and get progressively more challenging. We also wanted to explore the notion of playing against animated on-screen characters," explains executive producer Steve Lomas. "The concept for *Monster Lab* came about while our team was at a trade show. One of the graphic artists commented on how tiring it was to see so many morphing applications. My comeback was, 'I bet kids aren't tired of it.' As we walked the rest of the show, we started designing the game."

Ghoulish Games

There are three activities in this high-tech monster lab: Meetum, Matchum, and Morfum. In Meetum, meet the cast of 12 animated monsters and morph them into creepy new characters.

In Matchum, play against these ghoulish creatures in a fun memory game. Earn points by matching pairs of monster tiles.

In Morfum, above, four monster screens randomly light up as each sounds a different tone. Mimic the light and sound pattern correctly to earn points and advance to a more difficult sequence. Miss, it's a strike. Three strikes, the game is over.

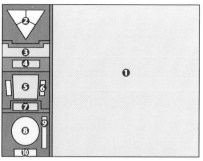

1. Game window 2. Color-coded game buttons 3. Name of active game, also opens credits 4. Player scoreboard 5. Monster door 6. Buttons to open and close Monster door 7. Monster scoreboard 8. Help door 9. Volume slider 10. Exit button

In the introductory screen, you'll meet the animated help agent. Click the Help door at the bottom of the control panel and out flitters the bat to explain whatever the cursor is on top of. Click anywhere on the screen to send him back.

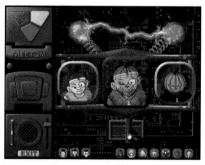

In Meetum, monsters are lined up below the Meetum Morfum machine. Click and drag pictures of any two monsters to the small side screens. For an animated introduction, drag the lever all the way to either side and click on the corresponding screen.

Drag the Morph lever in Meetum to morph two monsters into a new creature. When the lever is in the center, both monsters are equally blended. When it's all the way to one side no morphing takes place and an unmorphed image is shown.

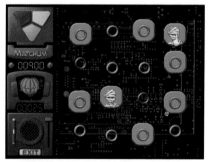

In Matchum, the monster shown in the monster door is the current opponent. Green rings represent matches found by the monster and red ones represent matches found by the player. The scores are also color-coded green and red. Note the monster's hand is the active cursor when it's the monster's turn. The player's hand cursor is not active here.

STATS AND SOFTWARE

It took a 12-member team 9 months to complete *Monster Lab*. The software used includes AfterEffects, DeBabelizer, Director, Excel, MacProject, Word, MovieShop, Now-Up-To-Date, Photoshop, Premiere, SoundDesigner, SoundEdit 16, and various proprietary tools, XObjects, and DLLs.

One of the main challenges, especially with Matchum, was how to communicate to children when it was their turn and when it was their on-screen opponent's turn. Preliminary prototyping and user testing provided helpful feedback. The solution was to add a second cursor in the shape of the monster's hand when it was the monster's turn and to follow its action with a verbal response when the turn was over.

Dividing Up the Screen

The interface is made up of two sections: a game window and a control panel that clusters the navigation buttons, game title bar, scoreboards, volume lever, and interaction controls. The control panel is always visible and accessible on the left. The game window changes when a different game is selected.

The game window is based on a square shape and the control panel on a vertical rectangle. Using different shapes reinforces the different purposes. Color also helps: The game window background is gray—subdued and monochromatic. In contrast, the main components of the control panel are bright blue with red, yellow, and green buttons that add accent color.

The buttons offer audio feedback too. Roll over a button and a voice of one of the characters states the name and function of the button. The response is programmed to randomly pick the voice so the player doesn't know which character to expect, resulting in a fun audio play toy, as well.

Lots of Animation

"This title has something like a thousand animated clips!" remarks Lomas. An entire QuickTime-based animation system was developed that allowed for an efficient and cost-effective method of creating the animated elements of a character and then processing each sound bite to get multiple performances. Custom tools were also developed to build movies, to perform lip synching, and to view the results of the processing.

Click the MegaMorf game button to get to the credits screen. Click any of the green tiles to get an animated reaction from the creators of *Monster Lab*. In the Monster door, Nyte Byter introduces them and describes the role each played.

High scorers are listed on the Matchum High Scores screen and the Morfum High Scores screen. The small pictures of the monsters show the three opponents that the player played against in one game.

Making the Internet Easy for Teachers and Students

Overview *Through this Web site, CCCnet, Computer Curriculum Corporation (CCC), a leading provider of educational software and services for K–12 and adult learning, offers teachers an easy way to integrate Internet projects into their curricula and uses bright colors, amusing graphics, animation, and audio to appeal to students.*

"Teachers were feeling a lot of pressure to make use of the Internet, so we created a Web site with lesson plans for teachers and interactive projects for students."

–Denise Daniels, producer/
creative director

Helping Teachers

Developed and maintained by Computer Curriculum Corporation, CCCnet provides teachers of grades K–12 with the structure they need to incorporate the Internet into their classrooms. In addition to thematic instructional units that include a main project, a mini-project, and interactive games based on national curriculum standards, the site offers detailed instructions and lesson plans for each of the accompanying projects and activities, an online forum where teachers can communicate with other teachers around the world, and "Webmentors"—former teachers who serve as online advisors.

Adding Value

The instructional projects of CCCnet are interdisciplinary, and unique technologies allow students to take full advantage of the communication and networking capabilities of the Internet. They can research by gathering information from a wide variety of online resources, communicate with participants from all over the world, collaborate with them on projects, and document and share results by publishing them on the World Wide Web.

In Energy Flow in Amazonia, for example, students explore the concept of food chains and energy pyramids in the ecosystem of the Amazon region. Clicking on the colorful objects on

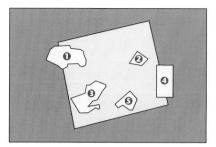

1. Electronic Safari button 2. Energy Pyramid button 3. Species List button 4. Energy Challenge button 5. Pyramid Page button

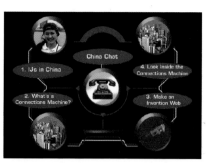

The discussion and video-conferencing area called China Chat presents material collected when students communicated with writers, photographers, video artists, and new media experts, referred to as "Internet jockeys" (or IJs) as they traveled through China.

In the main interface, shown here on the home page, brightly colored, clickable illustrations represent the different areas of the site. At the bottom of the page, the oval-shaped navigation buttons are made from details of the illustrations.

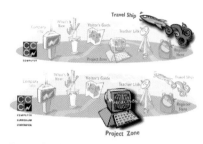

The navigation illustrations also appear at the top of the section pages to show you where you are and to link back to the home page. The illustrations that are not active are smaller and screened back while those that are active retain their full color, as do the Project Zone and Travel Ship sections above.

In Shapes Around the World the dimensional navigation buttons are available from every page within the unit. The CCCnet button at the top leads back to the site's home page.

STATS AND SOFTWARE

It took a 6-member team 6 months to develop the site: 6 weeks for planning and design, 12 weeks for asset production, and 6 weeks for programming and testing. Primary software included Director, Illustrator, Photoshop, Streaming Audio, and Streaming Video, with CGI/PERL, and Shockwave. Hardware included 12 Macintosh computers, 2 PCs, and one Silicon Graphics workstation. **cccnet.com**

the opening screen, shown on the opposite page, leads to the section's five different activities. Students link to other relevant sites to search for information on the Amazon, then create a Web page where they can publish their results.

Developing and Designing Content

Projects within instructional units are created during a 3-month development cycle that includes 3 weeks for planning and design, 6 weeks for asset production, and 3 weeks for testing. After a concept treatment is written, three different creative options are presented, then one is selected to be developed. Since art and navigation are integral interface components, both are considered from the outset of the design process, along with the important issues of file size and download speed.

CCCnet art and technology standards and navigation guide-lines provide consistency while allowing each project to have its own distinct interface and navigation elements that relate to the theme of the study unit. For example, each project has its own homepage, the CCC logo appears at the bottom of every page, and a navigation bar leads to the first-level areas within a project and links back to the project's home page. All projects are developed for a 14-inch monitor (640 x 480 pixels), and to maximize download speed, pages are no larger than 40K.

"We do usability testing on all of our projects with both teachers and students," says producer/creative director Denise Daniels. "All of our projects are student-driven and student-focused, so the copy and navigation elements are geared toward students." To appeal to today's media-savvy students, bright color palettes and playful graphics are encouraged.

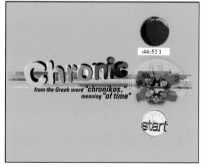

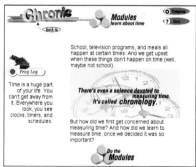

In the Chronic project, left, students investigate the origins of timekeeping and develop collaborative timelines. Throughout the interface, circles, spheres, and curvilinear shapes make reference to watches and clocks. To make it easier for students to digest written information presented on-screen, the text is broken up into small amounts, typeset large, and formatted in paragraphs with short lines, which Daniels refers to as "chunking."

S E P T E M B E R   1 9 9 7

WWW. **FONTSITE** .COM
DIGITAL TYPOGRAPHY & DESIGN

feature
A R T I C L E S

THE STYLE GUIDE: USING LATIN TERMS

The Style Guide is intended for writers and documentation specialists. (In the words of Ralph Wiggum, "Me fail english? That's unpossible!") This month we take a look at Latin abbreviations and terms.

i.e.
VERSUS
e.g.

How to use
Latin terms
Correctly

THE PRODUCTION ARTIST SURVIVAL GUIDE

The **Survival Guide** is a regular series written for computer graphic artists. This section demonstrates techniques used by production artists on a daily basis, and includes step-by-step instructions on how to make your job easier.

RULES OF TYPOGRAPHY: PART I

Setting
Your Type
Aglow!

Perhaps "guidelines" would be a better word, but there are some things in typography that you really oughta do, as well as some other things you really ought notta do. The goal of these rules (we'll present a few in each issue) is to create good-looking documents that bespeak the professionalism and attention to detail that went into creating them.

See Production Artist
Survival Guide

fontsite
B O O K S T O R E

The FontSite Bookstore offers a huge selection of books on typography and design, hand-picked and annotated by FontSite booknerds. Most of the books are available at discounts of 20% off the cover price, many at discounts as high as 30%.

font & file
D O W N L O A D S

Fonts for sale, fonts for free. Come visit our library of professional-quality typefaces in PostScript and TrueType formats for Mac OS and Windows. And some other cool stuff too.

annotated
L I N K O G R A P H Y

Our goal is to eventually build the world's most complete list of links to things typographic, annotated of course. A work in progress, we enthusiastically welcome all input.

about the
F O N T S I T E

Information about the FontSite including a discussion of the tools and fonts we used to build it.

FONTSITE

THE
RULES
OF
TYPOGRAPHY
PART I

Latin Terms

Production Artist
Survival Guide

FontSite Bookstore

Font & File Downloads

Linkography

About the FontSite

Main Page

The Rules of Typography are
reprinted from the book

Well, except one. While not necessary, it is acceptable and often more readable when composing e-mail (text that will be read online and not printed) to insert two spaces after periods, question and exclamation marks, and colons. See Chapter 8 for an introduction to e-mail typography. (Studies have shown that two spaces is approximately one too many.)

Francisco. It was Sunday
night and he'd had six or
seven. Turning to the guy on

TWO SPACES BETWEEN SENTENCES

Francisco. It was Sunday
night and he'd had six or
seven. Turning to the guy on

ONE SPACE BETWEEN SENTENCES

2 Use proper em and en dashes where appropriate.

Also a throwback to the days of typewriters, two hyphens—like these—were used to make a dash because true dash characters are not available on a typewriter. But this is a major no-no in typesetting and desktop publishing, where em dashes?like these?should be used instead. An em is a unit of measure equal to the point size you are using. For example

---

FONTSITE

GLOWING
TEXT (AND WHATEVER ELSE)

THE
PRODUCTION
ARTIST
SURVIVAL
GUIDE

TIP
If you use Illustrator, convert the type to outline paths before placing it into Photoshop. Sometimes Illustrator can't place it into Photoshop into less ascenders or descenders (see Fig 1). This falls under the category of "not a good thing."

TIP
If you prefer to use QuarkXPress®, any XPress EPS file can be placed with complete accuracy into Photoshop 4. But watch out, Photoshop 3 has problems with XPress EPS files.

With the premiere issue of **The FontSite** we're starting a series of articles showing techniques in computer art production. The series will mostly cover print graphics but as you may know, print graphics can be converted to web graphics quite easily. Over the past several years we've come across countless techniques for creating virtually all types of graphic. We hope to share some of these techniques with you in this series.

The first item up for discussion is making text glow. This example focuses on text but can be used on graphics as well. We're going to use **Adobe Photoshop**™. Photoshop is the one and only image manipulation program to use. It doesn't matter if you're using **Macintosh**® or **Windows**®, purchase a copy and learn how to use Photoshop.

Glowing text can be accomplished with a multitude of plug-ins. But doing it yourself allows for much more control and actually gives you better results.

First you need to create some type. This can be done directly in Photoshop but we prefer to use **Adobe Illustrator®** and then place the text into Photoshop (see the Tips at the right). After the type is created, make sure you have a transparent background. Go to **File > Preferences > Transparency** and set Grid Size to Small, Medium or Large. If you have a transparent background you will be able to see a checkerboard pattern around the type. If you don't you will need to recreate the type in a layer that has a transparent background.

g
g
Watch for
sections of
letters
disappearing.

FIG 1

Once your text is created properly we need to create a background color so we can see the glow. Create a layer just below the text layer. Set your Foreground Color to a dark color. Don't use the same color that's used for the type or you won't be able to see the type after you create the background. Select the entire background by choosing **Select > All** and then type **Option-Delete** (Macintosh) or **Alt-Delete** (Windows). This should fill the entire layer with the foreground color.

We now wish to turn the type layer into a selection. The shortcut for this is while holding down the **Command key** (Macintosh) or **Control key** (Windows), click on the text layer in the Layer Palette (see Fig 2). You should see the selection come up around the text.

Layers
Normal   Opacity: 100%
☐ Preserve Transparency
g g Stuff
& Things

The cursor will
change to look
like this when
loading the layer
as a selection.

Latin Terms

Rules of Typography

FontSite Bookstore

Font & File Downloads

Linkography

About the FontSite

Main Page

Visitors to The FontSite (**fontsite.com**) can find a wealth of information delivered as illustrated feature articles and tips on all aspects of type—from pointers on style and usage for those who write, to typesetting tips for production artists, to special effects using type for graphic designers, to the history of type and the fine points of typography and type design for those who want to put the desktop revolution in context. In addition, visitors can download free fonts and buy others from a collection of 1500 faces. The FontSite also provides annotated links to other sites that cover typography.

The site uses a clean, black-type-on-white-page approach. Not only is this metaphor familiar to type aficionados, says Ken Oyer, who developed the site with partner Sean Cavanaugh, but "it also downloads really quickly."

Winner of several awards for its robust content, The FontSite earns its keep through banner advertising, the marketing of The FontSite 500 type collection on CD-ROM, and book sales through a link to the online bookstore **amazon.com**, an option open to any site that recommends books. The FontSite receives a percentage of the sale of any book order that comes in to amazon.com via the link with The FontSite's recommended list.

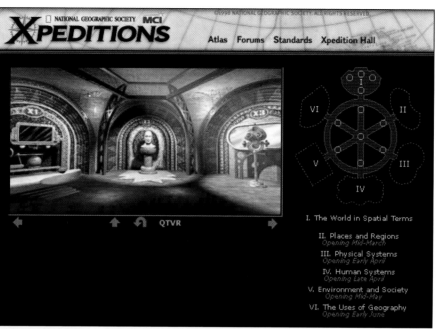

NATIONAL GEOGRAPHIC SOCIETY **MCI**
XPEDITIONS

Atlas Forums Standards Xpedition Hall

QTVR

I. The World in Spatial Terms

II. Places and Regions
Opening Mid-March

III. Physical Systems
Opening Early April

IV. Human Systems
Opening Late April

V. Environment and Society
Opening Mid-May

VI. The Uses of Geography
Opening Early June

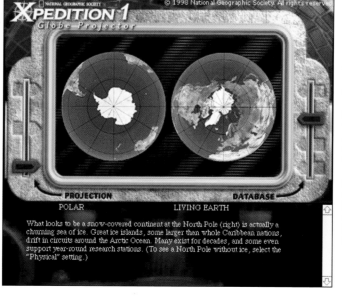

XPEDITION 1
Globe Projector

PROJECTION   DATABASE
POLAR   LIVING EARTH

What looks to be a snow-covered continent at the North Pole (right) is actually a churning sea of ice. Great ice islands, some larger than whole Caribbean nations, drift in circuits around the Arctic Ocean. Many exist for decades, and some even support year-round research stations. (To see a North Pole without ice, select the "Physical" setting.)

Through a partnership between MCI and The National Geographic Society, students of all ages can experience geographical, cultural, and historical material on the Xpeditions Web site (**nationalgeographic.com/ xpeditions**) whose goal is in part to advance the appearance of the U.S. National Geography Standards for grades K–12. The four components of the site—Atlas, Xpedition Hall, Standards, and Forums—are designed to stimulate thinking about the world we live in, its borders, and its diverse inhabitants.

To make the experience exciting for students and to engage their spatial senses as part of the learning process, Annex 1 in Xpedition Hall, above, leads them on a walk through the space. A floor plan of Xpedition Hall, a device familiar from real-world museums, serves as a site map and navigation system. Rolling the cursor over the plan identifies the different areas of Xpedition Hall, and clicking takes students to the selected area. A prerendered flythrough from the rotunda to the center of the lobby of Xpedition Hall is accomplished with a GIF animation. The site uses several HTML frames, but the continuous black background blends the frames seamlessly so the page seems unified and the whole presentation feels consistent from page to page.

Annex 1 has three areas to explore: X1, X2, and X3, each with an enticing gadget whose switches, dials, and levers invite interaction. For instance, the X1 globe projector, at right, shows different ways of representing the world in polar and planar maps. At left, the X3 world viewer shows maps of the world based on language, surface temperature, population growth, and other planetary statistics.

Another way the site engages students is by allowing them to interact with one another. "In Forums the students can exchange ideas about geography," says Julie Beeler of the design firm, Second Story, that helped National Geographic develop the site.

After the hands-on experience of exploring the various wings of the museum, visitors can extend the exploration in the classroom away from the computer. Teachers can download a variety of maps, and parents can learn about family activities that can help students achieve the goals set by the National Standards.

8 Publishing

Turning the pages in a printed magazine is self-explanatory but finding your way around a virtual publication can be intimidating and confusing unless good organization and design principles are put into practice.

MOST PRINTED PUBLICATIONS ARE DESIGNED AS A SERIES of pages to be read in sequential order. But on-screen publications allow readers to choose a nonlinear approach and to find information through linked concepts. As you'll see in the case studies that follow, this offers new challenges and provides new opportunities for the designer.

One of the most dramatic differences between designing a printed publication and designing for the screen is screen resolution. The resolution of a computer screen is typically a coarse 72 dpi (dots per inch) and requires that close attention be paid to layout and typography to ensure good readability. Another challenge for the designer is to determine how the reader will get from one page to another or from one section to another easily, while maintaining a clear understanding of where he or she is within the whole program.

This section includes electronic publications—magazines, encyclopedias, newspapers, and journals—that have been adapted from existing printed publications, such as *Verbum, the Journal of Personal Computer Aesthetics* (page 164), *Surfer Magazine* (page 162), and the *Star Tribune Online* (page 160), as well as some that have been conceived and designed entirely as electronic publications, such as *Just Think* (page 158), *Encarta 97 Encyclopedia* (page 150), *EnviroLink* (page 152), *epicurious.com* (page 154), and *Interact, the American Center for Design Journal* (page 156). When motion graphics and sound are combined with good design principles, the result can provide readers with an engaging and rewarding experience.

In Search of Information

Overview *The well-organized and visually appealing interface of the Microsoft® Encarta® 97 Deluxe Encyclopedia makes it easy to access a wealth of information through hypertext, illustrations, photos, animation, sound, video, and links to the World Wide Web.*

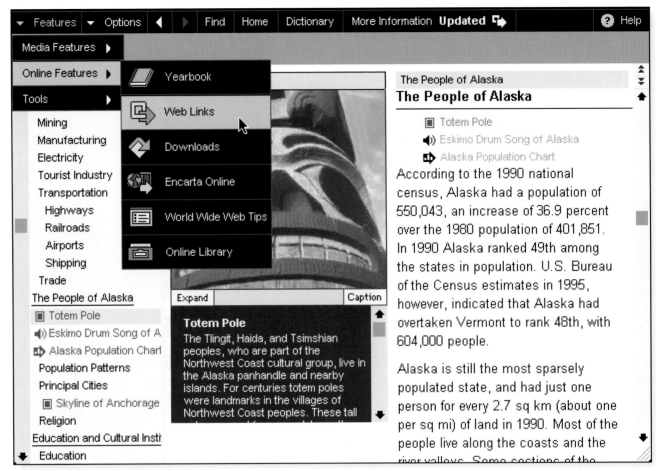

"We've created an environment that invites exploration and, through exploration, enhances learning."

–Bill Flora, designer

Digging Into Information

In the *Microsoft® Encarta® 97 Deluxe Encyclopedia*, a well-designed interface and the nonlinear electronic format of CD-ROM make searching for information much easier and more exciting than in a printed encyclopedia. Keyword searches, hyperlinking, sound, video, and animation greatly extend the kinds of information an encyclopedia can present. Updates, which in printed encyclopedias are limited to annual yearbooks, can be offered monthly through a link to the Web, and a Preferences dialog box lets users customize how information and navigation choices are presented.

Clear Organization and Easy Navigation

Encarta 97 is organized into four main sections: Encyclopedia Articles, Media Features, Online Features, and Dictionary. Clicking on a section title in the table of contents on the Home screen, left, leads to that section, but the sections can also be reached from many other places within the publication. For example, on the Article screen, above, the black navigation bar at the top allows access to other sections by way of buttons and drop-down menus that are hidden until needed.

Information can be viewed in four different ways on the Article screen: text only, text and outline, text and media, or all three, as shown above. The outline, left, shows where you are in the article, media and captions are displayed in the center, and text on the right. The title of the portion of the article or media type currently displayed is highlighted in the outline. Clicking

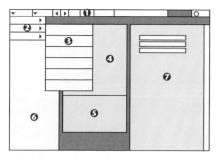

1. Navigation/Menu bar 2. Features menu
3. Online Features menu 4. Article media
window 5. Caption window 6. Article
outline 7. Article

To avoid having too many elements on-
screen at one time, captions are hidden
until you click the caption button below
the media window. Clicking the expand
button enlarges the picture to full screen.
Clicking on colored text in the article
jumps to related articles.

In the Media Features Timeline, the beginning of an era in history is marked with a
vertical green line and the end with a red
line. Clicking on a picture or timeline bar
opens an essay. Clicking on a globe opens
a map. Clicking on an event in the Find an
Event window locates it on the Timeline.

Navigation screens introduce Media Features and Online Features. Colorful background graphics distinguish these pages
from the neutral gray interface of the
Article screens. Large serif type in the title
contrasts with the smaller sans serif text
type. Clicking an image begins an activity.

Colored icons are displayed in the Online
Features menu, shown on the Articles
screen on the opposite page.

Media Features also has its own set of
colored icons that are found in the Media
Features menu of the Articles screen.

on a title in the outline displays that part of the text. Clicking
on a media icon in the article or outline displays media.

Color Adds Clarity

The black and warm gray interface components create a neutral
background for colorful media and hypertext. Shades of gray
behind text indicate selected items. Clicking colored text jumps
to a related article or form of media. The default color of the
hypertext is red, but it can be changed in the Preferences dialog
box to green, blue, or orange to suit the user.

User Feedback Provides Control

Sound and subtle visual changes on-screen provide feedback
and offer a sense of control and reassurance. Flat buttons pop
out or recede, the cursor changes form, type changes color, and

menus automatically swoop down when the mouse passes over
the menu marker. No more clicking, holding, and sliding to
reach menu items—the menu stays open until the cursor is
moved away. To avoid opening menus unintentionally, most
menu markers are positioned on the outskirts of the screen and
are programmed to open menus only when the cursor lingers on
the marker. Furthermore, the menu-opening feature can be
turned off in the Preferences dialog box. *Maw*

A consistent layout and clearly labeled buttons characterize the
Online Features Yearbook. Clicking on the Directory button on the
title screen, left, leads to the Yearbook Directory, center, where
you can select monthly updates from the World Wide Web. Selecting an area of interest changes the background color. Choosing
an article from the List of Updates, changes the type color. Clicking on the download button leads to the Download screen, right.

In the Media Features section, multimedia collages reveal dramatic
panoramas full of photos, colorful graphics, animations, sounds,
and links to related articles. Rolling the cursor over Famous Buildings in the contents on the Collages screen, below left, displays a
preview. Five screens long, the collage is viewed by scrolling.

STATS AND SOFTWARE

Software included Canvas, Photoshop,
and Studio 32. Hardware included
both Mac and PC. *Encarta 97* ships
on 2 CD-ROM disks. **encarta.com**

Screen shots reprinted with permission from Microsoft Corporation.

Just the Right Touch

Overview *The EnviroLink Web site offers the latest news, information, and resources about the environment in the context of a vivid interface that uses depth, texture, and lighting to create a strong tactile impression.*

"We deliberately avoided lots of high-tech images in the interface, because our site is about nature and the environment."

–Josh Knauer, executive director

For the Purpose of Connecting

One of the first 15 public Web sites on the Internet, EnviroLink has grown from a small mailing list of 20 student activists to become one of the world's largest environmental information resources, reaching more than 5.2 million people in over 130 countries every month. A major part of EnviroLink's mission is to encourage discussion and distribution of information about environmental issues. From the home page, above, users can access a library database, *OneWorld* magazine, a list of environmentally responsible businesses approved by EnviroLink, daily environmental news updates, an online forum of opinions and ideas, a gallery that features earth-conscious art, a rating of other sites and events based on their impact on the environment, and a search feature to locate information about specific topics.

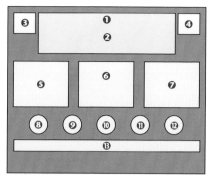

1. **EnviroLink symbol 2. EnviroLink logotype 3. About This Site button 4. Search
button 5. Library button 6. EnviroNews
button 7. Business Network button
8. Online Forum button 9. Online Gallery
button 10. About EnviroLink button
11. Awards button 12. Sites and events
rating button 13. Hypertext links**

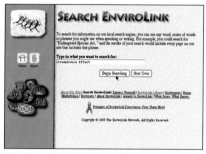

The icon that represents the search feature builds on the familiar animated run-
ner who's sent to find files on most computers. Based on a post-prehistoric cave
painting called *Marching Hunters*, found in
Casulla Gorge, Spanish Lavant, the icon
uses a spontaneous drawing style appropriate to the theme of the interface.

STATS AND SOFTWARE

A 10-member team worked about 13
weeks to complete the Web site—
planning and design took 8 weeks, asset
production, 4 weeks, and programming,
less than a week. Software included
BBEdit, DeBabelizer, and Photoshop.
Hardware included Mac, Unix, and
Silicon Graphics Indigo workstations.
envirolink.org

Pages are divided into a navigation panel
on the left and an information area on the
right. The stone representing a particular
section is shown at the top of the navigation panel. The remaining stones are clustered at the bottom. When a stone is at
the top, it is temporarily removed from
the cluster. Clicking on a stone in the cluster goes to that section.

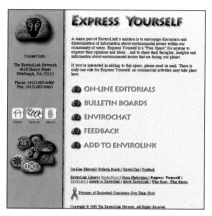

Each section is identified by a different
color, which is applied to the background
of the navigation panel on all of the pages
in that section. The light gray texture of
the information area creates a neutral
background for the colorful type and the
small stones that are used as bullets to
emphasize parts of the text.

Based on ancient Mayan artwork, the
mandala used in the icon for the
Envirolink Library symbolizes wisdom.
The library database is organized by subject under the main areas of earth, air,
fire, and water (the earth elements) and
flora and fauna (all living creatures), as
shown above by the five icons.

When Concept and Design Are in Harmony

The interface concept, developed by The EnviroLink Network and Immediate Access, was to create the perception of a natural environment on-screen. In support of the concept, the designer used texture, depth, and earth tones, in combination with organic objects and basic archetypal images. Straight lines were avoided, the designer opting instead for soft curves and unrefined edges. On the home page, artifacts that represent the sections of the site appear to be sitting on a sandy surface, or on clay tablets, or to have just been unearthed during an archeological dig. The titles are designed to look chiseled in stone or to float, like clouds, above the surface, casting shadows on the ground below. The typeface Lithos was selected for its irregular character.

From the Shores of the Puget Sound

Where do ideas come from? Well, the idea to use stones as the site icons came while Andrew Fry, the visual interface designer, was walking along the rocky shores of the Puget Sound. Fry carefully selected each stone for its size, shape, and flatness, placed the stones on a flat-bed scanner, scanned them, and then opened the scanned images in Photoshop, where they were colored in a palette of earth tones. Highlights were added to imply reflections from the sun, and shadows were created for depth. The icons, which are all based on ancient symbols and artwork from indigenous cultures, were debossed to make the stones look like artifacts or fossils. To retain detail and to keep file size small, the graphic objects were saved in JPEG format. The objects average around 10K.

Consideration for the Visitor

Out of consideration for users, executive director Josh Knauer suggests, "On the first page of a Web site people should have a choice between a high-graphics and a low-graphics version of the site, because there are people with everything from slow modems to fast T3 lines." The familiar duo, the tortoise and the hare, shown here, represent the two versions of the EnviroLink site: a text and low-graphics version for visitors with slower transmission capability or who prefer text-dominant files, and a high-graphics version for those who have faster transmission and who enjoy the graphics.

Two Sites in One

Overview *Take your pick between Epicurious Food and Epicurious Travel. Then follow a trail of eye-catching layouts full of fashionable colors, typography that's to-the-point, eclectic illustrations, and award-winning photographs.*

"I don't use an actual grid but there's an implied grid—a carry-over from my print background. If things should line up, I want them to line up; and if they don't line up, there needs to be a reason for it—to create visual tension, for instance."

–Steve Orr, design director

Companion Content

This CondéNet site is like a fork in the road: Visitors choose between two different content directions—Epicurious Travel and Epicurious Food—both of which draw on Condé Nast publications: *Condé Nast Traveler, Gourmet,* and *Bon Appétit.* Certain content from the magazines is adapted to the interactive online format and combined with new material developed specifically for the site. As shown above, the Epicurious Food site is divided into three sections: Eating, Drinking, and Playing with Your Food. Epicurious Travel also has three sections: Places, Planning, and Play, as shown at left.

Alike But Different

To show a relationship between the two sites, the layouts of the home pages for Epicurious Travel, left, and Epicurious Food, above, are similar. The word *epicurious*, set in Snell Roundhand and positioned flush left above *travel* and *food*, helps portray the connection. The hierarchy of information is clearly shown on each home page: The site's name is placed at the top of the page, like a magazine masthead, typeset large, but each name is treated differently to make a distinction between the sites. The feature box, on the left side of each home page, showcases a topic. The contents, to the right of the feature box, are clickable navigation buttons.

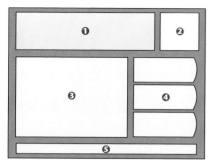

1. Masthead 2. Menu button 3. Feature box for promoting articles 4. Contents of the sections in the site 5. Word of the day

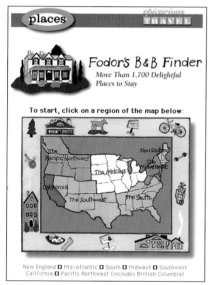

In the Places section of Epicurious Travel, clicking on the interactive map, or on the hypertext below, links to information on places to stay in that locale. Using a colorful illustration communicates a concept quickly and creates a cheerful atmosphere.

STATS AND SOFTWARE

A designer, an art director, 10 editors, and 10 to15 programmers work to maintain the Epicurious site and keep articles and information current. Software includes BBEdit, Illustrator, PhotoGIF, and Photoshop on Macs and Sun workstations. **epicurious.com**

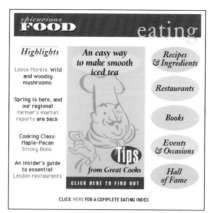

The colorful book cover, on the left of Epicurious Food's home page, calls attention to the featured topic. Clicking on the image opens the article. The article's title and the section names are typeset in Helvetica Extra Compressed to save space and to contrast with the thick and thin strokes of the serifed Berkeley Oldstyle Bold Italic used to typeset the smaller text sizes. The solid shapes of flat color and the typography are saved in GIF format.

Clicking on Eating on the home page opens the Eating section's main page where the contents are clearly organized in three columns with emphasis on the feature article in the center. For consistency, the contents of the Eating section are also positioned on the right side.

This *Gourmet* magazine main page uses a foreshortened image of a yellow bell pepper to draw the eye toward the title of the feature article. For convenience, a tool bar and a hypertext navigation bar appear at the bottom of every page.

Ongoing Maintenance

"Keeping the site fresh is probably the biggest part of the job," says design director Steve Orr. "Every day something on the site changes, and on alternating weeks we redo the home pages of Epicurious Travel and Epicurious Food by changing the color palettes and adding new art work to represent the topics in the feature boxes. These visual changes let readers know right away that there's new information."

Creating an Atmosphere

To brighten up the main pages and give the site a friendly face, lively spot illustrations and photographs are used in combination with color to direct the eye to certain topics and add interest to the page. The colors, says Orr, are inspired by palettes from contemporary fashion and interior design or sparked by associations. For example, the colors and pattern used to focus readers on Cookbook Catch, an article on community cookbooks showcased above in the feature box on the Food home page, are reminiscent of kitchen towels and provide an appropriate homey, country-kitchen feeling.

Colors are selected from a palette of 216 colors common to most browsers that Orr keeps handy on his desktop. Using

PhotoGIF, a Macintosh color-reduction plug-in for Photoshop, he creates highly optimized, Web-ready GIF images that are the smallest files possible for fast download.

From the Center Out

Both the Epicurious Food and the Epicurious Travel sites are organized like a wheel, with their respective home pages creating a hub in the center. As you move away from the center and into the areas where information is more concentrated, there are fewer graphics, and pages download more quickly. Pages are organized hierarchically, from top to bottom, and size and shape are used to emphasize information. For example, square versus oval: making interface elements oval sets them off because they have more white space around them. "It also keeps the layout from getting too blocky," adds Orr.

A Place To Meet and Make Friends

A strong sense of community has formed around the casual friendly style of this Web site. Like sitting around the kitchen table, visitors to Epicurious Food join in on forums to swap recipes and cooking tips, and many have become friends.

Mapping Out an Interface

Overview *In the interactive CD-ROM portion of this edition of* The American Center for Design Journal, *a celestial map metaphor is used to dynamically present the material, and icons that appear as locations on the map represent the articles.*

"*In publication design, editing and effective communication go hand-in-hand; the designer needs to be selective with the content in order to communicate a compelling message.*"

–Peter Spreenberg, IDEO

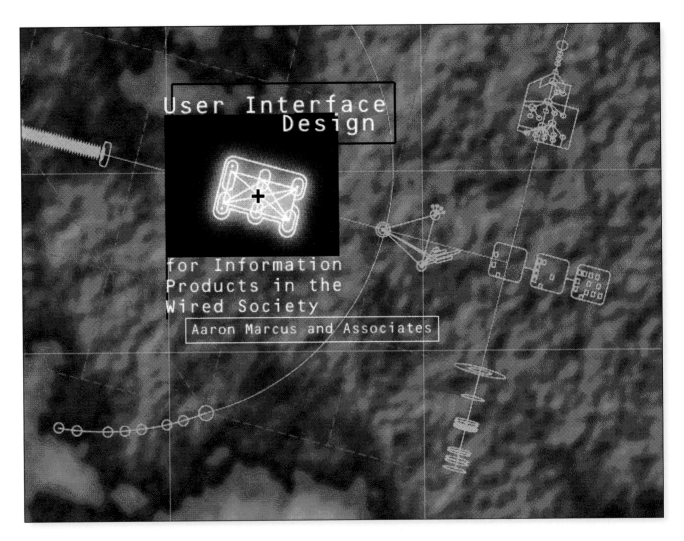

The Organization and Its Journal

The American Center for Design, a national organization of design professionals, educators, and students, publishes an annual journal of articles and essays devoted to a particular design-related theme. *Interact*, the 1994 edition of the journal, offered the audience two ways to explore the content: A printed booklet, designed by Tanagram in Chicago, featured essays on interaction design, and a complementary CD-ROM, edited by IDEO in San Francisco, provided illustrations and interactive demonstrations of the 11 different projects in the journal.

The Design Challenge

The editing process included developing a navigational interface and integrating content supplied by a variety of contributors. The interface, a portion of which is shown above, is basically a map of the table of contents of the projects featured on the CD-ROM. "It would have been easy to simply create a single static screen with titled buttons that users could click on to launch each associated piece, but that would have been boring," says IDEO's Peter Spreenberg. "Since the journal's readers are primarily designers, we realized that they already had a basic

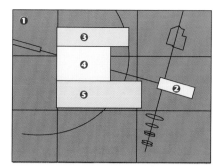

1. Section detail of contents map
2. Article icon 3. Title of selected article
4. Icon of selected article 5. Subtitle and
byline of selected article

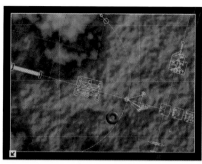

Pressing the spacebar while viewing the contents screen shows the available controls: a black border appears around the map and the yellow Quit icon shows up in the lower left corner. Click on the "i" or "o" of the *Interact* logo as they randomly cross the screen to see an animation.

Pressing the spacebar while within an article displays the navigation controls. The white arrow in the left corner takes you back to the contents map. Using the icons in the right corner, you can return to the article's title page, and go backward and forward. A caption appears at the top.

The self-running tutorial shows how the interface works. Clicking on an article icon on the contents screen turns the icon white and the background around it black. The title and author appear in white. The typeface OCRB contributes to the electronic feeling of the interface.

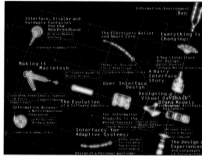

A complete version of the map provides an overview of all the authors and titles (top). An animated sequence scopes the map from a distance, then zooms in to define the main interface (bottom).

STATS AND SOFTWARE

Software included Capture, Director, FreeHand, Illustrator, Photoshop, SoundEdit Pro, and SwivelPro. Macintosh computers were used.

understanding of the Macintosh user interface, and we felt it was essential to create an interface that would be engaging—something that would allow for exploration and discovery."

Integrating Content

Contributors were invited to submit articles and interactive materials. The only submission requirements for the interactive projects were that the files needed to be Macintosh-compatible Director files, if possible, with 8-bit color at a screen resolution of 640 x 480 pixels. Some projects were delivered complete and ready to go, while others had to be digitized, animated, and edited into more complete presentations. "We didn't want to create too many submission restrictions for the authors, but that meant that we were then responsible for getting all the pieces to work together," says Spreenberg. "We received material in many different formats: 35 mm slides, print photos, interactive files, bitmapped images, text files, paper diagrams, and audio tapes. Piecing it all together and getting it to play smoothly on low-end platforms—like the Macintosh IIci—was the greatest challenge."

Navigating the Contents

"Although maps are still not universally understood, we felt that it was a fairly easy-to-grasp metaphor that most designers would understand after a few clicks. The icons that depict the sites on the map are subtly representative of the navigational structure of the associated article. For example, the icon for an article that uses a linear navigation structure is interpreted as a linear pattern and an article that is based on a more networked and hierarchical structure is represented by a more complex pattern." Moving the cursor to the edge of the screen causes the map to scroll in that direction, revealing more of the map. Double-clicking on an icon opens that project.

The *Interact* Logo

The *Interact* logo is prominently displayed on the front and back covers of the printed journal, shown on the facing page, and an animated version of the two separate parts of the logo randomly crosses the interactive map. Designed by Tanagram, the logo evolved from the vertical stroke and dot of a lowercase i. "The resulting objects are not just independent entities, but *counterparts*," says Eric Wagner of Tanagram. "Like the male/female metaphor, or the 0 and 1 of binary code, these objects convey the essential idea of interaction: the power and potential of the union." The back cover shows a magnified section of the front cover, indicated on the front cover by the dashed line and the magnifying glass icon, shown on the opposite page. The scale of the logo on the back cover was determined by the size of the CD-ROM disk that cleverly replaces the circular portion of the logo.

Interactive Journalism

Overview Animation, video, music, and sound effects support editorial illustrations and expand original story content in this interactive multimedia journal created by ad•hocINTERACTIVE.

"The text was initially input in Word. Then we took it into Illustrator to lay out the page, then brought it into Photoshop to be rasterized. Once it was composited, we took it into Director. It was important to catch typos early in the process. If we found one at the end, it was very upsetting—we had to go back a lot of steps to correct it!"

–Megan Wheeler, principal

Realizing an Idea

Megan Wheeler and Aaron Singer, partners in ad•hoc, could see the potential of incorporating sound and movement into the static medium of magazine publishing. In 1994, they developed *Just Think*, a quarterly interactive, digital magazine dedicated to news, entertainment, and information.

Using Media Effectively

The challenge in using multimedia is to determine which medium best suits a particular purpose. For example, instead of designing typographic pull quotes, ad•hoc presented the quotes in video format. "Actually seeing a person speak communicates the intent much more strongly than just reading text," explains Wheeler. "So we felt video was a much more powerful tool for this purpose."

In a story entitled *Virtual Violence,* digital media allowed the authors to re-create the experience of receiving offensive email. Virtually experiencing the eery situation makes it easier for the reader to understand the story and to empathize with recipients of this kind of email.

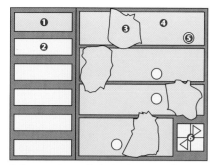

1. Screen name 2. Active contents button
3. Animated illustration/article button
4. Article title 5. Information button
6. Navigation cube

The start-up screen was influenced by magazine cover design. It showcases a bold image, displays the publication name, and lists key articles. Note the Tools pop-up menu with Bookmark selected.

To get more information about an article before making a selection, click the information icon beside the title on the Contents screen to read a summary of the article. Click the icon again to close the window.

This article about Stephen Spielberg's *Schindler's List*, uses movie clips to expand on the text. To play a clip, click on the film reel icon, left, or on the still image in the video window, upper right.

All six sides of the navigation quebe (pronounced "cube") are shown here. The design team's goal was to create a dynamic object that didn't take up much space on the screen and was always accessible.

Supporting a Concept with Visual Metaphors

Since intolerance is the focus of this issue, a wall is used in the background of the start-up screen and the Contents screen as a metaphor for the barriers that separate us. As shown on the opposite page, the subject categories are listed on the left of the Contents screen on individual stones, which are active buttons. Click a category, such as Features, to select it; the stone button is depressed as the article titles appear on the right.

Animated illustrations call attention to article titles. To go to a specific article, click on the animated illustration. The first screen of an article, like the title page in its printed counterpart, identifies the title, author, and illustrator.

Need Help? Spin the Quebe

A compact six-sided device that ad•hoc calls the *quebe* (pronounced "cube") was developed for storing controls and tools and is available on every screen. To save space, only one face of the animated 3D object is seen at a time.

Move the cursor to any of the four edges until it changes to an arrow. Click and the quebe rotates to reveal buttons for the Contents and start-up screen, as well as buttons for Exit, Forward/Backward, Help, and Tools with a pop-up menu for Print, Bookmarks, and Set-up. The quebe is smart, too. At the end of an article it spins to the Contents button in anticipation of the user making another selection.

STATS AND SOFTWARE

It took 3 months for a team of 20 to produce this hybrid CD-ROM, including researchers, writers, artists, and programmers. Software included Director with custom XObjects, FreeHand, Illustrator, Photoshop, SoundEdit, and Word. Development was done on the Mac and the product was ported to Windows.

The bright green title stands out against the dark, somber background illustration. The title is animated on-screen as if it were being input on a keyboard. First, the cursor blinks, then the letters show up one at a time accompanied by a pecking sound.

To ensure good on-screen readability, the designers selected a bold typeface and colored the text white so it would contrast with the dark background in this page from "Virtual Violence."

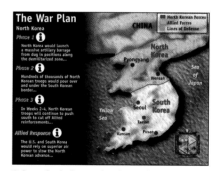

Select the information icons for additional text and for graphics on the map that illustrates the anticipated route of a North Korean invasion into South Korea. Note how hanging indents and color are used to emphasize subheads.

An AIDS Memorial

Overview *Through the honesty of black-and-white photography, the directness of journalism, the emotional impact of audio, and the interactivity of the Web, this project chronicles the toll AIDS took on the life and spirit of one family.*

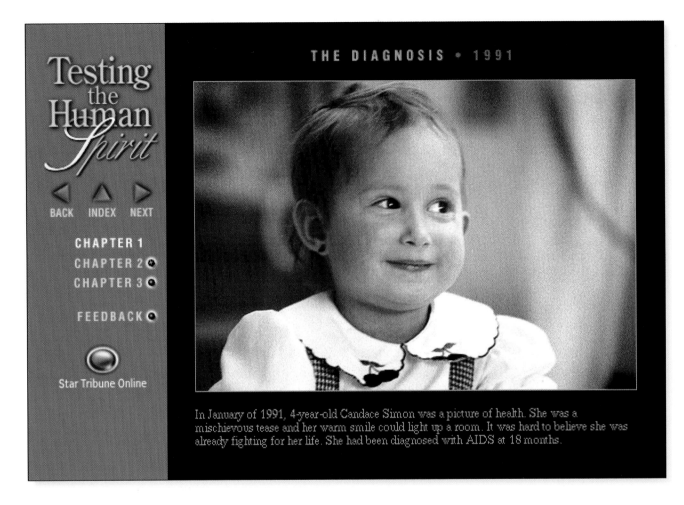

THE DIAGNOSIS • 1991

In January of 1991, 4-year-old Candace Simon was a picture of health. She was a mischievous tease and her warm smile could light up a room. It was hard to believe she was already fighting for her life. She had been diagnosed with AIDS at 18 months.

"Because of the Web site this story lives on and continues to touch people around the world, and that would have made Nancy Simon very happy."

–Brian Peterson, photographer

Telling Their Story

Assigned to document the daily struggles of a family living with AIDS, Brian Peterson, a staff photographer at the *Star Tribune* in Minneapolis, ended up taking more than 18,000 photographs of the Simons over a six-year period. Although parts of *Testing the Human Spirit* have been published periodically in the *Star Tribune*, left, the online version presents the entire story, with 100 of Peterson's dramatic photos and a moving audio narrative of Nancy Simon talking about dealing with an illness that her husband unknowingly transmitted after he was infected by a blood transfusion during emergency surgery and which she unknowingly passed on to their daughter during pregnancy.

The Contents

Testing the Human Spirit is divided into three main chapters: "The Diagnosis, 1991," shown above, "Death of a Child, 1994," and "A Mother's Farewell, 1996." Each chapter begins with an index of thumbnails of all the images in that section. You can select any image from the index or follow a predetermined sequence based on the story written by reporter Kimberly Hayes Taylor. Clicking Aids Resources in the table of contents on the article's home page opens a listing of Internet resources with links to other sites where information about AIDS and HIV can be found. A Photographer's Perspective and About This Project, also listed in the contents, offer background information.

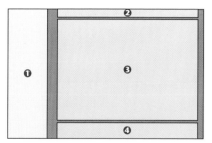

1. Table of contents and navigation controls 2. Chapter title 3. Photograph 4. Caption

When the first photograph in a chapter is displayed, only the Index and Next arrows are available on the control panel on the left, indicating that you may return to the index to select another image or proceed to the next image in the series.

Once you're beyond the first image in a chapter, the Back arrow also becomes available, indicating that you may return to the preceding image. The button to the right of each chapter title in the Contents disappears when you're in that chapter.

When you view the final photograph in a chapter, the Next arrow disappears, indicating that the photo being displayed is the last one in the series. The button at the bottom of the navigation panel links to the *Star Tribune*'s home page.

Using a thumbnail version of each photograph in the chapter index allows the images to load quickly and offers an overview of the entire chapter. Clicking the Begin button on the control panel opens the first page of the chapter. Clicking on a specific image goes directly to that page. Clicking on The Story connects to the *Star Tribune* Web site's text-only version of the story.

The Interface

Designed by Jamie Hutt, design editor of Star Tribune Online, the understated interface is divided into two main areas: a navigation panel on the left and a large display area on the right where the photographs are presented. Above each photo a title identifies the chapter and, below, a caption tells the story. To complement the black-and-white pictures, the color palette of the interface was limited to black, white, and grays.

Typography

The *Testing the Human Spirit* title design is a combination of Century Expanded and Berthold Script. The type was set and composited in FreeHand, converted to paths, then placed in Photoshop where shadows were added. Helvetica Condensed Bold was chosen for the title, table of contents, and navigation text because its simple sans serif style complemented the more elaborate typography of the title. The type appears in shades of gray so it doesn't compete with the highlights in the photographs, and contrasts with the background just enough so it can be easily read.

Preparing the Photographs

When the *Star Tribune* started printing color in its newspaper in 1987, staff photographers stopped using black-and-white film and switched to color film, which provides the newspaper with the option to reproduce pictures either in black-and-white or in color. For the *Testing the Human Spirit* newspaper articles, the 35mm color negatives were scanned using a Kodak 2035 at 2000dpi, the scanner's maximum setting. For the Web site,

Peterson opened the original 16 MB high-resolution color scans in Photoshop, converted them to grayscale, then sharpened and cropped all the images. After evaluating how each photo looked on-screen, Peterson adjusted the contrast and brightness so they would all have a similar appearance. Then he resized them to 5 x 7-inches at 72dpi and saved them in JPEG format, which reduced the file size down to a manageable 10 to 50K each.

Color Versus Grayscale

Although some color images were used in the periodic newspaper articles to project a feeling of hope, the images in the online version are all grayscale, which Peterson feels not only suits the subject matter but provides balance in the indexes where all of the photos are viewed at the same time, and offers consistency from page to page. Also, the grayscale image files are one-third the size of their color counterparts and download a lot faster.

Meeting a Tight Deadline

Following planning meetings during which site content, theme, interface metaphor, and navigation structure were mapped out, actual production took only 2 days. Producer Jackie Crosby orchestrated production and stayed on top of all the details, leaving Peterson to prepare the photos, while Hutt concentrated on the interface design and navigation, Ben Welter did final coding, and Will Outlaw edited and compressed the audio. Final production began on Thursday, and after working through the night on Friday, the team had the site ready to go online by Saturday—a quick turnaround even for a newspaper!

A Swell Site

Overview *In this Web site from Surfer magazine, spectacular action photos, GIF animations, and QuickTime movies of world-class surfing are as popular as the site's online bulletin board, which provides a forum for surfers to interact in ways that they've never been able to before.*

"If you're thinking about building a Web site, carefully consider what you're going to be able to offer that's different from the product that you have right now, and whether you're willing to devote the resources needed to get it going, and to keep it going until it starts showing a profit of its own."

–Chris Dixon, online editor

Catching the World Wide Wave

Surfer magazine had been documenting the sport of surfing for 36 years when Surfer Publications decided to develop a Web site. A major design goal was to make the online version, which would include similar content, look like an extension of the printed magazine by adapting its unconventional graphics style. Research had shown that typical *Surfer* readers, who are in their teens and 20s, like the magazine's photo issues, travel stories, and profiles of *ocean* surfers, and are fascinated by anything to do with big waves. In addition, the site could take advantage of online opportunities: QuickTime movies, GIF animation, audio playback of interviews with surfers, links to related sites, and an interactive bulletin board.

Understanding Client Goals

Consultants Sean Strauss and Ian Wynne of Vandelay Industries were chosen to develop the site, and to train online editor Chris Dixon of *Surfer* to update and maintain it. Surfers themselves, Strauss and Wynne share a love for the sport, and their understanding of the audience and knowledge of surfing meant that the client didn't have to do a lot of explaining—which translated into getting the site completed quickly.

A Fresh and Responsive Interface

To keep the site fresh, three random CGI scripts were designed to provide a different experience each time a reader logs on. The program randomly selects options from banks of stored data so

1. Message and identification frame
2. Main information frame 3. Navigation
frame 4. Hypertext links

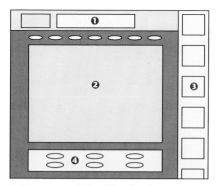

The Surf Shop

Hats | Library | T-shirts | The Surf Report

Kookmeyer Stuff | Music | Prints | Sale Items | Videos

home   interaction   magazine   gallery   linkage

Clicking on the Surf Shop icon, takes you
to the Surf Shop page, shown above,
where a cartoon illustration by Bob
Penuelas depicts the inside of the shop.
Selecting a yellow label takes you to that
department where purchases can be made
by calling a toll-free number or filling out
an online order form.

STATS AND SOFTWARE

To complete the Web site, a team of 3
worked 3 months—a total of 700 hours.
Software originally included Photoshop
and Simple Text, but now CyberPress,
PageMill, and Premier are also used. All
the design and construction was done
on the Mac and testing was done on different PC computers. **surfermag.com**

Over the 36 years that Surfer magazine
has been documenting the world of
surfing, Surfer Publications has accumu-
lated extensive archives of images,
articles, and quotes from some of the
most notable surfers in the history of the
sport. Every time a visitor logs on, the site
randomly displays a different classic quote
from its archives at the bottom of the
home page. The navigation objects are
shown in the navigation frame on the
right and also at the bottom of the main
information screen in case a browser
doesn't support frames.

Surfer Publications doesn't have to upload new content every
day. One script delivers the publication logo and a different
dramatic photograph, like the ones shown below on the two
versions of the home page. Another script presents a classic
quote culled from the *Surfer* archives, and the third script shows
an updated greeting with current time and date.

Three-Frame Format

Frames are used to divide the space into three distinct areas. The
top frame identifies the site and carries a brief message or
advertisement, the navigation frame is on the right, and the
larger central frame contains the main information and links to
other sites. The navigation buttons are photographs that represent the main sections and allow users to easily get to any

Clicking on the Interaction icon in the
navigation frame or at the bottom of the
main frame leads to the Interaction home
page, where the title is reversed out of yet
another cool surf shot. Underlined words
link to other pages in the section, including the popular Bulletin Board that
attracts visitors from all over the globe.

location within the site. Using multiple frames lets the reader
stay at *Surfer* even when the main frame opens another site.

An Idea Is Born

The site is based on a flexible hierarchical structure that allows
for easy modification. Changes to the site are influenced in part
by a detailed analysis produced by Net Count, a software
product that keeps track of the number of visits a page receives
within a given time period. Also helpful is feedback from visitors
via the site's email and popular bulletin board, which continuously receive email from all over the world. The idea for another
bulletin board called The Surf Doc, a forum dedicated to surf-
related health issues, grew out of an online discussion among
readers when a doctor who happened upon the conversation
replied with healthful advice.

From Photo to JPEG

The photos for the printed magazine are shot as color transparencies, scanned at different resolutions, and stored on CD. The
typical resolution for print quality averages about 4 MB per
image—too large for the Web—so when an image is selected, it
is sized as needed, then saved as a low-resolution JPEG.

Some of the articles in the printed magazine are also featured in the Web site.
CyberPress, a QuarkXPress plug-in, is used
to convert the magazine layouts to Web
pages, including converting the headline
typography from type to a GIF graphic.

Art Magazine Switches to Multimedia

Overview Verbum Interactive, *the world's first integrated interactive multimedia magazine, includes columns, art galleries, program demos, feature articles, a database, and an order section for products.*

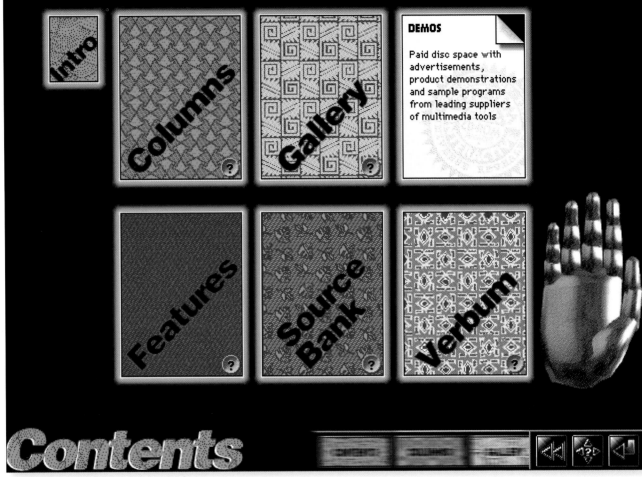

DEMOS

Paid disc space with advertisements, product demonstrations and sample programs from leading suppliers of multimedia tools

"Navigation tools don't have to stay static—they can grow or shrink, become dormant or get up and dance."

—Jack Davis, art director

The Communication Challenge

When *Verbum, the Journal of Personal Computer Aesthetics*, moved from the printed page to the computer screen, the challenge was to maintain the magazine's design integrity while incorporating the instructional and entertainment benefits of multimedia.

Verbum was already known for presenting content in imaginative ways. According to publisher/editor Michael Gosney, each printed issue was intended to be "a fresh design experiment." Even the logotype on the cover was redesigned for each issue. When designer Jack Davis developed the interface for the magazine's CD-ROM version, he combined text with audio, video, and 2D and 3D animation to achieve a dynamic presentation of the content.

Hierarchy of Information

An informational splash screen leads to a short introductory animation and then to the Contents screen, above. This screen establishes a home base and branches to an introduction/information screen, a directory that provides a bird's eye view of the contents, and the six main sections of the magazine.

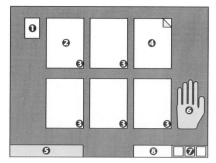

1. Intro/Info button 2. Main section buttons 3. Button to access sticky notes
4. Descriptive sticky note 5. Section title
6. Hidden Easter egg: animated signing hand 7. Navigation buttons 8. Animated navigation Power Bar

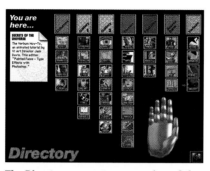

The Directory presents an overview of the content of each of the main sections. A sticky note to the left is revealed by rolling over any of the topic squares. The creative nature of the magazine allowed each layout to be treated in a unique way.

The Look and Feel column is one of the options that can be selected from the Directory. Note that the navigation buttons, right, are gray but still clickable when the control panel in the text window is active.

The Santa Fe Christian School article was selected from the Look and Feel screen. Here you can see an active text panel and the expanded navigation Power Bar, which was accessed by clicking on the double arrow icon on the lower right.

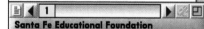

The text window control bar lets you print the article, turn the pages, play an animation, and access related sticky notes. The number represents the current page and slides along the bar to show where the current page falls within the article. If an animation is available, the running man icon jogs in place.

STATS AND STUFF

It took 10 team members 9 months to complete *Verbum Interactive*. It was developed for the Mac using Director, Illustrator, Photoshop, and an early 3D program called Swivel.

The Page as a Visual Metaphor

The familiar shape of a printed page is used as the visual metaphor for the control elements on the Contents screen. Each page-shaped button is distinguished from the others by bold colors and exciting patterns. When the user clicks the small round button with the question mark on any of the page elements, a sticky note presents an overview of the information to be found in that section (see Demos, opposite). This "know before you go" information allows the user to decide whether or not to proceed, thus saving unnecessary time in the wrist watch zone.

Getting Around

The three navigation buttons in the lower right corner of all *Verbum Interactive* screens (see below, far right) provide a way to return to the last screen visited (right), go to the Directory (center), and open and close the Power Bar (left). Click on a main section button on the power bar and a menu pops up to take you from the active screen to any other section in the electronic publication. Note that the same color- and pattern- coding used on the Contents page is repeated on the matching buttons of the power bar. Consistency helps users feel comfortable and understand where they are. When not in use, the power bar defies physics and nests neatly into the panel of three buttons.

Secrets Revealed

The two Galleries show projects produced by different designers and created with different authoring tools. Although it is a great collection, integrating the different elements was a nightmare. If you have a choice, when using off-the-shelf programming software, it's a lot easier if everyone involved in production is working in the same program and version.

One of the hundreds of spot illustrations created for *Verbum Interactive*.

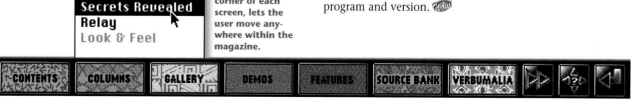

The Power Bar, anchored to the lower right-hand corner of each screen, lets the user move anywhere within the magazine.

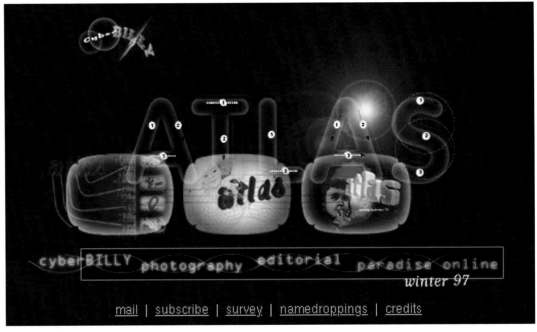

Oliver Laude's *@tlas Magazine,* a San Francisco–based webzine of photo-journalism, graphics, and illustration **(atlasmagazine.com),** has already been tapped to be part of the permanent collection of the San Francisco Museum of Modern Art. In its second year of existence *@tlas* was collected by the Museum for its graphic design—"the appearance of the thing on the screen"— says Aaron Betsky, curator of the Museum's Department of Architecture and Design, in an interview with *The New York Times.* Originally, the Museum requested only the three most current issues of *@tlas,* but because each issue includes hotlinks to back issues and references to other material, Laude persuaded Betsky to take the entire Web site. The site will be archived by the Museum on CD-ROM.

The relatively low-tech GIF animations that liven up the *@tlas* home page are intriguing and appealing enough to encourage visitors to explore further. So when visitors encounter art that pushes Web technology—in the CyberBilly section of the site, for instance—they are likely to make the effort to download the browser plug-ins needed to experience the higher-tech sound and video segments that characterize the interactive artwork.

The Editorial section of *@tlas* includes serialized fiction, delivered by screenfuls, and Cybordello, a listing of sites that make the best use of the Web. Although a completely new issue of the webzine appears only two to four times a year, the content of each issue is developed over time. For instance, Cybordello is updated weekly, drawing visitors back to the site to see what's new.

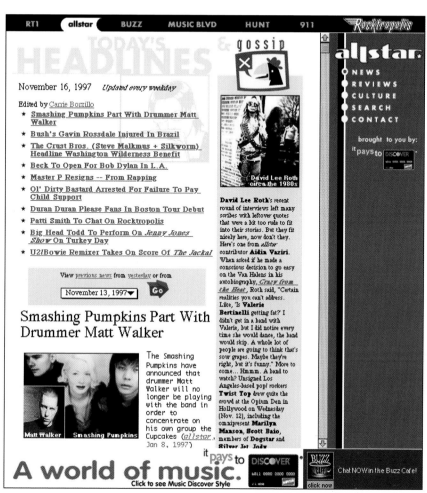

Content is key with *Allstar* magazine. This online music entertainment site (**allstarmag.com**) is "built around the writing of excellent music journalists," says Robert Lord, executive producer. And apparently others in the industry agree, as the site won the 1997 Best Music Journalism award, after being in existence less than a year.

Targeting college-age music aficionados, *Allstar*'s designers first decided what the content would be and how it would be organized. Then they worked out a flow diagram of how the content would be navigated. Only then, with those decisions made, did they approach the design of the user interface, "to make a bridge from the

eyeballs to what we were trying to present," says Lord. "Breaking it down into a three-step process worked very well."

To make the site not only a good read but a real resource, *Allstar* provides two ways for readers to "dig in" to more of the content. The Index, similar to the index of a book or the annual index some periodicals provide, is organized alphabetically by subject. Alternatively, in the Search section, which can be limited to search any combination of the sections of the magazine, readers can type in keywords to find the information they seek.

The *Allstar* site doesn't use a lot of "high technology," but one somewhat techy design element that works well is

the advertising banner. Separated from the content and located at the bottom of the window, the ad can play continuously as the user navigates the site. "To make this work by means of frames," says Lord, "we had to hack a number of solutions." Lord would advise staying away from frames, since the technology isn't fully compatible with the search engines that are so important for getting people to visit your site: "Nowadays, with improvements in HTML, you probably don't need frames."

9 Portfolios and Presentations

As location, location, location is to real estate agents, presentation, presentation, presentation is to creative professionals.

COMMUNICATION PROFESSIONALS promote themselves by showcasing work that they've already done. And thanks to new media, it's now possible for designers, photographers, and illustrators to show off their work in more intriguing and more immediate ways than in the acetate sleeves of the standard black leather portfolio case. These new media offer the advantage of blending still and moving images, text, and sound, with the added benefit of interactivity that provides a more engaging way to tell others about yourself, your company, and your creative potential.

This section features portfolios and presentations that were designed to be displayed on 72 dpi monitors and were delivered on floppy disk, CD-ROM, over the Internet via a Web site, or sometimes all three. Each example is a unique solution to a distinct set of challenges. Many are intended for a very focused audience, specifically potential clients who have an appreciation for conceptual uniqueness, design subtleties of color, typography, photography, and illustration, and the technical innovation that puts it all together.

Designed originally as a floppy disk promotional but now downloadable from a Web site, *Pinch* (page 178) demonstrates the power of good storytelling and the success of a strong visual metaphor. Take a look at how Mackerel's company presentation and portfolio (page 172–175) evolved from a HyperCard stack on a floppy disk to a Web site. The *Qaswa* Web site (page 180) achieves great depth and sense of space. Photographer Michel Tcherevkoff's Web site (page 184) achieves beauty and balance through a harmonious use of image, white space, and expressive typography. And check out the cool contraption designed to navigate the original mFactory Web site (page 176).

Brainpower

Overview *The EchoLilnk Interactive Web site uses different functions of the brain as metaphors for the company's capabilities, along with a unique color palette, and 3D wireframe and texture-mapped models for navigation.*

"The Web sites that I appreciate the most are the ones that treat the site as a space, make creative use of the dynamic possibilities of HTML, and make an environment that's interesting to explore."

–Gabriel Watson, multimedia artist

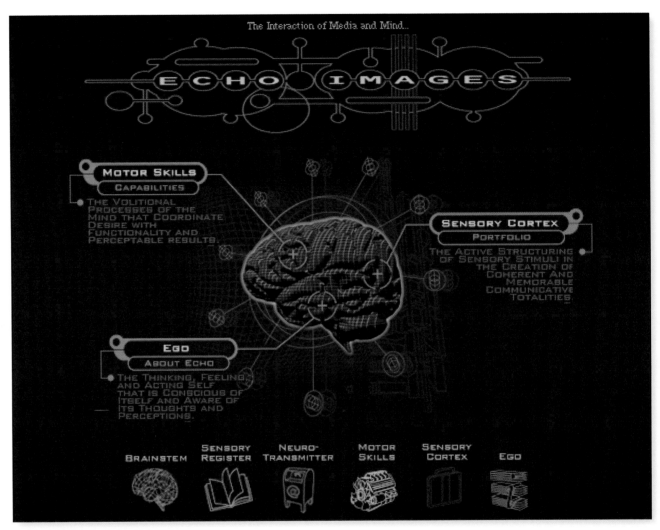

Metaphorically Speaking

To provide potential clients with easy access to information about the firm, interactive multimedia developer EchoLink produced a Web site that uses the central nervous system as a metaphor for the company. Shown above on the home page, three aspects of brain function represent the site's main areas.

Visualizing the Metaphor

The model of the brain on the home page was purchased from Viewpoint Data Labs, a 3D stock imagery resource. Textures, created in Photoshop, were applied to the model in Electric Image. The modified model was composited in Photoshop with line renderings created in FormZ, and futuristic graphics and typography designed in Illustrator.

The Color Palette

The site uses a unique combination of colors and takes advantage of the illuminative quality of the screen, with intense colors that contrast well against the muted brown and black backgrounds. Bright yellows and oranges are used to emphasize titles

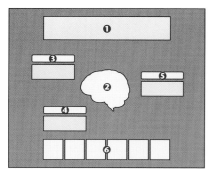

1. Masthead 2. Brain rendering 3. Capabilities section 4. About Echo section 5. Portfolio section 6. Navigation icons

Select Motor Skills on the home page to learn more about the firm's capabilities. The Motor Skills page carries the brain metaphor further by using the left and right hemispheres to represent the business and creative aspects of the company.

Select Sensory Cortex on the home page to see samples of the company's work. An elaborate 3D rendering, a labeled diagram, and text identify the company's portfolio categories.

Select Ego on the home page to find out more about the company. The Echo Images logo is a key design element, shown here in blue. The three stacked letters of the word "ego" balance nicely with the three parts of the logo. The darker color values recede into the black background while the more intense colors advance, creating a keen sense of space.

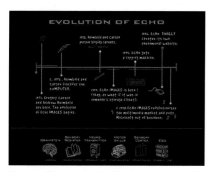

Choose History on the Ego page to see this colorful timeline that graphically charts the evolution of the company. The navigation icons appear across the bottom of every page and provide access to all of the main section pages within the site.

STATS AND SOFTWARE

A team of 2 worked 110 hours during a 1-month period to complete the Web site. Software included BBEdit, DeBabelizer, Electric Image, FormZ, Illustrator, and Photoshop, HVS PhotoGIF, JavaScript, and ProJPEG. Mac hardware was used. **echoimages.com**

and text and to provide good readability. The colors were selected from the Netscape cross-platform palette that offers 216 colors common to both Mac and Windows.

Choosing Typefaces
Headlines were typeset in Franklin Gothic small caps to provide solidity and a thick line weight. The horizontal character of Franklin Gothic works well with drop shadows added to achieve dimension. Subheads were typeset in OCR-A and OCR-B to add a futuristic and technical touch.

Creating the Navigation Icons
A series of six navigation icons, shown across the bottom of the home page, were developed to represent the different sections of the site, and the sections were named in accordance with the nervous system concept: Brainstem (home), Sensory Register (guestbook), Neuro-Transmitter (email), Motor Skills (capabilities), Sensory Cortex (portfolio), and Ego (company profile).

The icons were created in FormZ as "hidden-line" renderings, saved as EPS files, and placed in Illustrator where they were saved as Illustrator files, then opened in Photoshop. Using hidden-line rendering techniques, the 3D objects could be represented in a unique way that worked well with the limited color palette, and the wireframe objects required very little variation in color. It's interesting how the background color shows through the objects and optically mixes with the color of each one. Primary colors red, yellow, and blue and secondary colors orange, green, and purple were carefully chosen for similarity of color value and intensity so all of the icons would work together as a group.

These two screens show a subtle but effective way of indicating where you are within the Motor Skills section. When you visit pages that represent capabilities identified as belonging to the left hemisphere, the navigation panel is displayed on the left side of the screen and red is used to highlight the buttons. When you visit pages that represent capabilities identified as belonging to the right hemisphere, the navigation panel is displayed on the right side of the screen and blue is used to highlight the buttons.

The One That Didn't Get Away

Overview *Designed to show off the capabilities of Toronto's Mackerel Interactive Media,* The Mackerel Stack *is imaginative and full of surprises, activities, and fun facts—about fish!*

"The model for parts of this interface was the Fisher Price Activity Center—everything looks inviting to click.

–Kevin Steele, creative director

Holy Mackerel, What a Name!
In developing corporate identity, graphic designers dream of a company name that offers the creative potential seen in this interactive promotional. Once you've been digitally introduced, Mackerel is a hard name to forget. And that's the idea.

Good Design Mixed With Humor
The Mackerel Stack, a collection of explorations, positions Mackerel as a company with a good sense of humor and a strong sense of design. Screen areas, clearly defined by color and rectilinear shape, curious buttons, and arrows invite interaction.

Nothing Fishy About Mackerel
Following an introductory animation, the Main Menu screen above introduces the three main sections of the promotional piece, as well as the illustration of a mackerel that identifies the company. The round button in the lower left corner detours to the first of many surprises—"The Standard by Which Consistency Is Measured," an inspirational section on baseball's Lou Gehrig. His consistent batting average is used as a metaphor for Mackerel's success and the quality of the firm's work.

If there's any uncertainty about navigating from the Main Menu screen, click the button with the question mark. "Please

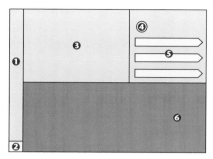

1. Screen name 2. Detour button
3. Project title 4. Help button
5. Contents buttons 6. Corporate identity

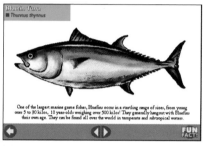

Select From Tuna to Wahoo on the Fun Facts About Mackerel screen at right to learn about mackerel and related fish. To delve deeper, click on the Fun Fact button, as above. Existing fish images were scanned, and used as templates to create bitmapped illustrations, then colored in Photoshop.

STATS AND SOFTWARE

Version 2.01 was produced in 16 weeks by a 6-member team. Software included Illustrator, Photoshop, SoundEdit, and SuperCard.

Modeled after Fisher Price's Activity Center, the What Do We Do? screen meets the design criterion that says: "If it looks like it *could* do something, it *should* do something." The title, graphic elements, and buttons at the bottom are all active. The three round red buttons lead to Virtual Bubble Wrap.

The Selected Portfolio screen features interactive multimedia projects developed by Mackerel. Select a project by clicking the active illustrations at the bottom. The back arrow is always accessible in the lower left corner, but to add visual interest, its style varies from screen to screen.

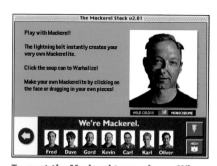

To meet the Mackerel team, choose Who Is Mackerel? on the Main Menu. Click and drag four photos to the large image to create a new Mackerelite. The button with the lightning bolt randomly mixes the four. The button with the soup can colors the composite á la Warhol.

Select" flashes red, and the hand icon points to each of the three section titles as they flash green and a tone sounds. Select a title to move on to that section.

What Do We Do? features a portfolio of interactive educational projects and marketing solutions that Mackerel designed as touch-screen kiosks or CD-ROM titles. In Who Is Mackerel? meet the people that make up the company, and get better acquainted by exploring a clever face-mixing activity. Mackerel Facts reinforces the company's name and builds on the identity. Accurate illustrations, animated fish, humorous sound bites, and colorful typography reveal everything there is to know about mackerel and the rest of the Scombridae fish family. Six printable recipes wrap up this fun and informative section.

The Stack's Life Cycle
The first version of *The Mackerel Stack* was released in December, 1989, as a 750K HyperCard stack. Over the years redesigns took

The Mackerel Facts screen is based on the Main Menu grid and illustrates how similar interfaces can be used for different content. The typeface Gill (no pun intended) is a favorite of the company because of the design opportunities offered by its many weights and styles.

advantage of improvements in technology and user awareness, and updated the company's portfolio. The version shown here, 2.01, is the tenth edition and was developed using SuperCard.

In 1996, the Mackerel Web site, mackerel.com (see page 174), replaced the floppy disk version of the promotional. *The Mackerel Stack 2.01* can now be downloaded to Macintosh computers from The Vault at the bottom of the site's home page.

Every Bit Counts
Mackerel's goal was to fit 2.01 onto a 1.4 MB high-density floppy disk. The portfolio samples and interactive graphics took up most of the space, with colors selected from the 8-bit Mac System palette. Simple electronic sound samples were created using SuperTalk tools. They required 80K, and 400K was needed by the SuperTalk player. With 100K still available, creative director Dave Groff came up with the idea for a unique activity called Virtual Bubble Wrap. At that point, a few pictures, a few sounds, and a little bit of code was all it took to complete *The Mackerel Stack*. When compressed, the 2.1 MB file just fits onto a single high-density floppy disk.

To play Virtual Bubble Wrap, click on the bubbles to hear them pop. Each popped bubble scores 1 point. The bubble artwork was created in Photoshop.

HyperCard to SuperCard to the Internet

Overview *Designers at Toronto's Mackerel Interactive Media built on the equity established by the firm's HyperCard stack, and the SuperCard stack, shown below, when they created their Web site.*

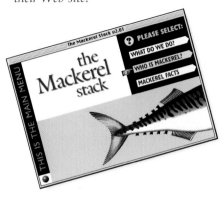

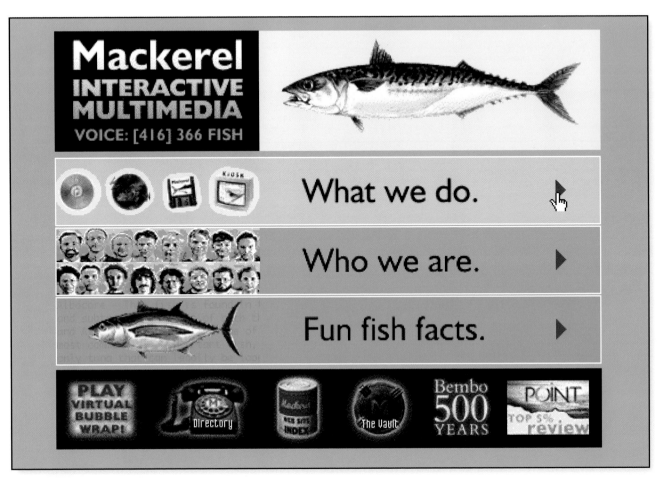

*"The main difference between **The Mackerel Stack** and our Web site is that the stack is a finished product and the site is a living entity with the potential to respond more quickly to business needs and our evolving goals."*

–Kevin Steele, creative director

Complementary Roles

The goal of the Mackerel Interactive Media Web site is to build on the equity established by *The Mackerel Stack* (see page 172) over the previous 6 years by continuing to promote Mackerel's creative and technical abilities and the company's expertise in interactive multimedia design. Even though the site has replaced the stack, Mackerel looks forward to creating another offline interactive promotional that will play a complementary role. While the site focuses on the business of multimedia design, such as research and development, employee recruitment, and consumer marketing, the independent piece will experiment with new designs for interactivity.

More and Less

When comparing *The Mackerel Stack* main menu screen, left, with the Web site home page, above, it's obvious that the home page builds on the design style, the visual structure, and the sense of humor that have come to be associated with the firm. The Mackerel designers took the best of the *Stack*, improved upon it, and adapted it to the design constraints of the Web.

From Page to Page

Linked pages are the structural foundation of Web sites. The home page, above, shows a clear overview of the contents and emphasizes the three main pages—What We Do, Who We Are,

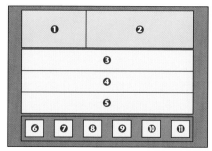

1. Web site name 2. Corporate identity
3. What We Do button 4. Who We Are
button 5. Fun Fish Facts button 6. Virtual
Bubble Wrap button 7. Employee directory button 8. Web site index button
9. The Vault button where the *Stack* can
be downloaded 10. Article button
11. Review of Web Site button

A page from the Online Portfolio features
the *Canadian Encyclopedia Plus* project.
Note that the home button at bottom
center uses the Mackerel illustration to
identify the home page. The clever 2¢ button to the left invites visitor feedback and
the one to the right links to a directory of
employee email addresses.

STATS AND SOFTWARE

During the conceptual stages all 25
employees were invited to give input.
A revolving site-development team
includes a creative director, an artist, a
programmer, and a technician. Software
included BBEdit, Illustrator, and
Photoshop. Graphics were created on
a Mac and tested on a PC. The site runs
on a Mac server using WebStar.
mackerel.com

The What We Do page, left, uses a graphic
banner to introduce the subsections, and
subtle embossed rules separate them. At
the top of the left column in Fun Fish
Facts, above, an animation flips through
illustrations of all the fish listed below so
they look like they're swimming.

To get to this page, Skipjack Tuna was
selected from the list of Scombrids on the
left side of the Fun Fish Facts page. The
fish illustrations are created as continuous-tone pencil drawings, then scanned,
colored in Photoshop, and saved in JPEG
format. Each is under 17K to allow for
speedy transmission. To maintain a feeling
of consistency when flipping through the
many pages in this section, Mackerel positioned the type and accompanying illustration within an area proportional to
a standard 640 x 480-pixel computer
screen, so visitors don't have to scroll.

and Fun Fish Facts—all carry-overs from the SuperCard stack.
Along the bottom, six buttons identify other pages by combining descriptive images, when possible, with text that lets visitors
know exactly what to expect. This is important because Web
access times are unpredictable. If visitors have to wait, it helps
if they know what they're waiting for.

Home
The aqua color on the home page highlights the main information areas and gives the impression that the mackerel are
swimming in cool waters. A darker blue serves as a background
for the secondary sections. Intense yellow was chosen to make
Interactive Multimedia stand out, which describes what the
company does, and bright red was used for the arrows that
indicate that more information follows. All flat colors were
selected from the 216 hues common to both Mac and Windows
System palettes.

Like the main screen of *The Mackerel Stack*, the home page is
a combination of rectilinear shapes, floating objects, and text

typeset in Gill. Everything on this
page is hot—if you click on any
rectangular field or any object, the
cursor changes to a pointing hand
and links to another Web page.

Hooked on Bubbles
Once a buried treasure in *The Mackerel Stack*, Virtual Bubble Wrap has
attracted over 70,000 visitors to the
Mackerel Web site. "When this
activity was ported over to Director

"Stubborn bubbles" are
difficult to pop. Hint:
Press longer on the
mouse.

and adapted as a tiny Shockwave movie, it was played by more
people in 3 months than saw the Stack in 2 years," says creative
director Kevin Steele. "Virtual Bubble Wrap is surprisingly the
most popular interactive diversion we've ever created. Some
visitors have submitted high scores approaching a million
popped bubbles! Just watch out for those 'stubborn bubbles,'
though," cautions Steele.

Cool Tool

Overview In this original Web site for mFactory, designed to promote the company and its product—multimedia authoring tool mTropolis—a retro-style gadget with bulging buttons, radiating lines, and hyper-typography invites participation, while the background color varies to distinguish the different topic sections.

"We wanted to create a tool that would be uniform throughout all the areas of the site so that people would get used to the interface, know what to expect, and feel comfortable moving from one place to another."

–Usok Sebastiann Choe, designer

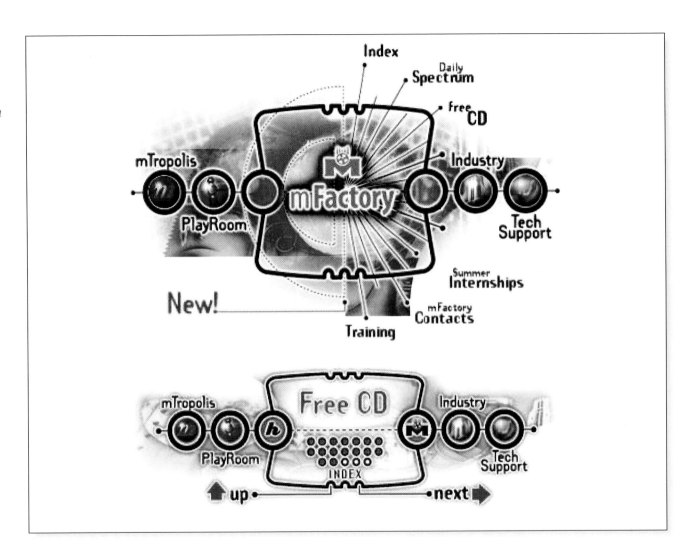

Building an Identity

The mFactory navigation devices, shown above, were created by Usok Sebastiann Choe to reflect the company's progressive attitude. He designed two basic versions of the gadget: the main one, top, found on the home page, and a more compact, space-saving design, bottom, found on all subsequent pages. The background photo imagery and purple color were inspired by the package design of mTropolis, left, the multimedia authoring tool developed by mFactory.

Designing the Structure

The clustered elements form a horizontal shape that fits nicely at the top of the screen, with the strong central area showcasing mFactory's symbol and logotype on the home page, and the section titles on the section pages. Colorful, bulging buttons identify the site's main sections, which are accessible from every page: mTropolis, PlayRoom, Industry, and Tech Support. The thin lines behind the right half of the larger structure, top, radiate from the center to titles of subsidiary areas, such as the

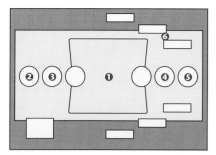

1. Hypertext title of the site 2. mTropolis section button 3. PlayRoom section button 4. Industry section button 5. Tech Support section button 6. Hypertext titles of the subsections

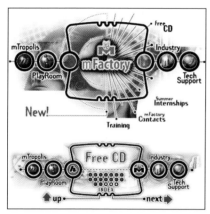

The navigation device found on the home page, top, was modified to save space on the section pages, bottom. The buttons are smaller and the shape in the center is more compact. The "up" and "next" arrows replace the leader lines and hypertext that identify the subsections on the home page.

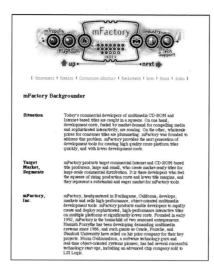

On the home page select mFactory in the center of the navigation structure to open the mFactory section, above, and find out more about the company. To make the subheads stand out, they were typeset bold and positioned in the left margin to take advantage of the left-to-right reading pattern.

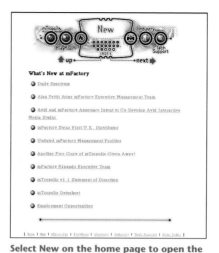

Select New on the home page to open the What's New section. Color is used to tie all the page elements together—the table of contents buttons and the hypertext are assigned the same color as the background behind the navigation device. The small round buttons in the table of contents mimic the larger navigation buttons at the top.

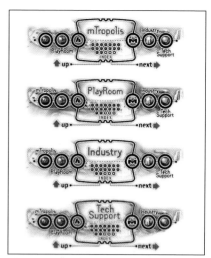

The navigation buttons of the four main sections are color-coded. Clicking on a button leads to that section's page where the corresponding background art is the same color as the button. To reinforce location within the site, the typography that identifies the button disappears when you're in that section.

Index. Choe's design provides a flexible system that supports expansion: More buttons and leader lines can easily be added as needed.

Size and Depth Cues

The designer used location, size, and depth to prioritize information. Larger objects and thicker lines appear to advance toward the viewer, while smaller objects and thinner lines appear to recede. The most important information, like the company name and section titles, is typeset large and placed in the center—the structure's main focal point—and the main section buttons are large and placed along the strong horizontal axis.

Color Shows Where You Are

The navigational elements float above a colorful background collage of photo imagery. The background color varies from page to page to identify the different sections and coordinates with the color of the corresponding section's navigation button.

Building the Structure

The type is set in Emigré Template Gothic, chosen for its open counterspaces, bold stroke weight, and high-tech character. Other typefaces were considered, but when tested their counterspaces filled-in after JPEG compression. Template Gothic's ascenders are tall in comparison to the descenders creating an interesting upward movement and emphasizing the strong line quality of the typeface that relates well to the linear structure.

The structure's framework was created in FreeHand and placed in Photoshop, where final color was added, graphic effects completed, and the graphics combined with the background photo collages. The artwork was saved in the JPEG file format because of the continuous-tone quality of the photographs, and the organic nature of the graphics. So that the viewer doesn't have to wait until the full image downloads to the home page, two versions were created: One with a Gaussian Blur that was compressed to 4K and downloads quickly serving as a placeholder until the 12K higher-resolution file loads after it. The first impression of the interface is soft, colorful, and out-of-focus: then it slowly transitions into a sharp image.

Pinch Power

Overview *In this self-promotional piece produced by Brad Johnson Presents, the design and strength of a clothespin are used as metaphors for the company's creative capabilities.*

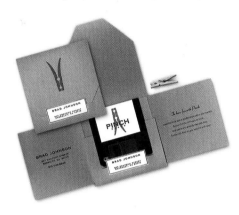

"**Pinch** *made my career. I used this project to learn the computer. One year later I was no longer working as a carpenter.*"

–Brad Johnson, director

Dramatic and Strategic

Pinch, a lighthearted and entertaining five-minute self-running multimedia presentation, was developed as a direct-mail promotional, ostensibly for prospective customers of a fictitious 1930's wooden clothespin manufacturer.

Although the user cannot interact with *Pinch,* the design metaphor, thematic graphics, and the efficient use of disk space are inspiring and relevant to interactive interface design. As *Pinch* dramatically touts the strength and reliability of the clothespin, it also strategically showcases the illustration, ani-

mation, and design expertise of its developer, Brad Johnson. Animated illustrations and typography introduce the company through a series of theatrical sets that lead to this typographic message: "Pinch Brand clothespins; we keep your clothes on the line with our design, our woods, and our reliability." The follow-up Design and Woods sequences use dynamic typography, illustration, and animation to describe the unique design features of the clothespins, from the taper of their arms to the special woods from which they're carefully cut.

An introductory animation pauses to iden-tify the fictitious company. Warm rich tones of color are used hierarchically to emphasize the Pinch brand name first, an illustration of the product second, and, finally, the product type—clothespins.

On the final screen of the opening mar-keting message, Design is represented by technical blueprints, Woods by a piece of lumber, and Reliability by the fabric hang-ing securely on the line. Bold Copperplate uppercase charaters emphasize key words.

This montage establishes a relationship between the map, The Woods, and the clothespin. For visual balance and overall file size management, the aspect ratio of the illustration is smaller than the screen but proportional to it.

The Woods section identifies different parts of the country where Pinch varieties grow. Dithering the map created an interesting grainy texture that suits the style of this project. The colored 1-bit background helps keep file size small.

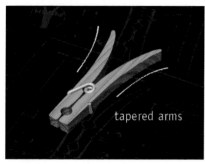

The Design animation points out unique features of the clothespin: longer body, tapered arms, double-gauge brass alloy spring, triple-coil construction, offset fulcrum, and consistent in-line tracking. The object is presented over an enlarged blueprint in the background to reinforce the concept.

Reminiscent of the Past

For compactness and ease of use, the presentation fits on a single floppy disk, which is imaginatively packaged with a miniature Pinch brand wooden clothespin, as shown on the opposite page. The theme and vintage mood of *Pinch* are initially established by the packaging, even before the multimedia presentation is seen. To accomplish this, the different packaging elements, including disk labels and stickers, were printed on a letterpress, a relief printing process widely used through the first half of the 20th century.

Johnson furthered the theme by choosing typefaces reminis-cent of earlier times: Copperplate, Coronet, and Officina Sans. And Jeff Stafford's upbeat tunes, recalling the jingles of 1950's television commercials, add the finishing touch.

Digital Backdrops

In *Pinch,* background graphics are an important unifying ele-ment. They provide design consistency within the interface, add richness and dimension, and communicate content. In the introductory scene, a red theater curtain sets the tone for the performance to follow. In the Design section, a blueprint tech-nical drawing fills the background. And a dark green map is used in the Woods sequence.

To maintain sufficient contrast between background and foreground objects, background colors are darker while fore-ground objects are lighter and brighter. To ensure legibility, type is usually white, or a light color, often with a dark drop shadow when the typography superimposes areas that contain both light and dark values.

Most of the backgrounds are 1-bit images made up of two colors selected from the 8-bit Mac System palette. They create a striking backdrop for the more detailed 8-bit art placed in the foreground. When saved in PICT format in Photoshop, the backgrounds are reduced in size to only 4K. The completed file weighed in at 2MB and compressed down to 1.36MB—just small enough to fit on a 1.4MB high-density floppy disk.

Backstage

The screen shown on the opposite page began with an outline of the clothespin shape drawn in Illustrator, then opened in Photoshop, where it was rasterized and used to create a pattern of clothespins. This pattern was saved in PICT format and later used as a texture map in StudioPro to create the background of the box label.

The same Illustrator line drawing of the clothespin was extruded in StudioPro to create the dimensional form. The wood-grain texture was generated, the spring modeled, and the final clothespin assembled. The 3D clothespin file was rendered as a PICT and then opened in Photoshop, where it was incorpo-rated into the box label design, which was then saved as a PICT. Back in StudioPro, the box was modeled, mapped with the PICT label from Photoshop, and filled with clothespins.

Designing Deep Space

Overview *In this Web site, designed to promote the multimedia capabilities of Qaswa Communications, imaginative dimensional controls lead visitors through the site. Background textures remind them where they are, and an alternate Shockwave version of the site offers sound and animation.*

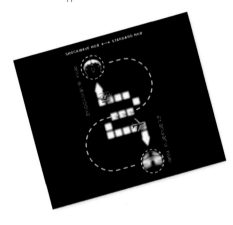

"Introducing a sense of dimension into an interface transforms the flat static surface of the screen into a believable space that draws people in and adds to the realism of the experience."

–Ammon Haggerty, designer

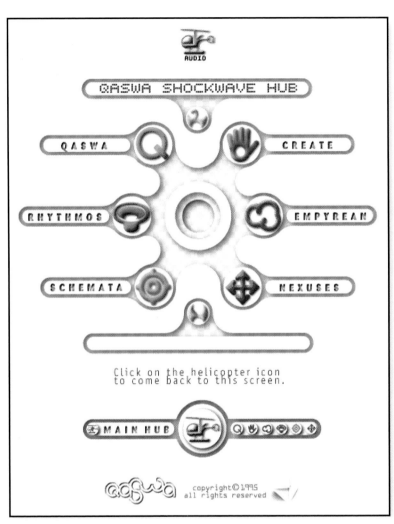

The navigation bar, shown above, uses multiple layers and shadows to create an illusion of depth. The airplane on the left of each bar indicates that the Standard hub, rather than the Shockwave hub, is open. The name of the section and the large icon in the center show which section is active. On the right the six color-coded icons represent all the sections of the site. Clicking on them links directly to those sections.

Exploring New Approaches to a New Medium

Ammon Haggerty of Qaswa Communications set out to produce a Web site to promote his artistic skills and design abilities, and to provide a global forum for his ideas and visions. Challenged by a personal goal to push the limits of the medium and create a sense of dimension on-screen, he ended up producing a Web site full of depth illusion and imaginative controls.

Developing a Metaphor

The theme of this Web site grew out of an idea Haggerty had to create a three-dimensional space that existed on another world and that was accessible only by spacecraft. The site's metaphor—an airport hub—the navigation controls, the section icons, and the copywriting are all influenced by this theme.

On the opening page, shown at the left, the participant has the opportunity to select the Standard or Shockwave version of the site. The icons and imagery reflect the metaphor: An airplane represents the Standard hub and a helicopter identifies the Shockwave interface. The following page builds on the theme: In the Standard version, a message from the captain

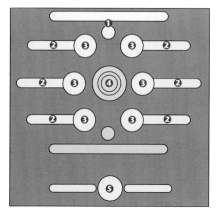

1. Hub identification 2. Section title buttons 3. Section icon buttons 4. Pattern window in Shockwave hub 5. Navigation bar

The detail of the Nexuses button found on the Contents page shows how the background pattern is also used to identify the section.

The message from the captain of the Standard hub, top, "please adjust your browser wingspan to match ours," and from the pilot of the Shockwave hub, bottom, "please adjust your browser so my chopper is flyin' centered," demonstrates how appropriate copywriting can enhance a concept.

STATS AND SOFTWARE

Designer Ammon Haggerty completed the design and implementation of the Qaswa Communications Web site in 6 days. Software included Director, Illustrator, Infini-D, Netscape Navigator, Photoshop, Shockwave, and StudioPro on the Mac. **qaswa.com**

The gray-and-white checkered background is used on all of the pages that relate directly to the company, such as the site's table of contents, above.

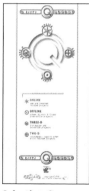

Selecting Qaswa from the Main Hub, left, leads to this page of color-coded portfolio categories: Three-D, Online, Print, and Offline.

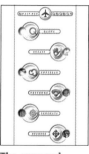

Selecting the Three-D button on the Qaswa page, left, leads to this display of work. Clicking on an example enlarges it to full-screen.

To identify specific locations within the site, the section icon is shown in the center of the navigation bar. Below the bar, either the airplane or helicopter icon identifies the hub.

The buttons on the Nexuses page link to other sites and are designed to reflect the meaning of the word *nexus*—connection or link. They also relate to the geometric look of the other controls.

instructs visitors to adjust the page width to the wingspan of the airplane, and the helicopter pilot on the Shockwave version asks that the page be adjusted to the blade of the helicopter. This is a clever way to maintain control over the width of the page so the participant sees the page as the designer intended.

Shaping the Interface

Most of the interface elements were created through experimentation with balance and geometric shapes, particularly circles. Haggerty designed several levels of depth within a single object to achieve a greater feeling of dimension. The controls and icons were constructed in Illustrator and then placed in Photoshop where the shadows and highlights were added and they were colored using custom palettes.

The concept of dimension is also used on the center panels that float above the patterned backgrounds and cast shadows on the surface below. The pattern establishes a border for the information area of the page, identifies the individual section, and creates a common thread that unifies the site. All the background tiles were created in Photoshop.

Synergy and Efficiency

For the Qaswa site, coding was an integral part of site design. "Understanding the potential of Lingo and HTML and doing the actual programming help me better conceptualize the design," explains Haggerty. "These two assembly languages are the glue that holds all the pieces together. Also, work flow can be very quick when all aspects of the project are conceived, executed, and implemented by the same person."

It All Began over Lunch

Overview *Visitors are attracted to The Speared Peanut Design Studio's Web site because of its catchy name, good clean design, and an original animated design award that owners Paul and Kristina Kremer created.*

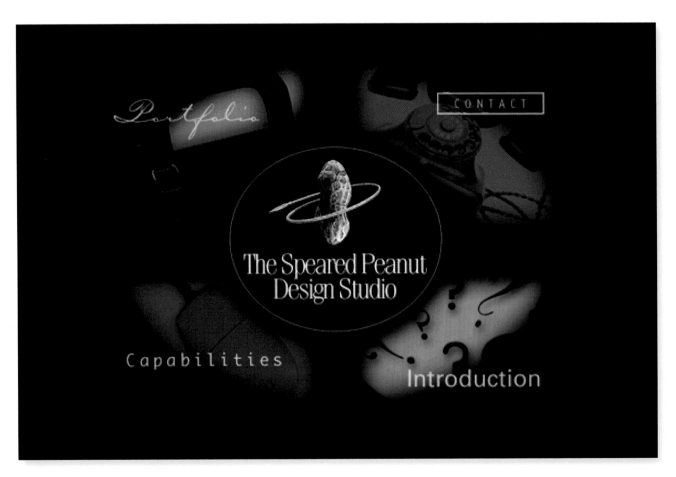

"The most common mistake that designers make when designing for the Web is thinking that more is better. If a site is cluttered and hard on the eyes, no one will want to explore its options."

–Kristina Kremer, creative director

Good Ideas Are Often Unexpected

Husband and wife design team Kristina and Paul Kremer of the Speared Peanut Design Studio in Houston, Texas, came up with the idea for the name of their company over lunch one day. Paul was enjoying a peanut butter sandwich and Kristina was crunching on a dill pickle spear. Seriously.

Start-up Animation

Curiosity over the name attracts visitors to the site, as well as the fact that the site is the home of the now famous Speared Peanut Design Award. "People are always curious about the speared peanut name," says Kristina, "and we wanted to make use of that curiosity, so Paul created a GIF animation of the speared peanut for the welcome page—the first view people get of the site."

To create the 3D version of the speared peanut, he scanned the shell of an actual peanut on a flatbed scanner at 300 dpi, then opened it in Photoshop, where he created a peanut-surface pattern. With the help of friend Chris Huffman, Paul built a model of the peanut in StudioPro. The scanned texture was pasted onto the 3D form and a GIF animation was created using GIFBuilder.

Design Goals

Since their company specializes in interface design, particularly Web site design, Kristina and Paul wanted an interface on their own site that was really different-looking and that would be appreciated by potential clients as well as their peers. They favored a clean, straightforward layout that provides a refuge from the visual bombardment of the Internet. "We can design

1. Title 2. Portfolio section 3. Contact section 4. Capabilities section 5. Introduction section 6. Hits-to-site counter

The introductory pages of the main sections, which represent the third level of the site, are designed on a three-column grid. The background color and duotone image that represent each section on the home page carry over to the introductory pages of the sections.

The image buttons on the black information panel lead to related topic pages. With this layout, new buttons can be added at any time without having to rework the site. The color-coded bands, right and left, vary in width depending on how the viewer's browser window is set.

Clicking on an image button on an introductory page of a main section leads to the individual topic pages, such as the Rates page above. These pages have their own colored background, intended to provide a quiet setting for the information.

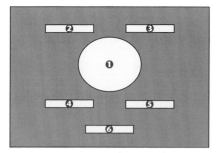

The Speared Peanut Award is presented to Web sites that are innovative, informative, and easy to navigate, and that demonstrate a great eye for typography, color, and composition. Award recipients are notified by email, then told how to retrieve the award, above, from the Speared Peanut Web site, and asked to create a link from their site to the Speared Peanut site.

for ourselves and for our peers by pushing design in new directions, but unless our work is accessible to everyone, we've failed. Likewise," adds Kristina, "if our work is not original, and doesn't contribute something to design, we have also failed."

Color, Metaphors, and Typography

On the home page, opposite, the peanut icon in the center of the screen is surrounded by clickable duotone images that lead to the site's four main sections. The graphics are distinguished by color, visual metaphor, and typography.

Yellow and a leather portfolio represent the Portfolio section. The script typeface Carpenter suggests a personal touch. Red, an electronic mouse, and the computerized look of the typeface Tekton represent the Capabilities section. The Contact section uses purple, a dial telephone, and the typeface Futura Condensed, reminiscent of the numbers on the dial. The color gray and question marks identify the Introduction section, where

information about the business side of the company is found. The straightforward design style of the sans serif typeface Univers represents the content of this section.

After selecting colors that would provide the harmony of primary colors without the intensity of pure hues, the designers converted them to Netscape's 216-color palette. The type was set in FreeHand and rasterized in Photoshop where it was combined with the duotone images. The portfolio is a scanned object, the mouse and telephone are from a stock photo CD, and the question mark art was created in FreeHand.

Keeping It Simple

When asked about design, Kristina suggests, "Keep it simple, so the work draws people in instead of hitting them over the head. A lot of sites are hard on the eyes because they use colored text on top of busy backgrounds and it's just impossible to read. That comes, I think, from a lack of design knowledge."

STATS AND SOFTWARE

With help from a writer and a 3D artist, Kristina and Paul worked off and on for 2 months to complete the site. Mac and PC hardware were used. Software included AfterEffects, Director Web Tools, FreeHand, GifBuilder, Illustrator, ImageMapper, PageMaker, Photoshop, PixelSpy, Premiere, SimpleText, and StudioPro. **spearedpeanut.com**

The understated design style of The Speared Peanut Design Studio is apparent not only in their own site but also in those of their clients (**kentwilliams.com**). The Web site, left, of draftsman and painter, illustrator and comics creator Kent Williams is elegant in its simplicity. The signature adds a personal touch and the colorful buttons stand out against the neutral gray background. Clicking a painting on the gridded image map opens a larger version.

A Masterful Impression

Overview *A straightforward layout with colorful backgrounds, expressive typography, and imaginative copywriting captures the essence of the avant-garde photography of Michel Tcherevkoff in this Web site designed to promote his work.*

"Rather than flood the site with unnecessary technology, we've used good design principles and sound layout techniques to bring focus and movement to the page."

–Blaine Graboyes, designer

Showcasing Photographers Online

The Master Series in the online version of *Photo District News* magazine showcases the work of outstanding commercial photographers, like Michel Tcherevkoff, whose site is sponsored by Kodak Professional, the professional products division of Eastman Kodak, and was developed, along with a companion floppy disk, by Wow Sight + Sound in New York. "Each site in the Master series is designed to give an impression of what the featured photographer is like, so each site is entirely different," explains Myrna Masucci-Kresh, executive director of Advertising Photographers of New York, "Michel's site is like him—light-hearted, irreverent, European, and unusual."

From One Page to the Next

Shaped by a strong commitment to design excellence, the eleven sequential pages are unified by a simple and consistent

One of the featured photographs is presented in the top portion of each page in combination with a unique headline treatment. In some cases text type follows, as shown here. The three forms of navigation used in this site are displayed on this full page: scrolling, clicking on the exclamation mark and downward-pointing arrow, which jumps to the next section of a long page, and clicking on the encircled "continue" which leads to the next page.

STATS AND SOFTWARE

A designer and a designer/programmer worked 5 days to complete the site: 2 days for planning and design, 2 days for asset production, and 3 days for programming and testing. Software included BBEdit, DeBabelizer, Photoshop, and QuarkXPress on Mac hardware. **pdn-pix.com/MasterMichel**

The handwritten character of the typeface and the unrestrained typographic treatment mimic the flowing line of the shoelace. The transition of the size of the letters from small to large in the word "second" creates an illusion of depth that relates to the perspective of the shoe.

The bold red lips in this photo inspired the background color. The strong central axis of the symmetrical photo guides its placement in relation to the background, and the curve of the film reel is repeated in the two lines of type that bracket the photo and focus attention on the image.

The alternating black-and-white background and the border around the photo reflect the pattern of the dalmatian and the soles of the shoes. Staggering the two lines of type and coloring one white and the other black ties everything together.

approach. Each page presents one of Tcherevkoff's photographs complemented by background and typography that build on the colors and forms in the photographs, and reinforce the expressive nature of the copywriting. To create interest on the page and to anchor the photo, the background space is defined in one of three ways: as solid color (like the home page shown on opposite page, left), divided vertically into two equal parts, or divided vertically into three parts, two of which are equal, with a narrow strip of color on the right side.

For example, on the page shown opposite, the background space is divided into three vertical parts. The yellow relates to the same color in the fish, and the rounded shape, which creates a niche for the image, reiterates the curve of the glass. The line of type, "He kicks up his heels, he stands on his head...," is rotated 270 degrees and reads down the full length of the page until it meets the concluding phrase, "like you now!" which is rotated 180 degrees to play off the idea expressed in the writing.

Maintaining the Integrity of the Photographs

The original color transparencies were scanned and stored on a Kodak Pro Photo CD, then manipulated and retouched with Barco Creator software on a Silicon Graphics Indigo workstation, and output on an LVT Digital Image Recorder. To accurately represent the color, sense of space, and density of the photo-

graphic medium within the limitations of the Internet, a custom palette was created in DeBabelizer for each of the images, and then each palette was edited individually to keep file size to a minimum while maintaining the integrity of the photographs.

The Process of Designing

Every project at Wow Sight + Sound begins with a meeting of all the participants involved in the project. Brainstorming and pencil sketches lead the way to one design idea to which the team feels committed. Blaine Graboyes, vice president of new media development, says, "All of us at Wow come out of traditional fine art or design backgrounds, which enhances our aesthetic sensitivity and influences our design style. We work a lot with traditional media—pencils and erasers, colored pencils, markers, crayons—to develop ideas and layouts before going to the computer, but once on the Mac a project like this one flows from QuarkXPress to Photoshop to DeBabelizer to BBEdit.

"We're most interested in exploring the strengths of different media and matching the goals of a project and the needs of the client to the appropriate medium," adds Graboyes, "The solution might be print, or an interactive floppy disk, a CD with packaging, or a Web site. Or the solution might span several media, like a CD-ROM, packaged with related print materials, that connects to a Web site." *Wow*

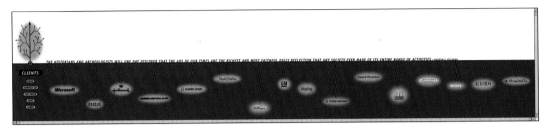

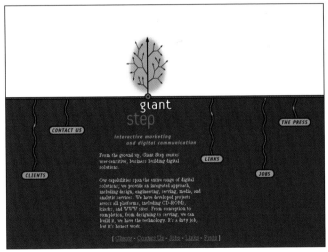

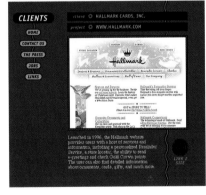

Besides showing Giant Step's prowess with various forms of online technology, the design firm's Web site (**giantstep.com**) also demonstrates a mastery of design fundamentals, translated to the Internet with great success. A GIF animation opens the site by "growing" the logo: Starting with a small circular seed, the logo sprouts and sends up branches; finally an oval of color appears behind the treelike structure. On the home page and in other areas of the site, a horizon divides the screen into sky and ground, with most of the content accessible by clicking glowing text buttons "rooted" in the ground. To unify the site, the organic colors of the home page are carried throughout, and buttons for the site's six main sections always appear on the left, with the active section highlighted at the top of the stack.

The site's horizontal scrolling advertises the firm's ability to innovate. Rather than providing instructions or arrows to tell visitors how to scroll in this naturally horizontal environment, the designers have used a long quotation from Marshall McLuhan at the horizon, so it's apparent that something extends off the screen, and the viewer will intuitively scroll to follow it through the "landscape."

Although the site does provide links to sites the firm has done for its largely high-profile clientele, the designers wanted to keep prospective clients at giantstep.com while they viewed the firm's work. So they created small demos that are contained within the site.

The design has successfully retained its simple look and feel, even as Giant Step has grown fairly dramatically in the number of clients it serves. Visitors can easily and quickly navigate from place to place without having to deal with a lot of text or extra navigational tools.

One addition to the site, however, is the Jobs section. Noticing that many of the visitors to the site came in from addresses ending in ".edu," the site designers deduced that these must be students looking for inspiration or, more likely, work. So they added a section that lists their needs for designers, programmers, and others.

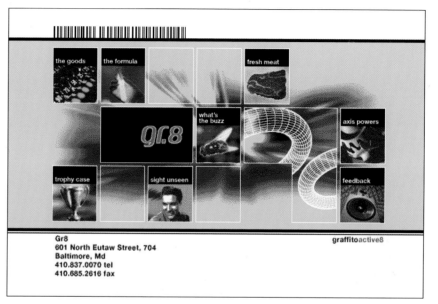

Gr8
601 North Eutaw Street, 704
Baltimore, Md
410.837.0070 tel
410.685.2616 fax

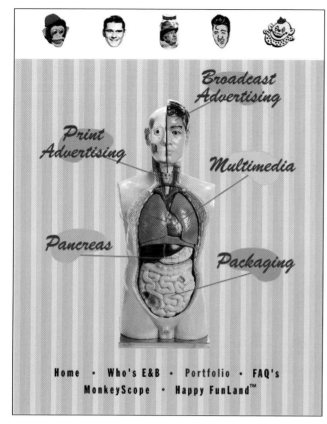

Elvis & Bonaparte's Web site (**elvisbonaparte.com**) promotes this "creative content" company's design experience and techno-logical competence, starting with a home page that takes a cre-ative, humorous approach to the firm's "anatomy." The happy—or bizarre in the case of Stumpy, the man in the jar—icons at the top of the page tempt visitors to click further into the site. An engag-ing and humorous Pop Quiz points out the differences between Elvis & Bonaparte and firms that do only online advertising, also taking the opportunity to demonstrate the firm's understanding of the key ways online advertising differs from print and to present the innovative solutions the firm has developed for attracting and holding an audience at a site and for developing and tracking leads. The Stumpy section is promotion with an atti-tude (see page 62). Through a Q&A format, Stumpy's "bobbing noggen" differentiates Elvis & Bonaparte from mere interac-tive multimedia studios, encouraging prospective cli-ents not to "blow all yer budjit on sompin' what's real perty and real stupid."

The goal of the Graffitoactive8 Web site (**gr8.com**) is to provide an interactive online portfolio that doubles as a marketing tool, to let clients know the firm offers a full range of print and new media services. As shown on the home page, above, samples from projects that Gr8 has com-pleted for clients are used as navigation elements that lead to other areas of the site.

A numbering system identifies the different content areas and a matrix of interconnected frames and pages allow for different ways to navigate, depending on where you are within the site. But the main navigation elements are always available in the horizontal bar that runs across the top of the page. Rollovers, highlighting, and section numbers helps users keep track of where they are.

The site also demonstrates that the firm has developed tools for the Web, such as the *communication core*, a project management tool that provides a secure environment for clients to review all project-related materials, including cor-respondence, schedules, and electronic design comps, online at any time from anywhere—a big plus when members of a project team are not in the same location.

"The Web's file size restrictions are limiting, but the chal-lenge is to push the boundaries as much as possible. We used standard formats to produce the site, but it's how the assets are put together and how they interact with each other that makes the site unique," says marketing assistant Jason Baranowski.

10 Sales

CSA Archive Sampler
A Tin Full of Illustrations **190**

harpercollins.com
Packaging a Product and Producing a Web Site **192**

imageclub.com
Browse or Buy: Clip Art, Photos, and Typefaces **194**

iqvc.com
From Surfing the Net to Shopping the Net **196**

NucleusOne Guide
Dancing on A Grid **198**

travelocity.com
Online Travel Takes Off **200**

Gallery **202**

Once a fringe experiment, virtual shopping is now helping businesses grow by providing powerful new ways to promote and sell products.

INTERACTIVE DESIGN AND MULTIMEDIA can be very effective in promoting and selling products. Each case study in this section incorporates a way to order or actually purchase featured products. Included are examples developed for distribution on floppy disk, CD-ROM, and the World Wide Web. The floppy disk and CD-ROM projects also have accompanying Web sites.

The Web certainly offers convenience to customers: Open 24 hours a day, it never closes, and customers don't have to leave home to do their shopping. Web sites also provide advantages for sellers. A mass audience can be reached, new products can be added and prices changed easily without the expense of reprinting sales materials. Visitors to the site can be counted, and online consumer questionnaires can quickly provide businesses with useful information and feedback from customers.

The case studies in this chapter show how graphics and typography can set an appropriate tone and how clear navigation systems can guide users through a document with ease. Supplemental animation, audio, and video enhance a company's sales message. For example, the graphic interface of the *CSA Archive CD-ROM Sampler* (page 190) complements the design style of the archive's product line; animation brings typefaces to life in the floppy disk *NucleusOne* (page 198); and the navigation elements of the HarperCollins Interactive Web site (page 192) provide a consistent look and feel, allow for easy expansion, and minimize the amount of time it takes to move through the site.

A Tin Full of Illustrations

Overview *The CSA Archive Sampler produced by the Charles S. Anderson Design Company delivers samples of illustrations, a product catalog, and an order form, all on a CD-ROM, uniquely packaged in a round tin can.*

"The challenge of designing this interface was to preserve the old feeling of the historic images and at the same time to put them in the context of contemporary media."

–Charles S. Anderson, creative director

Sampling the Archive

The *CSA Archive Sampler* provides an entertaining overview of the CSA Archive, a pay-per-use stock illustration resource of nearly a million historical and original line art images covering many subject categories. The CD-ROM *Sampler*, intended for advertising agencies, graphic designers, and desktop publishers, offers 100 illustrations and 80 typographic dingbats royalty-free, and a chance to order CSA Archive products, including a printed catalog of the complete Archive, and specialty items inspired by the extensive image collection.

Setting a Tone

The interface is designed to reflect the content of the collection. Unconventional, irregular shapes relate to the loose quality of the hand-drawn illustrations, many of which were originally created in the 1920s to the 1960s by untrained artists.

Since the illustrations and typographic dingbats are all flat, two-dimensional, black-and-white, high-contrast art, no gradations or three-dimensional modeling are included in the interface. Color is used sparingly for accent and feedback: Warm hues embellish backgrounds and when a section title in the table of

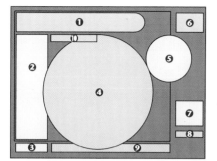   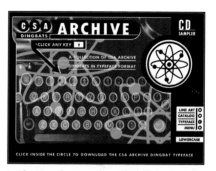

1. Section title 2. Section contents
3. Scroll buttons to flip through illustration details five at a time 4. Large window for full-view illustration. 5. Small window for animation 6. Product title 7. Table of contents 8. Information panel 9. Instruction panel 10. Full-View message bar

From the Main Menu, above, choose Slide Show, Skip, or Quit. Skip gives the option to bypass the slide show for those who want to go directly to Line Art to view the 100 sample illustrations or from there go to the Catalog or Typeface sections.

The Slide Show introduces the Archive, explains its origin, and gives a quick tour of the warehouse facilities. To move between screens, use the forward and backward arrows on either side of Next.

In the Typeface section, click the typewriter keys to show Archive Dingbats in the round preview window. For more choices, click the Shift key. To download a dingbat font as TrueType or Postscript Type 1, click anywhere in the round preview window.

To order specialty items, including the printed catalog of the full Archive, shown on the Catalog main screen, download and print the order form, which can then be faxed or mailed.

STATS AND SOFTWARE

The *Sampler* took one year to design and program and another three months to complete music and narration. Multimedia production was done by the Wanganui Polytechnic School of Design in New Zealand. **csa.com**

contents is selected, red fills the corresponding circular button.

Screens are accompanied by background music taken from stock drive-in theater intermission tapes. The scratchy, low-tech sound complements the tone of the illustrations.

The bold sans serif typeface, 20th Century, is characteristic of the time period. All caps are used to identify headlines, to label interface components, and to give instructions. The text in the sidebar on the left of the screen is set in upper and lower case, which saves space and makes text more readable. All of the type is set large so it's easy to read on-screen.

Adding Value
A design goal of the project was that the sampler would be more than just an index of images. The team wanted it to be fun to work with and to display how the illustrations and dingbats might be used by showcasing Archive images in logotypes and animations, and incorporating them into background patterns.

Scrolling Through the Line Art
There are 20 different screens in Line Art, the sampler's main section. Each screen, as shown on the opposite page, features a set of five illustration icons, a large viewing area where a selected illustration is showcased, and a small window where animations are shown. To move between sets of illustrations, use the two scroll buttons at bottom left that are invisible until the cursor rolls over them. The button with the arrow pointing

down goes to the next set of five illustrations. The button with the arrow pointing up leads back to the previous set.

Taking a Closer Look
As stated in the instruction panel at the bottom of the screen, "click on an icon to view the matching full image in the large round window;" a quirky sound heralds the enlargement. The Play button at the bottom of the small round window starts a vignetted QuickTime movie created in Director that features an animated composite of the five illustrations lined up on the left side of the screen.

The name (Flower Pot) and the reference number (34) of the enlarged image appears in the Full-View message bar. The small information panel below the table of contents, on the right side of the screen, shows the illustration's file size (144K), which is good to know when transferring images or placing them into other documents. To download an EPS or TIFF version of the royalty-free illustration or dingbat, click on the full image in the large round window. A dialog box reassures that the download was successful.

Fifteen of the illustrations included on the CD-ROM are for use as folder icons like the ones used here to identify folders in the CSA Archive Window.

Packaging a Product and Producing a Web Site

Overview *The navigation elements of the HarperCollins Publishers Web site, designed by San Francisco's Studio Archetype, are modular graphics that give the site its consistent look and feel. They minimize the time it takes to move through the site, and allow for easy expansion.*

"In order to create a navigational framework for a large corporation like HarperCollins that has many different divisions, we developed systems of global and regional navigation that serve as a superstructure to unite various sections of the site."

–Lillian Svec, information architect, Studio Archetype

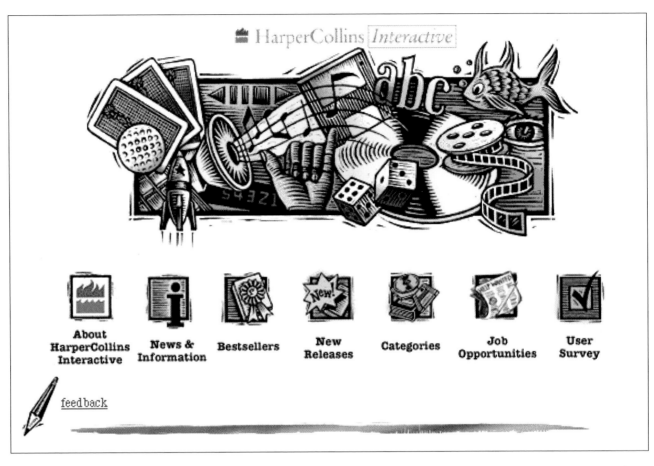

Assessing Need

To develop a master plan for the HarperCollins Web site, Studio Archetype began with an extensive needs assessment that they call the "information architecture phase." This study led to detailed diagrams that mapped out the entire site and clarified relationships between general information that pertains to the overall company and specific information that relates to the separate divisions. These diagrams served as blueprints for design planning, content development, and programming of the Web site shell.

The infrastructure and interface of the shell were designed to support the content and functions defined in the initial assessment, which included supporting marketing and promotion efforts, servicing field representatives, promoting relationships with customers, making it possible to order products, linking readers to authors by email, and providing news about recently released titles.

Designing Around Software Packaging

The Interactive division of the Web site was the first to be developed and served as the model for the remaining sections. It made sense to begin by promoting existing digital media titles on the Web, and the promotional material was already designed and available in digital format. So the packaging system that Studio Archetype had designed for the HarperCollins Interactive CD-ROM product line became the foundation for the publishing giant's Web site.

The packaging design incorporates the look of a book cover.

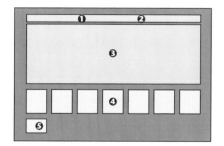

1. **Corporate symbol and logotype**
2. **Division title 3. Masthead illustration**
4. **Section buttons 5. Feedback icon**

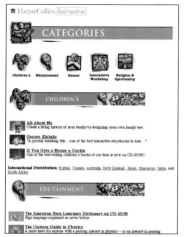

At the top of the Interactive Categories page, each of the five categories is defined by a color and an illustrated icon. Clicking on an icon brings that portion of the Interactive Categories page into full view. The background behind the white type in the title bars is the designated category color. The other icons are grouped on the right side of each title bar and, when clicked, conveniently bring a different category into view. This avoids visitors having to scroll to the top of the page to choose another category.

STATS AND SOFTWARE

Studio Archetype worked for 12 weeks to develop the HarperCollins Web site. Software included Illustrator and Photoshop. Macintosh computers were used. **harpercollins.com**

Clicking on the New Releases icon at the bottom of the corporate home page, left, or clicking on the featured book covers or the hypertext titles in the list of Selected New Releases leads to the page above.

Clicking on an illustrated icon on the New Releases page, left, takes you to a particular topic section where you can choose a title. Clicking on a title leads to a summary of the book and a picture of its cover. Scrolling to the bottom of the page reveals further linking options, including email to the author.

A color system and a series of illustrations created by Dave Danz identify the different product categories. Horizontal bands of alternating tints and shades of the appropriate category color wrap around the side of each package and showcase the title and author, like the spine of a book. The front of the package features an illustration that previews the product's content, a layout approach used extensively in book cover design. The category illustrations are placed at the top of the package to identify the product type, and computer compatibility and performance information is displayed at the bottom.

Adapting the Design to the Interface

The color system and illustration icons from the packaging were carried over to the Web site to identify the interactive categories. The icons are used beside each product in the Categories contents page, shown at the left. The color bands of alternating tints and shades become a band of buttons that link to other content areas within the Interactive division (see above). This concept of using illustrations and color to key content is continued throughout the site.

Under the Corporate Umbrella

The HarperCollins corporate symbol and logotype identify each page and are followed by the italicized name of the division, as shown on the Interactive division's home page, opposite. On the site's home page, as well as other main division home pages,

the name is centered over a masthead illustration. Below the colorful masthead are a series of illustrated buttons that lead to the division's main subdivisions. Clicking on the pencil connects to an area where visitors can offer feedback.

Studio Archetype designed a graphic hierarchy that lets users know how deep in the site they are and also provides a clear framework so new pages can be built to match. On subdivision pages the masthead illustration is reduced. Subdivision titles are set in all caps, like Categories, left, and New Releases, above. Topics titles within the subdivisions are smaller, like Children's and Edutainment, left.

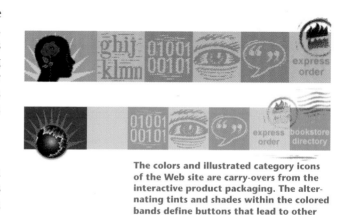

The colors and illustrated category icons of the Web site are carry-overs from the interactive product packaging. The alternating tints and shades within the colored bands define buttons that lead to other areas within the division.

Browse or Buy: Clip Art, Photos, and Typefaces

Overview *Browse through Image Club Graphics' online catalog of digital clip art, typefaces, and stock photographs; visit the Tips & Tricks section to see how to put the products into practice; place orders; and download purchases at the Web site's online store.*

"There's a synergy between the print catalog and the Web site—the print catalog drives traffic to the Web site and the Web site sends customers to the catalog."

—Grant Hutchinson, designer

Web Site Complements Printed Catalog

Through its 60-page full-color direct mail catalog that's sent to nearly a million customers each month, Image Club Graphics, a division of Adobe Systems, sells digital typefaces, stock photos, clip art images, Adobe applications and upgrades, and an array of third-party plug-ins and accessory software. The Web site supports the catalog by offering customers more options. Some customers prefer to browse online and have their purchases delivered via courier service; other customers want to place orders over the phone, then download their purchases; others prefer to do things completely online; and some prefer to take care of business completely over the phone.

Considering the Customer

When developing the site, designer Grant Hutchinson considered the needs of the customer in arriving at a 460-pixel width for the site's pages. "We have a broad customer base that uses different computer platforms and screen sizes," says Hutchinson. "Not all customers have 17- or 20-inch monitors so we used a page width of 460 pixels to accommodate all sizes."

And not all customers have the same graphics capabilities either. "It's extremely frustrating when you're required to have a plug-in to see some part of the information," adds Hutchinson. "Make sure that you've got something in place that allows people to bypass graphics if they don't have the capability."

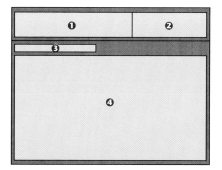

1. **Section title** 2. **Telephone number**
3. **Name of product shown** 4. **Product display area**

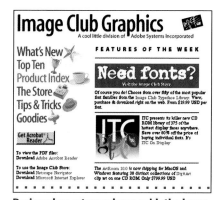

Designed on a two-column grid, the home page, shown above, is straightforward and sales-oriented. The colorful navigation index, on the left, shares screen space with product news and special product promotions, on the right. The section titles in the navigation index are typeset in Adobe Myriad Condensed to save space and to tie in with Adobe's Web site and product packaging, which also use Myriad.

STATS AND SOFTWARE

A 3-member team worked 2 months to get the Image Club Graphics Web site up and running. Software included BBEdit, DeBabelizer, HyperCard, Illustrator, Photoshop, PageMill, and Photo-Master on Macs. **imageclub.com**

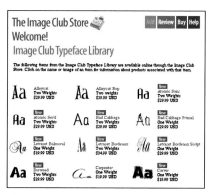

The Image Club Store lists the typefaces that can be bought and delivered online. To see a complete font, click on the name of the typeface shown in blue. Afterwards the name turns purple to show that you've already looked at the typeface.

Clicking on the name of the typeface on The Image Club Typeface Library page opens its product information page. Clicking the hypertext "add" or the button at the top adds this product to your online shopping basket.

To review your purchases, click on the Review button at the top to open the online shopping basket. The selected products, in this case typefaces, are displayed, along with the individual prices and the total price.

Interface

Section titles are color-coded, and a clip art image from the product line represents each section, as shown at left. For consistency, the same type color and image are used on the section pages as on the Product Info page, opposite, and on the Top Ten pages below. To accurately display clip art and stock photo collections, each collection of images is optimized to an 8-bit Adaptive palette using the batch conversion feature of DeBabelizer, which, according to Hutchinson, "is fast and offers good control over super palettes and file formats."

The Top Ten section features the ten most popular typefaces and ten bestselling clip art and stock photography collections. Clicking on the product title below the sample images opens the product's information page, such as the PhotoGear Skyscapes page, at far right, which displays 13 of the 85 images in the collection and provides ordering information. For customers who prefer not to order online, the telephone and fax numbers are on every page.

Presenting a Lot Without Overwhelming

Using thumbnails to represent extensive collections of stock photos provides customers with a clear overview, and showing a selection of the ten most popular collections in each product category offers a manageable place to start browsing. After an abbreviated look, as in the Top Ten pages shown below, customers can see more by clicking on a sample.

Electronic Shopping

Promoting and selling products via a Web site has the potential to provide a customized marketing approach based on individual customer needs and preferences. Dynamic promotions can be targeted to specific customers based on what they've looked at and what they've bought on the Web site, and what they've ordered through the catalog.

From Surfing the Net to Shopping the Net

Overview Tables of contents, hypertext, and color-coding help visitors shop and navigate through iQVC, the interactive online counterpart to cable TV's QVC shopping channel.

"We established two main areas of content: one for shopping and transactions, and another for information and entertainment."

–Eric Wilson, executive producer, Studio Archetype

Going Online

When QVC, the successful cable television shopping channel, decided to go online with its retail service, Studio Archetype in San Francisco worked closely with QVC to develop an interface and organizational structure that gives online shoppers the same level of service as TV shoppers are accustomed to.

Added Flexibility

The QVC shopping channel briefly introduces one product at a time on the air, and there's usually a limited supply available. Shoppers call to order the product during the presentation or write down the item number for later. With iQVC, shoppers not only have access to daily specials and products currently being presented on-air, but to a catalog of all items in stock—"anytime, anywhere." One of the design challenges was to figure out how to organize the extensive list of products and to develop an interface and navigational structure flexible enough for products to be easily added to or deleted from the list as they sell out.

The designers dealt with organization in a number of ways. To help find products, iQVC Shop departments are located at the bottom of the home page; a unique search feature allows products to be located by item number, manufacturer's name, description, or preferred price; and a directory of product groups links to a page where items are listed alphabetically by name and

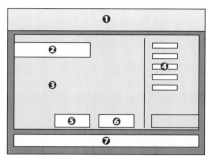

1. Header and site identity 2. Electronic Shopping button 3. Information area 4. Table of contents 5. Order Today's Special Value button 6. Order Current On-Air item button 7. Area for text links

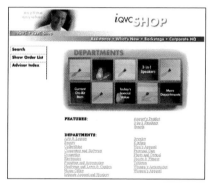

The drawers and cubbyholes on iQVC Shop's Departments page are a metaphor for the traditional storefront. Building on established merchandizing techniques, the images and text can be changed easily to display seasonal items or special values. Other pages can be selected by clicking the text in the cubbyholes or the underlined hypertext below. The table of contents, left of the drawers and cubbyholes, leads to other iQVC Shop sections.

STATS AND SOFTWARE

A 6-member team worked 11 weeks on 6 Macintosh and 2 PC computers to complete the Web site. Software included Illustrator and Photoshop.

iqvc.com

Product detail pages picture the item and provide a product description, as well as item number, price, and shipping and handling costs. Color, size, and quantity are selected in pop-up menus before adding the product to the order list.

To order an item, select "Add to Order List" on the Product Detail page. Make the necessary selections on the order list, then choose to keep shopping, update, or confirm the order. The online forms follow the same ordering procedure as QVC's toll-free telephone service, known for its speed, quality, and efficiency.

Assistance, What's New, Backstage, and Corporate HQ are organized like magazine layouts with headlines, subheads, body text, and vignetted photographs. Spot color enhances communication: Hypertext is yellow and the selected article is red.

price. For those who want to plan ahead, a programming guide offers dates and times of scheduled TV product presentations.

Inter-Linked

An elaborate interconnected structure of pages offers ease of navigation and thus ease of shopping. The site has five main sections as shown opposite on the iQVC home page in the table of contents on the right: What's New, Corporate HQ, Backstage, Assistance, and iQVC Shop.

All subsequent pages are based on a similar layout. A masthead at the top displays an identifying graphic and the section title. Two colorful bars divide the masthead from the information area. The first bar is orange-yellow, and links to the home page and the iQVC Shop, and the second one, colored maroon, links to the other four sections that offer help and entertain visitors with behind-the-scenes human-interest articles. Clicking a gray section name in a colored bar leads to that specific section and the name of the section turns white, indicating the visitor's location within the site.

The content options in a particular section are listed on the left side of the information area. On the two iQVC Shop pages, shown above, the contents are typeset flush left and separated by outlines to relate to the boxes in the forms found in this

section. In the editorial sections, the contents are flush right with no divider lines, in keeping with the editorial style, as in Backstage above.

What's New, Corporate HQ, Backstage, and Assistance were designed as a series of vertically oriented online magazines to take advantage of the Web's scrollable page feature. In a friendly and informative way, they present editorial material that leads viewers to the iQVC Shop. In one feature column, for example, an article on cooking is dotted with recipes, and useful product recommendations shown in hypertext link directly to product detail pages that in turn link to the order form.

Naming and Identifying

iQVC stands for "interactive" QVC, which is an acronym for quality, value, and convenience. The new logotype is introduced on the masthead of the home page, opposite, and heads all the pages in the iQVC Shop. The slant of the bold italic lowercase Bodoni "i" in combination with the color red symbolizes action and effectively represents the word "interactive." To distinguish the online magazine pages as corporate communication, they bear the company's standard QVC logotype set in Goudy Old Style (see Backstage above).

Dancing on A Grid

Overview *In* NucleusOne Guide, *a promotional demo for a font from the digital type foundry, Shift, overlapping layers display the collection of icons; animated icons double as navigation buttons; and contrast between color and grayscale, and sharp and blurred images helps to prioritize information.*

"The goal was to display the font in a dynamic way while keeping production and distribution costs down."

–Joshua Distler, creative director/ designer

Promoting the Font

NucleusOne, a collection of 73 industrial symbols and icons in Postscript Type 1 format, is showcased in this interactive font browser designed by Joshua Distler for Shift. Images of the symbols and icons that make up the font, contact information, and directions on how to order the font are presented on panels and positioned on-screen according to a grid.

Following the Path

Once past the introductory screen, there are two ways you can move from one panel to another: by clicking on animated *NucleusOne* icons, like the three shown above in the colorful squares, or by clicking on any visible part of a panel. None of the panels ever completely fills the monitor—at least a portion of each of the overlapping panels is always on-screen, making it easy to shuffle through them simply by clicking.

Contrast Creates Visual Hierarchy

The universal design principles of focus and implied depth are used to establish a hierarchy in the *NucleusOne* interface. The

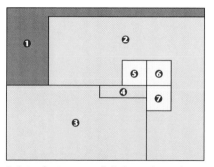

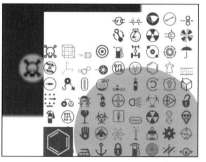

1. Introductory panel 2. Second panel showing the symbols and icons of the font
3. Ending title panel 4. Title area
5. Animated button for order information
6. Animated button for compatibility information 7. Animated button for trademark information

In the introductory screen the animated *NucleusOne* icon, second from the left, prompts the user to "click here." White "negative" space is used to emphasize the name *NucleusOne*, and complementary colors yellow and purple create a dynamic contrast.

Clicking on the *NucleusOne* icon on the introductory screen brings another panel to the foreground that features the symbols and icons. For continuity, the yellow circle fills in the white negative space of the purple shape on the preceding screen.

Clicking on the animated button on the font panel shows details from the font and offers a visual break from the horizontal and vertical grid by angling the rows of icons. Clicking on a blurred background panel brings it forward.

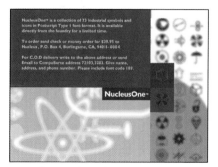

An ending *NucleusOne* title panel and three information panels revolve around a point where the four panels meet. Clicking on the *NucleusOne* title or on a colorful animated icon brings the corresponding panel to the foreground, such as the how-to-order panel above.

active panel appears to be in front of the others and its images and type are sharp. In contrast, the other panels appear to recede into the background because they're partially covered by the top panel and their images are blurred.

Color Plays A Part, Too

In addition to depth and focus, color also reinforces visual hierarchy. The bright colors of the foreground panel stand out against the monochromatic panels in the background.

The color palette is based on contrasting warm and cool colors that were selected, along with black and white, from the Macintosh System palette. The contrasts between warm and cool, light and dark, bright and dull provide good opportunities for combining the artwork, typography, and backgrounds: The dark images show up well against the light backgrounds and the light images show up well against the dark.

Some of the colors are close in value, or luminosity. This offers an additional design possibility: to combine the two similar values and achieve a dynamic interaction of color that creates a flickering effect, as shown in the purple-red animated buttons on the ending screen at the left.

Deciding To Publish on Disk

Besides wanting to present *NucleusOne* in a unique way, several cost-saving factors contributed to the decision to produce an

interactive demo to be distributed on floppy disk. First, the production costs of an on-screen promotional would be lower than for a comparable printed piece. Most of the cost of printing is in the initial press setup—the more you print, the lower the unit cost. Shift wasn't sure what the demand would be, and the interactive demo could be produced as needed in varying quantities. Second, the floppy disk is an affordable medium and costs no more to distribute by mail or courier service than a printed piece would. And there was an added bonus—the 924K electronic files could be easily distributed online from a Web site.

Creating the Artwork

The artwork was drawn in Illustrator, rendered in Photoshop, then placed in Director. Programming was done using Lingo, Director's scripting language. For example, the out-of-focus, grayscale panels were substituted for the sharp, color images and left on-screen using Lingo's "trails of sprite" option.

Online Travel Takes Off

Overview *The Travelocity Web site uses color-coding, an extensive system of illustrated icons, QuickTime videos, photos, animation, and Internet databases to assist the do-it-yourself traveler.*

"The only thing that's constant is change itself—particularly with a Web site. Web years are shorter than dog years!"

—B.D. Goel, vice president of product development, Worldview Systems Corporation

Providing a Service

Travelocity is a one-stop travel site from Worldview Systems Corporation and SABRE Interactive, which enables consumers to instantly reserve and buy airline tickets, book hotels and car rentals, browse the entire database of worldwide destinations, purchase unique travel-related products, and exchange travel experiences in real-time chat forums and via messages posted to online bulletin boards. The site's searchable electronic database includes weather forecasts, driving directions, a currency converter, and photos, videos, and maps of thousands of destinations around the world, including extensive up-to-the-minute calendar-of-events details for over 200 featured destinations.

Making Customers Feel Comfortable

Making travel arrangements and purchases over the Internet can be intimidating. To build credibility and instill confidence, the two most important design considerations were clarity and ease of navigation. The uncluttered layout, whimsical illustrations, straightforward wording of titles, and a clear system of color-coding help put customers at ease.

Identifying the Service

The Travelocity logotype, a clever combination of *travel* and *velocity,* combines roman and italic letterforms to imply "fast travel arrangements." The colorful symbol above the logotype portrays a skyline and an airplane at takeoff to reinforce the message. The four colors in the Travelocity symbol are the basis for the site's color-coding system that clearly organizes the comprehensive information and different media into four main categories. The four-color scheme makes it quick and easy to fit

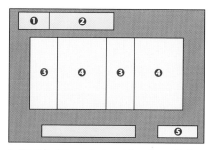

1. Travelocity symbol and logotype 2. Section title 3. Illustrated category icons 4. Category headings 5. Continue button

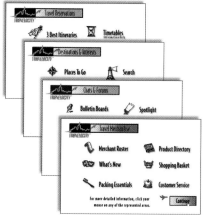

Color-coding is applied to the home pages of the four main sections.

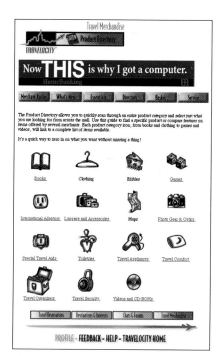

Hierarchical titling identifies where you are. Above, the section title (Travel Merchandise) appears at the top of the page and the subsection title (Product Directory) and its icon are shown in the rectangle just below it.

Some of the icons are representational, as in the case of Hotels & Cars, opposite, and others are metaphorical. For example, the lighthouse, above, is used as a metaphor for the Search feature. The four main sections are accessible via colorful buttons at the bottom of every page.

The Travelocity symbol and logotype appear at the top of each Web page. The colored panel to the right of the symbol is filled with a gradation of the color that represents that particular section. Section titles and category headings are typeset in Bodega Sans, whose condensed letterforms and short descenders save screen space.

new pages into the site's organization. But to add a fifth category would mean modifying the symbol and changing the existing graphics on every page.

A Picture's Worth

Throughout the site illustrated icons identify subsections and topics, and offer a friendly touch. And since people respond more quickly to pictures than words, they help speed customers to their destination. To unify the pages, the topic illustrations are equal in size and share the same hand-drawn style—ink drawings that were scanned, then colored in Photoshop. Drop shadows add dimension and show that the icons are clickable.

Keeping Up-to-Date

One of the biggest challenges of maintaining this site is the constant need to update time-sensitive information. An extensive network of correspondents continually gather information from around the world, writing and publishing articles on a daily basis. To deliver up-to-the-minute travel and entertainment information, many of the Travelocity pages are updated via access to other Internet databases that provide details on flight schedules, hotels, and car rentals, and the ability to search through thousands of events and activities, listings of restaurants, sights, and shops in hundreds of destinations around the world.

Photographs offer a peek at out-of-the-way destinations.

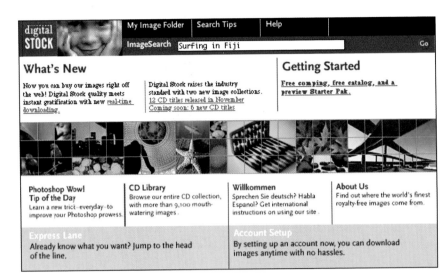

The primary goal of this prototype for the redesigned Digital Stock Web site (digitalstock.com) is to make it easy for visitors to find the single photo or CD-ROM image collection they want and buy it. Implemented with frame technology, a band appears at the top of every page, with the company logo, a personal "shopping bag" folder for accumulating images, and a search function. "We want our customers to be able to start an image search from wherever they are in the site, without having to backtrack to another screen," says Digital Stock's executive director Charles Smith.

Besides this band, the home page, shown above, offers the added value of tips and techniques for using Photoshop, a way to browse the entire Digital Stock library, and an opportunity for customers who know what they want—based on an earlier visit to the site or a search through the company's CD-ROM or printed catalog—to go straight to the ordering page.

To meet the needs of a broad audience, Digital Stock has provided a button on the home page that can bring up instructions in five languages. And site designers have made the image-acquisition process as language-independent as possible by supplying three buttons under each image that's located in response to a customer-

initiated search. Visitors can simply click the left button to add the high-resolution image to their shopping folder, the center button to download a low-resolution FPO (for position only) version, or the right button to expand the search to see images more loosely related to the search criteria, as shown above.

Tips adapted from the current version of *The Photoshop Wow! Book* add value to the site, encouraging visitors to return for the latest helpful hint; they also support sales by helping customers succeed with the images they buy. And a What's New section encourages site visitors to check on what's changed since their last visit.

Designed to deliver information quickly and efficiently, the Iomega site (iomega.com) uses a magazine metaphor—*iomegazine*. The main content of the site is information to help people buy products, customer support information to answer questions buyers may have after purchasing the product, and helpful ideas for getting full use from the products, using them in ways customers might not have thought about yet.

The site's home page (see page 58) serves as the magazine's cover, listing and providing links for a main feature and three other features under that. In addition, the cover holds the three most important buttons on the site: to get to the site Contents, above right, to the Tech Support section, and to Software Downloads.

A previous version of the site drew complaints that navigation wasn't clear. "But complaints have declined just about to zero," says Julie Vastano, editor-in-chief,

since the change to a magazine metaphor. "People understand what a magazine is. They understand the concept of a contents page." The magazine metaphor also supports the monthly schedule of updates to the site.

The site includes a product guide—a catalog of every product Iomega sells, with a clear organization maintained by a grid. Not yet ready to support a direct online ordering process, the company has created links to a partner whose site takes the orders for Iomega products.

To keep this utilitarian site lively and visually exciting, site designers use humor, bright colors, wide-angled photography, and some Shockwave and QuickTime animation. But the size and number of graphics files are strictly controlled. Says Vastano, "People will be much more satisfied with less on a page and faster loading." Animations are clearly sidelined, so that visitors can enjoy them by choice, not by accident.

Welcome to JOE BOXER® WWW V.6.9.

Before we start, are you wearing clean underwear?

 YES NO

That's what they all say. We at JOE BOXER® know a thing or two about underwear. To download a free pair of virtual underwear, please stand with midsection towards monitor now.

The primary goal of the Joe Boxer site is to position the brand in the online community as creative, enterprising, and unique (joeboxer.com). "The company's motto is 'a brand is an amusement park and the product is a souvenir,'" says vice president of marketing Denise Slattery. "We wanted to create online entertainment that would translate into more interest in the brand, so site visitors would then purchase the product when they see it in department stores."

Foregoing technological bells and whistles, site designers concentrated on clever navigation and minimal download times. Unlike the design goal of most sites, navigation at joeboxer.com isn't meant to be simple or direct. Part of the appeal for some users is that, in Slattery's words, "the site is intentionally weird and not easy to get through." Avoiding a "click here for information" approach, the site's designers are gratified by the comment they get most frequently from users: "That was fun!"

Appendix A: Project Contributors

Contact information for projects pictured in this book, listed alphabetically.

adobe.com
Adobe Systems
345 Park Avenue
San Jose, CA 95110
408-536-6000

www.adobe.com

adobemag.com
Dietz Design Co.
100 South King Street, #540
Seattle, WA 98104
206-621-1855
Fax: 206- 621-7146

robert@dietzdesign.com
www.dietzdesign.com

Art Director/Designer: Robert Dietz

Adobe Photoshop 3.0 Deluxe CD-ROM
Adobe Systems
1098 Alta Avenue
Mountain View, CA 94039

www.adobe.com

Producer: George Jardine
Art Direction/Design: Jonathan Caponi
Music/Sound: David S. Mash
Video: Mark Boscacci
Tutorials: Russell Brown, Luanne Cohen, Laura Dower

Alben+Faris, Inc., *see* **Making It Macintosh**

allstarmag.com
Allstar
4416 Finley Avenue
Los Angeles, CA 90027
213-666-6067
Fax: 213-666-0191

roblord@allstarmag.com
www.allstarmag.com

Executive Producer: Robert Lord
Art Director: Michele Comas
Interactive Producer: Victor Bornia
Design Consultant: Trevor Gilchrist

The American Center for Design Journal, *see* **Interact**

apple.com
Apple Computer
1 Infinite Loop
Cupertino, CA 95024
www.apple.com

Art Dabbler
MetaCreations Corporation
6303 Carpinteria Avenue
Carpinteria, CA 93013
805-566-6200

metasales@aol.com
www.metacreations.com

Macintosh Programming: Mark Zimmer
Windows Programming: Tom Hedges
Interface Design: John Derry
Interface Programming: Priscilla Shih
Engineering Management: Glenn Reid
Programming: Christina Hall
Project Management: Jon Bass
Asset Management: Tad Shelby

atlasmagazine.com
@tlas Magazine
Atlas Web Design
1201 Howard Street
San Francisco, CA 94103
415-553-4074
Fax: 415-552-6328

olivier@sirius.com
www.atlasmagazine.com

Creative Director: Olivier Laude
Senior Designer: Amy Franceschini
Technology Director: Michael Macrone

Barnes & Noble Promotional Animations
barnesandnoble.com
i/o 360° digital design, inc.
841 Broadway
New York, NY 10003
212-533-4467

www.io360.com

Producer: Ming Lau

The Bettmann Archive Screensaver
Carbone Smolan Associates
22 West 19th Street, 10th Floor
New York, NY 10011
212-807-0011
Fax 212-807-0870

Principal/Creative Director: Ken Carbone
Senior Designer: Justin Peters
Images from Corbis/The Bettman Archive

bluewaters.com
BlueWaters Production
350 Ninth Street
San Francisco, CA 94103

bluewaters@aol.com
www.bluewaters.com

Producer: Ming Lau

boxtop.com
BoxTop
10960 Wilshire Boulevard, Suite 1550
Los Angeles, CA 90024
310-235-3900
Fax 310-235-3999

acaldwell@boxtop.com
www.boxtop.com

Brad Johnson Presents, *see* **Second Story**

Brilliant Media, *see* **Xplora 1**

Bryce 2
MetaCreations Corporation
6303 Carpinteria Avenue
Carpinteria, CA 93013
805-566-6200

metasales@aol.com
www.metacreations.com

Senior Science and Design Officer: Kai Krause
Eric Wenger
MetaTools Design Team

bybee.com
Netjet Communications
585 Howard Street, Suite A
San Francisco, CA 94105
415-538-3370

info@netjet.com
www.netjet.com
www.bybee.com

Lead Designer/Developer:
    Matthew McGlynn
Patrick McGovern

Carbon, *see* **Paper machine**

The Cartoon History of the Universe
Human Code, Inc.
1411 West Avenue, Suite 100
Austin, TX 78701
512-477-5455

www.humancode.com

Producer: Chipp Walters
Project and Design Director:
    Lindsay Gupton
Visual Designer: Kyle Anderson
Programmer: Brian Brantner
Software Director/Interface Design:
    Gary Gattis
Audio Director: John Smith
Design Director: Lloyd Walker
Adapted from the book by Larry Gonick

cccnet.com
Computer Curriculum Corporation
1287 Lawrence Station Road
Sunnyvale, CA 94089
800-455-7910 x6155

wendy_huang@cccpp.com
www.cccnet.com

Classic Photographic Image Objects
Classic PIO Partners
87 E. Green Street, Suite 309
Pasadena, CA 91105
800-270-2746

ridgley@classicpartners.com
www.classicpartners.com

Clement Mok Designs CD-ROM
Studio Archetype, Inc.
600 Townsend Street, Penthouse
San Francisco, CA 94103
415-703-9900
Fax: 415-703-9901

www.studioarchetype.com

cooktek.com
Hanson/Dodge Design
301 North Water Street
Milwaukee, WI 53202
414-347-1266
Fax: 414-347-0493

postmaster@hanson-dodge.com
www.hanson-dodge.com

Creative Director: Clay Feller
Art Director: Leslie Worth
Designer: Sean Donnelly
Copywriter: Carol Polacek
Photographer: Mark Salewsky
Information Design/Producer:
    Thomas Gaudynski
Programming/Serving:
    Honeycomb Interactive

cow.com
cow.
1522 Cloverfield Boulevard, Suite E
Santa Monica, CA 90404
310-264-2424
Fax: 310-264-2430

vision@cow.com
www.cow.com

Lead Designers: David Lai, Kendrick Lim
Programmers: Diana Brickell,
    Jonathan Santos
Creative Directors: Mateo Neri,
    Bryan Dorsey

CSA Archive CD-ROM Sampler
CSA Archive
P.O. Box 581639
Minneapolis, MN 55458-1639
612-339-1263

csa@internet.com
www.csa-archive.com

Creative Director: Charles S. Anderson
Interface Designers: Tom Eslinger,
    Brian Smith
Writers: Lisa Pemrick, Renée Valois
Programmers: Tom Eslinger, Brian Smith
Graphic Designers: Charles S. Anderson,
    Paul Howalt, Tom Eslinger, Brian Smith
Photographers: Darrell Eager,
    Andy Kingsbury
Illustrators: CSA Archive
Animators: Tom Eslinger, Brian Smith,
    CSA Archive
Music Composer: Stock
Multimedia Production Company:
    Wanganui Polytechnic School of
    Design, New Zealand

CyberMom
Kuester Partners, Inc.
81 S. 9th Street, Suite 300
Minneapolis, MN
612-338-6030
Fax: 612-338-6175

kuester@kuester.com
www.kuester.com

designory.com
The Designory, inc.
Pinkhaus
211 East Ocean Boulevard
Long Beach, CA 90802
562-432-5707
Fax: 562-491-5225

lannon.tanchum@designory.com

Art Director: David Glaze
Designer: Chip McCarthy
Copywriter: Frank Cunningham,
    Rich Conklin
Photographer: Walter Urie and various
Programming: Genex Interactive
Client: The Designory, inc., and Pinkhaus
Executive Creative Director:
    Lannon Tanchum
Producer: Jason Deal

Digital Facades, *see* **icsla.com, lynx.com**

digitalstock.com
Digital Stock, a Division of Corbis
    Corporation
750 Second Street
Encinitas, CA 92024
800-545-4514
760-634-6500
sales@digitalstock.com
www.digitalstock.com

discovery.com
Discovery Channel
7700 Wisconsin Avenue
Bethesda, MD 20814

www.discovery.com

dockers.com
Levi Strauss & Co.

www.dockers.com

echoimages.com
Echo Images, Inc./EchoLink
4747 Morena Boulevard, Suite 100
San Diego, CA 92117
619-270-4300
Fax: 619-490-0324

gcarson@echolink.net
www.echolink.net

Executive Producer/President: Gregory
    Carson
Creative Director: Angela Lester
Art Director/Creative Writer/Programmer:
    Gabriel Watson
Metaphor/Interface Designer: Paula Klein
Graphic Designers: Tiffany Caliva,
    Eric Altson

theedisongroup.com
The Edison Group
60 South 6th Street, Suite 2800
Minneapolis, MN 55402

tdupont@martinwilliams.com
Project Manager: Alan Lewis

elvisbonaparte.com
Elvis & Bonaparte
115 NW First Avenue, Suite 300
Portland, OR 97209
503-226-0999
Fax 503-226-0777

www.elvisbonaparte.com

Web Designer: Mike Olson
Creative Director/Designer/Illustrator:
    David Helfrey
Photographer: Steve Beals

entier.com
Gr8
2400 Boston Street, 3rd Floor
Baltimore, MD 21224
410-837-0070

info@gr8.com
www.gr8.com

Creative Director: Morton Jackson
Designer: Kurt Thesing

envirolink.org
EnviroLink Network
4618 Henry Street
Pittsburgh, PA 15213
412-683-6400
Fax: 412-683-8460

info@envirolink.org
www.envirolink.org

epicurious.com
CondéNet, Inc.

www.epicurious.com

© CondéNet, Inc. 1997

Fantastic Forest
nationalgeographic.com/features/
96/forest.html
National Geographic Interactive
1145 17th Street NW
Washington, DC 20036

echristenberry@nationalgeographic.com
www.nationalgeographic.com

fontsite.com

Sean Cavanaugh
seanc@fontsite.com

Ken Oyer
keno@Fontsite.com

giantrobot.com
Giant Robot

grobot@deltanet.com
www.giantrobot.com

giantstep.com
Giant Step
820 W. Jackson, Suite 400
Chicago, IL 60607
312-470-2700
Fax: 312-470-2770

melisa@giantstep.com
www.giantstep.com

Designers: Xavier Wynn, Sheau Hui Ching,
    Sean Moran
Programmers: Kerry O'Donnell,
    Adam Heneghan
Copywriter: Gregory Galloway

thegolfchannel.com
The Golf Channel Online
7580 Commerce Center Drive
Orlando, FL 32819

www.thegolfchannel.com

WebSite Partner: CBS Sportsline
www.cbs.sportsline.com

gr8.com
Gr8
2400 Boston Street, 3rd Floor
Baltimore, MD 21224
410-837-0070

info@gr8.com
www.gr8.com

Creative Director: Morton Jackson
Designer: Kurt Thesing

grants.com
Landor
1301 Fifth Avenue, Suite 1600
Seattle, WA 98101
206-505-7500
Fax: 206-505-7501

www.landor.com

Creative Director: Bill Chiarvalle
Lead Designer: Scott Curtis
Designer: Alvin Fong
Electronic Production: Mike Synoground
Copy Editor: Erica Jorgensen
Back End Coding: Incommand Interactive

Gyro Interactive Pty Ltd, *see* **Museum
of Victoria, Victoria Buildings and
Builders, Waypoint 1**

hallmark.com
Giant Step
820 W. Jackson, Suite 400
Chicago, IL 60607
312-470-2700
Fax: 312-470-2770

melisa@giantstep.com
www.giantstep.com

Designers: Xavier Wynn
Programers: Kerry O'Donnell,
    Adam Heneghan
Project Managers: Colin Costello,
    Melisa Vázquez
Hallmark Cards, Inc.

Hanson/Dodge Design, *see*
cooktek.com

harpercollins.com
Studio Archetype, Inc.
600 Townsend Street, Penthouse
San Francisco, CA 94103
415-703-9900
Fax: 415-703-9901

www.studioarchetype.com

Information Architecture: Lillian Svec
Design Direction: Claire Barry
Design: Jennifer Anderson, George Chen
Illustration: Dave Danz
Implementation: Sheryl Hampton,
    Emma Ainsworth, Kathleen Egge

Headlight Media, *see* **myrrh.com**

Herman Miller Aeron Chair
Herman Miller Shapes
Studio Archetype, Inc.
600 Townsend Street, Penthouse
San Francisco, CA 94103
415-703-9900
Fax: 415-703-9901

www.studioarchetype.com

HiRez Audio
Geno Andrews
2354 Ocean Avenue
Venice, CA 90291
310-827-8991

digitalrlm@earthlink.net

How Your Body Works
Mindscape
88 Rowland Way
Novato, CA 94945
415-897-9900
Fax: 415-897-7166

bholmes@mindscapes.com

Health
Producer: Barc Holmes
Art Direction/3-D: Imagine This
Art Directors: Rich Hone, Bob Hone
Project Manager: Teri Rousseau

Universe
Producer: Barc Holmes
Art Direction: M/W Design
3D: Digital Artworks
2D: Intervision
Project Manager: Maya Draisin

Human Code, Inc., *see* **Cartoon History
of the Universe**

Hybrid CD-i
GTE Interactive Media,
a division of GTE Vantage, Inc.

CyberIsland
2916 Commercial Avenue, #307
Anacortes, WA 98221
360-293-3114
Fax: 360-293-8665

www.cyberisland.com

Executive Producer: Mark Dillon
Designer/Director: Steve Lomas
Lead Engineer: Mark Armendariz
Chief Engineer: Steven Blumenfeld
Business Director: Lauren Callaby
Tools Engineer: Danny Aijala
Data Manager: Tim Tembreull
UNIX Administrator: Michelle Jannette
Programmer: Robin Ashley
Production Managers: Jeanne Juneau,
    Jennifer Johnston
Artists: Stephen King, Kory Jones,
    Tommy Yune, Marvin DeMerchant
Encoding Engineer: Dave Salizoni
Audio Engineer: Dom Wiedey
Video Editor: Terry Barnum

icsla.com
Interstate Consolidation
Digital Facades
1750 14th Street, Suite E
Santa Monica, CA 90404
310-581-4100
310-581-4105

www.dfacades.com

Creative Director: Oliver Chan
Lead Programmer: Jane Lin
Graphic Production: Owen Jiang
Project Manager: Steve Klinenberg

imageclub.com
**Image Club Graphics (Adobe
    Systems, Inc.)**
833 4th Avenue SW, Suite 800
Calgary, Alberta, Canada T2P 3T5
800-661-9410
Fax: 403-261-7013

info@imageclub.com
www.imageclub.com

Grant Hutchinson
Blake Springer

**Interact: The American Center for
Design Journal CD-ROM**
IDEO
Pier 28 Annex
San Francisco, CA 94105
415-778-4700

spreenberg@ideo.com
www.ideo.com

Interactive Roundtable
GTE Interactive Media,
a division of GTE Vantage, Inc.

CyberIsland
2916 Commercial Avenue, #307
Anacortes, WA 98221
360-293-3114
Fax: 360-293-8665

www.cyberisland.com

Producer: Allan Pinkus
Designer/Director: Steve Lomas
Programmer: Dan Spirn
Tools Programmer: Danny Aijala
Graphic Artists: Stephen King, Tom Yune
Video Editors: Terry Barnum,
    Tim Tembreull
Executive Producer: Mark Dillon
Audio Engineer: Dom Wiedey

**Internal & External Communcation,
Inc.,** *see* **Leave It To SEEMIS**

i/o 360° digital design, inc. see
barnesandnoble.com

iomega.com
www.iomega.com

iqvc.com
Studio Archetype
600 Townsend Street, Penthouse
San Francisco, CA 94103
415-703-9900
Fax: 415-703-9901

www.studioarchetype.com

Information Architect: Clement Mok
Design Director: Samantha Fuetsch
Executive Producer: Eric Wilson

Designer: Brian Forst, Paula Meiselman
Information Design Director: Lillian Svec

joeboxer.com
Joe Boxer
1265 Folsom Street
San Francisco, CA 94103
415-882-9406
Fax: 415-882-7940

joeboxer@joeboxer.com
www.joeboxer.com

Johnson, Brad, *see* **secondstory.com**

Joshua Distler Design, *see* **NucleusOne**

The Journeyman Project®:
Pegasus Prime™
Presto Studios, Inc.

presto@presto.com
www.presto.com

©1996 Presto Studios, Inc.
©1996 Bandai Digital Entertainment Co.,
    Ltd.

Executive Producer: Michel Kripalani
Producer/Director/Art Director: Jack Davis
Project Manager: Patrick Rogers
Conceptual Designer/Special Effects:
    Tommy Yune
Lead 3D Animator: Kory Jones
Lead Video Specialist/Graphics Mechanic:
    Tim Tembreull
Lead Progammer/Pippin and Macintosh
    Version: Bob Bell
Lead Programmer/Sony Playstation
    Version: David Black
3D Animator: Shadi Almassizadeh
Lead 3D Modeler: Leif Einarsson
3D Modeler/Animator: Andrew Heimbold
3D Modeler/Texture Artist:
    Michael Jackson
Image and Audio Processing/Localization:
    Lauren Morimoto
Music Composer/Sound Designer:
    Bob Stewart
Assistant Programmer: Monika Weikel

The Journeyman Project® 2:
Buried in Time™
Presto Studios, Inc.

presto@presto.com
www.presto.com

©1995 Presto Studios, Inc.
Sanctuary Woods Multimedia

The Journeyman Project® 3:
Legacy of Time
Presto Studios, Inc.

presto@presto.com
www.presto.com

©1997 Presto Studios, Inc.
Broderbund Software, Inc.
Red Orb Entertainment™

Just Think 2
ad•hoc Interactive, Inc.
221 Caledonia Street
Sausalito, CA 94965
415-332-0180
Fax: 415-332-0182

info@adhoc.com
www.adhoc.com

Executive Producer: Aaron Singer
Creative Director: Megan Wheeler
Vice President of Technology:
    Shawn McKee

jwtworld.com
J. Walter Thompson
4 Embarcadero Center, Suite 800
San Francisco, CA 94111
415-955-2042
Fax: 415-955-2199

carrell.mccarthy@sf.jwtworld.com
www.jwtworld.com

kahlua.com
Lois/E.J.L. (Year 2K)

cow.
1522 Cloverfield Boulevard, Suite E
Santa Monica, CA 90404
310-264-2424
Fax: 310-264-2430

vision@cow.com
www.cow.com

Lead Designer: Bryan Powell
Lead Engineer: Samuel Goldstein
Programmer: Jonathan Santos
Creative Directors: Mateo Neri,
    Bryan Dorsey
Agency: Lois/E.J.L. (Year 2K)

kentwilliams
Kent Williams
Fax: 919-968-1530
kentwilliams@earthlink.net
www.speared peanut.com/artist/
    kentwilliams.html

King Cobra
nationalgeographic.com/features/
97/kingcobra.html
National Geographic Interactive

www.nationalgeographic.com

Producer: Laura Carter
Designers/Developers: Julie Beeler,
    Brad Johnson
Snake Illustrator: Paul Krafter
Writer: David Taylor

King, Stephen
King Design
1097 Oceanic Drive
Encinitas, CA 92024

kinghome@aol.com

klutz.com
455 Portage Avenue
Palo Alto, CA 94306
650-857-0888
klutz@mediacity.com
www.klutz.com

Web site design by Studio Verso

Illustrator: Lou Brooks

**Kristine Hyejung Hwang
Floppy Disk Portfolio**
Kristine Hyejung Hwang
321 Annie Lane
Rochester, NY 14626
716-723-9236

hwang@kodak.com
www.rit.edu/~hjh5787

kuester.com
Kuester Partners, Inc.
81 S. 9th Street, Suite 300
Minneapolis, MN 55402
612-338-6030
Fax: 612-338-6175

kuester@kuester.com
www.kuester.com

Creative Director: Kevin Kuester
Designer: Bob Goebel
Designer/Programmer: Eric Kreidler,
    Jeff Siegel
Copywriter: David Forney

landor.com
Landor
1001 Front Street
San Francisco, CA 94111
415-955-1400
Fax: 415-955-1358

more_info@landor.com
www.landor.com

WebMaster: Chris Jones
Creative Director/Designer: Dean Wilcox
Designer/Coding: Colin Johnston
Executive Director/Worldwide Marketing
    Communications: Peter Allen
Production/Coding: Kai Banser
Designer/Production: Carlos Oropeza
Photography: Michael Freil
Director of Interactive Branding:
    Dean Fernandes

Leave It to SEEMIS
Internal & External
Communication, Inc.
310-827-4464

marketing@iec.com
www.iec.com

Leave It to SEEMIS was developed by
Internal and External Communication, Inc.
(IEC) for Chevron Corporation © 1991.

Lost & Found
GTE Interactive Media,
a division of GTE Vantage, Inc.

CyberIsland
2916 Commercial Avenue, #307
Anacortes, WA 98221
360-293-3114
Fax: 360-293-8665

www.cyberisland.com

Designer/Director/Idea Mechanic:
    Steve Lomas
Art Director: Kory Jones
Software Designer: Farshid Almassizadeh
Software Engineer: Dan Spirn
Xobject and Tools Programmer:
    Danny Aijala
Jr. Software Engineer: Lynn McCarty
Audio Engineer: Terry Barnum
Host: Zachary Lomas
Photographer: Glynn Jones
Voice-Over Talent/Writer: Lani Minella
Writer/Music: Beth Wood
Production Assistant: Dana Eber
Video Editor: Tim Tembreull

lynxgolf.com
Lynx Golf Inc.
16017 E. Valley Boulevard
City of Industry, CA 91749

www.lynxgolf.com

Lynx Golf Inc.
DDB Needham Los Angeles
Digital Facades

mackerel.com
Mackerel Interactive Media
416-366-FISH
mackerel@mackerel.com

www.mackerel.com

Creative Directors: Kevin Steele, Dave Groff
Art Director: Cindy Dubis
Webmasters: Bones Richardson,
    Ryan Murphy
Additional Concepts: the whole Mackerel
    Team

The Mackerel Stack
Mackerel Interactive Media
416-366-FISH
mackerel@mackerel.com

www.mackerel.com

Creative Directors: Kevin Steele, Dave Groff
Concepts and Creation: Mackerel
Programming: Karl Borst, Kevin Steele
Team: Karl Borst, Dave Groff, Kevin Steele,
    Oliver Meurer, Gord Gower,
    Fred Williamson, Kat Cruickshank

Making It Macintosh
Apple Computer, Inc.
1 Infinite Loop
Cupertino, CA 95014

Team Leader/Interface Design/Instructional
    Designer/Writing/Programmer:
    Harry Saddler
Graphic Designers/Interface Designers/
    Illustrators: Lauralee Alben, Jim Faris
Instructional Designer/Writer:
    D. Leah Antignas
Animators/Illustrators: John B. deLorimier
    Jr., Alice Griffin Garber
Animator: Matthew Siegel
Media Producers/Technical Support:
    Henri Poole, Sheryl Hampton
Editors: Laurel Rezeau, Jeanne Woodward
Writer: Lori Kaplan
Content Advisor: Bill Fernandez
Administrative Support: Miki Lee
Production Manager: Martha Steffen
Project Manager: Trish Eastman

Alben+Faris, Inc.
317 Arroyo Seco
Santa Cruz, CA 95060
408-426-5526

mail@albenfaris.com
www.albenfaris.com

manslife.com
Real Life Publishing
116 W. Jefferson Street
Mankato, KS 66956
913-378-3772
Fax: 913-378-3772

info@manslife.com
www.manslife.com

MegaMorf Monster Lab
GTE Interactive Media,
a division of GTE Vantage, Inc.
CyberIsland
2916 Commercial Avenue, #307
Anacortes, WA 98221
360-293-3114
Fax: 360-293-8665

www.cyberisland.com

Executive Producer/Idea Mechanic:
    Steve Lomas
Project Lead/Graphic Designer:
    Marvin DeMerchant
Graphic Designer: Kory Jones
Industrial Design: Son Dao
Principal Software Engineer: Tim Bank
Xobjects and Tools Programmer:
    Danny Aijala
Software Manager: Dan Spirn
Audio Engineers: Terry Barnum,
    Dom Wiedey
Production Manager: Sal Parascandolo
Writer/Voices: Lani Minella
Music: David Siebels
Animation and Character Design:
    Michelle Light

Melbourne Water Corporation
Rankin Bevers Associates
502 Albert Street
East Melbourne, Victoria 3002 Australia
613-9-662-1233

design@rba.com.au
www.rba.com.au

Design: Wayne Rankin
Production/Navigation: Michael Kratofil
HTML: David Cox

mFactory.com
mFactory, Inc.
susan@mfactory.com
www.mfactory.com

Production Manager: Susan Deering
Web Guru: Shashank Parasnis
Designer: Usok Sebastiaan Choe
HTML Programmer: Andy Chu
CGI Scriptors: Christopher King,
    Andrew Flir

Microsoft® Encarta® 97
Deluxe Encyclopedia
Microsoft Corporation
One Microsoft Way
Redmond, WA 98052-6399

Sheila Carter
Diane Shambaugh
Kanchen Rajanna
Kathleen Kincaid
Michael Forney
Susan Lally
Adrienne O'Donnell
Bill Flora

Museum of Victoria
Gyro Interactive Pty Ltd
502 Albert Street Pty Ltd
East Melbourne, Victoria, 3002 Australia
61-3-9662-1027
Fax: 61-3-9663-8805

gyro@gyro.com.au
www.gyro.com.au

Design: Wayne Rankin

myrrh.com
Headlight Media
920 Woodmont Boulevard, Suite G-9
Nashville, TN 37204
615-463-9366

headlight@home.com
www.headlightmedia.com

Art Direction: Joseph Moore
Design/Programming: Headlight Media

Myst
cyan.com

All Myst, indica, sounds, images and text
© 1993 Cyan, Inc. All rights reserved.
Myst® Cyan, Inc.

nationalgeographic.com, *see* **Fantastic**
Forest, King Cobra, Xpeditions

netjet.com
Netjet Communications
585 Howard Street, Suite A
San Francisco, CA 94105
415-538-3370

info@netjet.com
www.netjet.com

John Hersey
Dina Harp
Matthew McGlynn
Patrick McGovern

Nissan Interactive
Nissan Motor Corp., USA
18501 S. Figueroa Street
Carson, CA 90248
310-532-3111

nissan-usa.com

NucleusOne Guide
Joshua Distler Design
1221 Oak Grove Avenue, Suite 105
Burlingame, CA 94010
415-343-3940
Fax: 415-343-3498

www.shiftype.com

Creative Director/Designer/Programmer:
    Joshua Distler

Paper Machine
papermachine.com
Carbon
info@carbon.com.au
www.carbon.com.au/paper/

Creative Direction: John Lycette,
    Mark Lycette
Design/Production: John Lycette

pdn-pix.com/MasterMichel
WOW Sight + Sound
520 Broadway 2nd Floor
New York, NY 10012
212-941-4600
Fax: 212-941-5927

wownet@aol.com

Tcherevkoff Studios Ltd.
15 West 24th Street
New York, NY 10010
212-229-1733
Fax: 212-229-1937

www.tcherevkoff.com

Creative Director: John Fezzuoglia

Pinch
Brad Johnson Presents
937 Grayson Street
Berkeley, CA 94710
510-649-8444

bradj@bradjohnson.com
www.bradjohnson.com

Design/Illustration/Animation:
    Brad Johnson
Sound: Jeff Stafford

pivotdesign.com
Pivot Design, Inc.
223 W. Erie, 4th Floor
Chicago, IL 60610
312-787-7707

staff@pivotdesign.com
www.pivotdesign.com

pmdraid.com
cow.
1522 Cloverfield Boulevard, Suite E
Santa Monica, CA 90404
310-264-2424
Fax: 310-264-2430

vision@cow.com
www.cow.com

Lead Designer: Bryan Powell
Creative Director: Bryan Dorsey
Programmers: Tammy McKean,
    Carl Brinkman, Jonathan Santos
Photography: Syko Song

polygram.com
p2
input@p2output.com
www.p2output.com

Design: Christopher Pacetti,
 Matthew Pacetti

presto.com
Presto Studios
presto@presto.com
www.presto.com

Designer: Tommy Yune
©1998 Presto Studios, Inc. All rights reserved.

The Program
Kuester Partners, Inc.
81 S. 9th Street, Suite 300
Minneapolis, MN 55402
612-338-6030
Fax: 612-338-6175

kuester@kuester.com
www.kuester.com

protozoa.com
Protozoa
415-522-6500
Fax: 415-522-6522

info@protozoa.com
www.protozoa.com

Web Design: Marilyn Novel
Creative: Tracey Roberts, Dan Hanna

qaswa.com
Qaswa Communications
423 Washington Street, Floor 5
San Francisco, CA 94111
415-399-9895
Fax: 415-986-7594

qaswa@hooked.net
www.qaswa.com

Interface Designer: Ammon Haggerty

Quattro Formaggi
Nu.millenniaIInc.
E. J. Dixon III
1044 Passiflora Avenue
Encinitas, CA 92024
760-942-3940

Executive Producer: Don Doerfler
Producer/Creative Director: E.J. Dixon III
Lead Programmer: Scott Bancroft
Art Director: Kyle Huston
Audio & Video Director: Hans Fjellestad
Tour Photography: Joe Charbanic,
 Kenny Funk

Radius Rocket Home Companion
Presto Productions
presto@presto.com
www.presto.com

Rankin Bevers Associates, *see*
Melbourne Water Corporation,
 Sydney Design '99 ICOGRADA

rezn8.com
ReZ.n8 Productions, Inc.
6430 Sunset Boulevard #100
Hollywood, CA 90028
213-957-2161

webmaster@rezn8.com
www.rezn8.com

Saatchi & Saatchi Pacific, *see*
toyota.com

sbg.com
SBG Partners
1725 Montgomery
San Francisco, CA 94111
415-391-9070
Fax: 415-391-4080

d.cunaan@sbg.com
www.sbg.com

Design Director: Phillip Ting
Designer: Martina Lui

scifi.com/The Dominion
The Dominion/Sci-Fi Channel
1230 Avenue of the Americas
New York, NY 10020

feedback@scifi.com
www.scifi.com

All pages: Copyright Sci-Fi Channel/USA
Networks; "Caption This!" also copyright
Best Brains, Inc.

sdge.com
San Diego Gas & Electric
SDGE Executive Producer: David Brown
Echolink Interactive Executive Producer/
 President: Gregory Carson
Echolink Interactive Creative Director:
 Angela Lester
Echolink Interactive Lead Designers:
 Gabriel Watson, Paula Klein,
 Tiffany Caliva

secondstory.com
Second Story
239 NW 13th Ave. #214
Portland, OR 97209
503-827-7155

Designer: Julie Beeler
Designer: Brad Johnson

julie@secondstory.com
www.secondstory.com

smucker.com
Giant Step
820 W. Jackson, Suite 400
Chicago, IL 60607
312-470-2700
Fax: 312-470-2770

melisa@giantstep.com
www.giantstep.com

Designers: Mark Rattin, Tim Irvine
Programmer: Kerry O'Donnell

spearedpeanut.com
The Speared Peanut Design Studio
Houston, TX
713-527-9909

over@spearedpeanut.com
www.spearedpeanut.com

Paul Kremer
Kristina D. Kremer

startribune.com/aids, *see* **Testing the**
Human Spirit

studioarchetype.com
Studio Archetype, Inc.
600 Townsend Street, Penthouse
San Francisco, CA 94103
415-703-9900
Fax: 415-703-9901

www.studioarchetype.com

sundancechannel.com
sundancefilm.com
Viacom Interactive Services
Creative Director/Executive Producer:
 Kathleen Wilson
Managing Producer: Adam Pincus
Producer/Designer: Michael Welles
Manager Production and Graphics:
 Dave Griffith
Director Software Development:
 Paul Mackles
AA Director: Barry Deck
Graphics Integrator: David Harth
Sundance Channel Media Coordinator:
 Lisa Van Dyne
Sundance Channel Chief Financial Officer:
 Rob Sussman
Sundance Channel Executive Producer:
 Susan Levovsky
Media Integrator: Adam Toll
Software Development: Joel Spolsky
Database/CGI Programming: Sajeev
 Joseph, Kit Lynes
HTML Programmers: Kirk Membry,
 Chris, Larsen
Special Thanks: Les Woodbury,
 Doug Cooper, Alex Maghen,
 Jon Cooper

surfcheck.com
Ted Deits
5942 Edinger Avenue, Suite 113
Huntington Beach, CA 92649
1-800-445-1099
714-840-3800

cyberkahuna@surfcheck.com
www.surfcheck.com
timchandler@ocean5
ocean5.edgeis.com

surfermag.com
Surfer Publications
P.O. Box 1028
Dana Point, CA 92629
714-496-5922
Fax: 714-496-7849

surfermag@earthlink.net
www.surfermag.com

Vandelay
Consultants: Ian Wynne, Sean Strauss

Surfer
Publisher: Doug Palladini
Magazine Editor: Steve Hawk
Advertizing Director: Kevin Meehan

Surfology 101
Internetwork Media Inc.
411 7th St.
Del Mar, CA 92014-3013
619-755-0439
Fax: 619-481-8181

www.in-media.com

Sydney Design '99 ICOGRADA Conference
Rankin Bevers Associates
502 Albert Street
East Melbourne, Victoria 3002 Australia
613-9-662-1233

design@rba.com.au
www.rba.com.au

Design: Wayne Rankin

tcherevkoff.com, *see* **pdn-pix.com/ MasterMichel**

Testing the Human Spirit
Star Tribune
startribune.com/aids
425 Portland Avenue
Minneapolis, MN 55488
Fax: 612-673-7973

www.startribune.com

Designer: Jamie Hutt
Producer: Jackie Crosby
Photographer: Brian Peterson
Audio Editing: Will Outlaw
Editing/Technical Support: Ben Welter

theedisongroup.com
The Edison Group
60 South 6th Street, Suite 2800
Minneapolis, MN 55402

tdupont@martinwilliams.com

toyota.com
Saatchi & Saatchi Pacific
3501 Sepulveda Boulevard
Torrance, CA 90505
310-214-6000
Fax: 310-214-6361

dvanetc@saatchipac.com

Creative Director: Dean Van Eimeren
Associate Creative Director/Designer:
  Alan Segal
Designers: Harjanto Sumali, Chris Ray
Writer: Freddy Nager
Multimedia Production Company:
  Noyo Media Group, San Francisco
Producer: Philip Dzilvelis

tradeinfo.com
cow.
1522 Cloverfield Boulevard, Suite E
Santa Monica, CA 90404
310-264-2424
Fax: 310-264-2436

vision@cow.com
www.cow.com

Lead Designer: Bryan Powell
Creative Director: Mateo Neri

travelocity.com
Worldview Systems Corporation
114 Sansome Street, Suite 700, S
San Francisco, CA 94104
415-391-7100
Fax: 415-616-9982

www.travelocity.com
www.wvs.com

Neal Checkoway
B.D. Goel
Meyer & Johnson
Anette Auyang
Marcy Gordon
Pamela Malpas
Aaron Puritz
Ann Harrington
Dan Larkin
Dave Kinsfather
Scott Mueller
David Grimsby
Ruth Gumnit
Daniel Malson
Mason Jones
Ron Klatchko

treacyfaces.com
Treacyfaces, Inc.
P.O. Box 26036
West Haven, CT 06516-8036
203-389-7037
800-800-6805, orders

treacyfa@ix.netcom.com
www.treacyfaces.com

Designer/Floppy Presentation: Joe Treacy
  and Gary Eckstein, Falls Church, VA
Designer/Web Site Store: Joe Treacy and
  Innovative Systems, Oxford, CT
Designer/Typefaces: Joe Treacy, along with
  various designers, under license

ussenioropen98.com
cow.
1522 Cloverfield Boulevard, Suite E
Santa Monica, CA 90404
310-264-2424
Fax: 310-264-2430

vision@cow.com
www.cow.com

Lead Designer: Bryan Powell
Creative Director: Mateo Neri
Programmers: Jonathan Santos,
  Samuel Goldstein

vfs.com
Vancouver Film School
vfsweb@griffin.multimedia.edu
www.multimedia.edu

Administrator: Susan Janzen
Art Director: Melissa Lee
Project Manager: Bonnie Robb

Verbum Interactive
Verbum, Inc.
P.O. Box 78067
San Francisco, CA 94107
415-777-9901

mg@verbum.com
www.verbum.com

Design and Graphics: Jack Davis
Programming: Michel Kripalani
Creative Direction: Michael Gosney

Victoria Buildings and Builders
Gyro Interactive Pty Ltd
502 Albert Street
East Melbourne, Victoria, 3002 Australia
61-3-9662-1027
Fax: 61-3-9663-8805

gyro@gyro.com.au
www.gyro.com.au

Design/Imaging: Wayne Rankin
Programming/Producer: John Swales
3D Modelling/Animation: Scott Bilby
Project Manager: Rebecca Szwede

Waypoint 1
Gyro Interactive Pty Ltd
502 Albert Street
East Melbourne, Victoria, 3002 Australia
61-3-9662-1027
Fax: 61-3-9663-8805

gyro@gyro.com.au
www.gyro.com.au

Producer: John Swales
Principal Designer: Wayne Rankin
Production Manager: Allistair Ebeli
InterNET Solutions: Amanda Ierace
Visual Designers: Beata Vitas,
    David Trewein, Melissa O'Brien
Production Assistant: Careta Brace,
    Gregory Kleiman, Rebecca Szwede,
    Sean Doyle
Video Special Effects: Chris Reynolds
Evaluation: Elizabeth Molyneaux,
    Kirsten Mann, Tim Anderson
Resource Manager: Kayt Edwards
Proofreader: Kate Fooke
System Designer: Natasha Dwyer
Administrator: Ruth Rankin
3D Animator: Scott Bilby, Troy Mortier
2D Animator: Trace Balla

WebVise
Auto F/X Corporation
P.O. Box 1415
Main Street
Alton, NH 03809
603-875-4400
Fax: 603-875-4404
shayne@autofx.com

Xpeditions Hall
National Geographic Interactive

www.nationalgeographic.com

Producer: M. Ford Cochran
Producer and Designer: Julie Beeler,
    Second Story
Creative Director and Designer:
    Brad Johnson, Second Story
Senior Engineer: Ken Mitsumoto,
    Second Story
3D Illustrator: Jim Ludtke
Writer: Ted Chamberlain

**Xplora 1, Peter Gabriel's
Secret World**
Interplay Productions
714-553-6655

www.interplay.com

Brilliant Media
450 Pacific Avenue, First Floor
San Francisco, CA 94133

info@brilliantmedia.com
www.brilliantmedia.com

Interactive Director and Producer for
    Xplora: Steve Nelson

Appendix B: CD-ROM Software Contributors

Contact information for software contained on the accompanying CD-ROM.

BBEdit
Bare Bones Software Inc.
P.O. Box 1048
Bedford, MA 01730
781-687-0700
Fax: 781-687-0711

www.barebones.com

BladePro
Flaming Pear Software
#3, 7157 Quinpool Road
Halifax, Nova Scotia
Canada B3L 1C8
902-455-2357

lloyd@kagi.com

ccn.cs.dal.ca/~aa731/blade.html

ccn.cs.dal.ca/~aa731/feathergif.html

Claris Home Page
FileMaker, Inc.
5201 Patrick Henry Drive
Santa Clara, CA 95052-8168

www.filemaker.com

Dreamweaver
Macromedia, Incorporated
600 Townsend Street
San Francisco, California 94103
415-252-2000
Fax: 415-626-0554

www.macromedia.com

FeatherGIF
Flaming Pear Software
#3, 7157 Quinpool Road
Halifax, Nova Scotia
Canada B3L 1C8
902-455-2357

lloyd@kagi.com

ccn.cs.dal.ca/~aa731/blade.html

ccn.cs.dal.ca/~aa731/feathergif.html

Flash
Macromedia, Incorporated
600 Townsend Street
San Francisco, California 94103
415-252-2000
Fax: 415-626-0554

www.macromedia.com

Fusion
NetObjects, Inc.
602 Galveston Dr.
Redwood City, CA 94063
650-482-3200
Fax: 650-562-0288

info@netobjects.com

www.netobjects.com

GifBuilder
Yves Piguet
Av. de la Chablière 35
1004 Lausanne
Switzerland

piguet@ia.epfl.ch

GIFConstruction Set
Alchemy Mindworks Inc.
P.O. Box 500, Beeton,
Ontario, CANADA, L0G 1A0.
905-936-9501
Fax: 905-936-9502

These software titles included with this publication are provided as shareware for your evaluation: GifBuilder, BladePro, FeatherGIF and GIF Construction Set. If you try this software and find it useful, you are requested to register it as discussed in its documentation and in the About screen of the application. The publisher of this book has not paid the registration fee for this shareware.

www.mindworkshop.com/alchemy/
    gifcon.html

Hot Dog Pro
Sausage Software
Level 25
150 Lonsdale St
Melbourne VIC 3000
Australia
Fax: 61 3 96631096

www.sausage.com

HoTMetal Pro
SoftQuad Inc.
20 Eglinton Ave. West, 13th Floor
P.O. Box 2025
Toronto, Canada
M4R 1K8.
617-229-2924
617-272-4876

SoftQuad Boston
168 Middlesex Tpk
Burlington, MA 01803
416 544-9000
Orders: (N. America only):
800-387-2777
Tech Support: 416-544-8879
Fax: 416-544-0300

www.softquad.com

Internet Explorer
Microsoft
One Microsoft Way
Redmond, WA 98052-6399
425-882-8080

www.microsoft.com

Netscape Communicator
501 E. Middlefield Road
Mountain View, CA 94043
650-254-1900
Fax: 650/528-4124

home.netscape.com

PageMill Acrobat
Adobe Systems Incorporated
345 Park Avenue
San Jose, California 95110-2704 USA
408-536-6000
408-537-6000

www.adobe.com

RealPlayer
Real Networks, Inc.
1111 3rd Ave, Suite 2900
Seattle, WA 98101
206-674-2700

www.real.com

Shockwave
Macromedia, Incorporated
600 Townsend Street
San Francisco, California 94103
415-252-2000
Fax: 415-626-0554

www.macromedia.com

Stuffit Expander
Aladdin Systems, Inc.
165 Westridge Dr.
Watsonville, CA 95076
408-761-6200
Fax: (408) 761-6206

www.aladdinsys.com

Index

Y

Yahoo Web site, 29
Yakima Brewing and Malting
    Company, 70
Yamamoto Moss, 206
Yune, Tommy, 98

Z

Zoo Entertainment, 100